PRAISE FOR *THE COUPLE'S RETIREMENT PUZZLE*

"We spend a large fraction of our lives in retirement, but, unlike career or marriage, we don't prepare for it, except by saving money. *The Couple's Retirement Puzzle* helps us all make retirement less of a puzzle and more of an opportunity."
—*Harry R. Moody, director of academic affairs, AARP*

"There is nothing easy about figuring out the future, and when you're a couple, it's twice as challenging. Roberta Taylor and Dorian Mintzer offer practical, thought-provoking advice as they help you put the puzzle together. Read it before you retire and save yourself some pain!"
—*Jeri Sedlar, coauthor,* Don't Retire, REWIRE!

"*The Couple's Retirement Puzzle* is a book that every couple in retirement transition needs to run out and get, pronto. It is practical, inspiring, and insightful—a real gem in a field where we all need more resources to read and think about!"
—*Olivia Mellan, author of* Money Harmony

"Roberta Taylor and Dorian Mintzer have written an indispensable guide for couples who look forward to years of living and loving together. The wise, compassionate conversations in this book turn the fears and dilemmas of growing older into rich and challenging adventures."
—*Gina Ogden, PhD, author of* The Heart and Soul of Sex *and* The Return of Desire

"Every baby boomer couple should own this terrific, couple-friendly guide to successfully navigate the retirement transition.

Filled with must-have conversations, real-life examples, and a boatload of invaluable tips and techniques for productive communication, this is the book I wish I had written."

—*Lin Schreiber, Encore Career coach and speaker*

"*The Couple's Retirement Puzzle* offers both a clear glimpse of the challenges we all face in our ever-longer lifetimes and a blueprint for a successful quality of shared life and relationships in retirement. The authors are among a very few experts on the subject. If you read one book about the subject, let it be *The Couple's Retirement Puzzle.*"

—*Carleen MacKay, author of* Plan "B" for Boomers *and* The 50,000 Mile Career Checkup, *coauthor of* Boom or Bust *and* Return of the Boomers

"This book will encourage and support many couples who—reluctant to confide in friends, or even each other—had imagined they were the only ones challenged by the retirement transition. A must-read that teaches couples to work together as a team... Roberta Taylor and Dorian Mintzer are great life coaches...They know how to bring couples together on a question that often divides them: 'What's it all about in the next part of our lives?' Their understanding of and attention to the purpose part of the retirement puzzle really gets the dialogue rolling!"

—*Richard Leider, bestselling author of* The Power of Purpose: Find Meaning, Live Longer, Better *and* Repacking Your Bags: Lighten Your Load for the Rest of Your Life

"If you and your partner are questioning how you can experience a fulfilling life in retirement, then here is the book you've been waiting for. Your journey forward in the second half of life is not a solitary venture. Couples need to support each other's growth with mutual understanding and encouragement. Dorian Mintzer and Roberta Taylor have drawn on years of professional practice, personal experience, and research in shaping exercises that will launch you on new adventures together."

—*William Sadler, PhD, author of* The Third Age: Six Principles of Growth and Renewal After Forty, *director of research for the Center for Third Age Leadership, and professor of sociology and business at Holy Names University*

"Relationships are the most overlooked subject in planning for the future. Financial security, good health, and meaningful activities are important but not sufficient. The authors present useful examples and tools to make the average retirement a fabulous one by approaching the subject of relationships with knowledge, experience, humor, and compassion. Take special note of the exercises and tips, and have fun with the puzzle!"

—*Helen Dennis, coauthor,* Los Angeles Times *bestseller* Project Renewment: The First Retirement Model for Career Women

"*The Couple's Retirement Puzzle* is a much-needed and eloquent addition to a growing field that has tended to ignore the importance of couples working together to plan and create the post-midlife they want. Roberta Taylor's and Dori Mintzer's wise advice, compelling stories, and practical exercises will help to improve your communication, sharpen your individual and joint decision-making, and ease your transitions into this promising life chapter."

—*Margaret (Meg) L. Newhouse, PhD, principal, Passion and Purpose LifeCrafting, and founder of the Life Planning Network*

"*The Couple's Retirement Puzzle* deals with second-half-of-life dilemmas and choices from a unique perspective that I haven't encountered before—the couple's angle. I welcome this fine book, which offers practical, sensible, and useful information for honestly and openly exploring 'what's next.' Life transitions are indeed a puzzle, but a solvable one!"

—*Connie Goldman, author of* Late-Life Love: Romance and New Relationships in Later Years

"From the beginning of our work in the 'powerful aging' movement eleven years ago, we have noticed time and again couples out of alignment when one or both are transitioning from full-time work to their next chapter. We are delighted that Roberta Taylor and Dorian Mintzer, both experienced professionals and 2Young2Retire certified facilitators, have taken on this important project. *The Couple's Retirement Puzzle* is a much-needed resource."

—*Marika and Howard Stone, coauthors,* Too Young to Retire: 101 Ways to Start the Rest of Your Life

"*The Couple's Retirement Puzzle* begins with the puzzle that is retirement but ends up being a pathway for those seeking a sensible, self-renewing, and mutual approach to this next stage of life. Surprisingly, there are few resources available for couples seeking help in figuring out how to address the many pieces of the puzzle together. Roberta Taylor and Dori Mintzer each have the deep experience, sensitivity, and personal insight to guide couples through the maze of issues, challenges, and opportunities related to what comes next. *The Couple's Retirement Puzzle* is a treasure trove of practical wisdom for those just beginning the journey and even for those who have already stepped into it."

—*Fred Mandell, PhD, coauthor of* Becoming a Life Change Artist: 7 Creative Skills to Reinvent Yourself at Any Stage of Life

"What an achievement! Your ten upbeat conversation starters hit all of my buttons! After living separately for the last fifteen years, my life partner and I have just moved together into a shared home across the country from familiar faces and places. Old attitudes and differences plus new needs and issues have shown up quickly and caused me to wonder where we could find a counselor to help us 'get to yes.' With your book in hand, we don't need a counselor! We hope to create a fertile environment for both personal freedom and sustained togetherness. Thanks for your help in guiding our transition."

—*Janet M. Hively, PhD, gerontologist, educator, and cofounder of the Vital Aging Network, the Minnesota Creative Arts and Aging Network, and the SHIFT Transition Network*

"If you and your spouse, or you and your children, are ever at a loss for topics of conversation, read 'Relationships with Family: The Theory of Relativity' in Dorian Mintzer and Roberta Taylor's book *The Couple's Retirement Puzzle*. The topics they cover are all-important and are 'musts' for strengthening your family relationships."

—*Ruth Nemzoff, EdD, resident scholar, Brandeis Women's Studies Research Center, and author of* Don't Bite Your Tongue: How to Foster Rewarding Relationships with Your Adult Children

"Dorian and Roberta's book adds breadth and depth to the topic of couples living well in retirement. This is a book I can give to my financial life planning clients to help them address the range of issues and possibilities to consider as they engage in the adventure of 'life after jobs.'"

—*Elizabeth Jetton, CFP, senior adviser, RTD Financial Advisors and cofounder of Directions for Women*

"*The Couple's Retirement Puzzle* is the only book that puts it all together for couples dealing with retirement, exploring the need to still earn money and the desire to be engaged meaningfully in life and work while remaining a happy couple. I highly recommend it for all couples grappling with these important and complex issues!"

—*Edward G. Rogoff, coauthor of* The Second Chance Revolution: Becoming Your Own Boss After 50 *and Lawrence N. Field professor of entrepreneurship, Baruch College, City University of New York*

"*The Couple's Retirement Puzzle* reveals that, in the context of married lives, the traditional issues related to retirement are far more complex and difficult than is generally recognized. But Roberta Taylor and Dorian Mintzer also show us that satisfactory resolutions are possible once the issues are properly understood. In five years, there will be a dozen books imitating *The Couple's Retirement Puzzle*, because it is such a critically important and highly useful guide. Although other books may appear, this is the book we will surely want to use and recommend to others."

—*Chuck Yanikoski, president of RetirementWORKS, Inc., and founder of the Association for Integrative Financial and Life Planning*

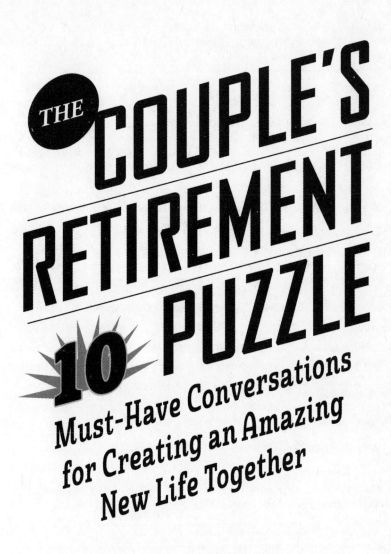

THE COUPLE'S RETIREMENT PUZZLE

10

PUZZLE

Must-Have Conversations for Creating an Amazing New Life Together

Roberta K. Taylor, RNCS, MEd *and*
Dorian Mintzer, MSW, PhD

sourcebooks

Sourcebooks and the colophon are registered trademarks of Sourcebooks, Inc.

The vignettes in this book are both composite and actual stories of individuals and couples. In some cases, names have been changed for purposes of anonymity.

This publication is designed to provide accurate and authoritative information in regard to the subject matter covered. It is sold with the understanding that the publisher is not engaged in rendering legal, accounting, or other professional service. If legal advice or other expert assistance is required, the services of a competent professional person should be sought. —*From a Declaration of Principles Jointly Adopted by a Committee of the American Bar Association and a Committee of Publishers and Associations*

Published by Sourcebooks, Inc.
P.O. Box 4410, Naperville, Illinois 60567-4410
(630) 961-3900
Fax: (630) 961-2168
www.sourcebooks.com

Originally published in 2011 in the United States by Lincoln Street Press, LLC.

Library of Congress Cataloging-in-Publication Data

Taylor, Roberta K.
  The couple's retirement puzzle : 10 must-have conversations for creating an amazing new life together / Roberta K. Taylor, RNCS, MEd, Dorian Mintzer, MSW, PhD.
    pages cm
Includes bibliographical references and index.
(trade : alk. paper) 1. Retirement. 2. Retirement—United States. 3. Retirement—United States—Planning. 4. Retirees—United States—Life skills guides. 5. Quality of life. I. Mintzer, Dorian. II. Title.
HQ1062.T395 2014
306.3'80973—dc23

                                    2014021420

Printed and bound in the United States of America.
                        VP 10 9 8 7 6 5 4 3 2 1

From Roberta Taylor

For Bruce, with love, as we travel together
and share our life path. —Roberta

And for Bari and Jonathan, my wish for you is to fully embrace
your lives, discover your many gifts, and define your own
meaning of success. —Love, Mom

From Dori Mintzer

This book is dedicated with deep gratitude and love to David
and Louie, two special people who are helping my second half
of life be the best years of my life.

For David, with love: I cherish our life and journey
together. I couldn't have written this book without your
love, support, and belief in me. —Dori

For Louie: You have brought joy, love, laughter, and happiness
to my life. At times you are wise beyond your years. I hope
you'll allow yourself to find your passion and purpose as you
continue to grow. I love being your Mom. —Love, Mom

Contents

Foreword

The vast majority of people who are about to retire are going to do so with someone else. Yet there is surprisingly little in the literature on retirement that provides an explicit framework for how to go about making important retirement decisions together.

That gap is now thankfully and skillfully filled with *The Couple's Retirement Puzzle: 10 Must-Have Conversations for Creating an Amazing New Life Together*. Roberta Taylor and Dori Mintzer give us a practical, no-nonsense guide brilliantly organized around ten critical conversations. The thought of having such conversations may seem daunting to some, even while they recognize the importance of doing so. That is why Roberta and Dori not only frame the topics, but also coach the reader on how to have those conversations to get the most out of them.

The Couple's Retirement Puzzle is chock-full of useful information. In fact, given the wide territory covered by the ten conversations, the amount of information marshaled within this book is quite impressive. Roberta and Dori also do a wonderful job of interweaving real-life situations with marvelous insights and get-to-the-heart-of-the-matter conversation starters. But the cumulative effect of the book is greater than these elements. As you move through the book, you'll realize you are making connections and building relationships, not only with your partner as you engage in these important conversations, but also with the authors, who gently reveal parts of their own histories. Roberta and Dori serve as wise guides to the next chapter in our lives. The overall effect is one of being caringly shepherded over unfamiliar terrain.

This is also a book you will have a long-term relationship with—you will find yourself coming back to it. Interestingly, the "10 Must-Have Conversations" truly apply to any stage of life. I can envision giving the book as a gift to a newly married couple or to a couple with teenage kids—and, of course, to those on the cusp of this new stage of life called retirement and to those who have already embarked on the journey.

As Roberta and Dori remind us in the introduction, the times they are a-changin'. They speak about the way the baby boomer age wave and the longevity revolution are beginning to radically change the way we think about that stage of life we call retirement. This next stage isn't going to be your mother's or father's "retirement." Those living this next stage will be doing the changing.

Roberta and Dori are like great artists who show us how to see ourselves and the world around us in new ways. With their help, we have the opportunity to reimagine our future and our relationships with renewed vitality and commitment—one couple at a time, together. They have given us a marvelous gift.

—Fred Mandell, PhD, coauthor, *Becoming a Life Change Artist: 7 Creative Skills to Reinvent Yourself at Any Stage of Life*

From the Authors

Coauthoring a book is exhilarating, exhausting, and an opportunity to learn things about yourself that you probably needed to know but might not have wanted to see. As challenging as the process may be, what you learn along the way is invaluable. And, of course, when the labor is over and the manuscript is finally ready for printing, there is a wonderful sense of shared accomplishment and relief.

We met at a meeting of the Life Planning Network, a multidisciplinary organization for professionals working with people in the second half of life. Although we hardly knew each other, there was a feeling of connection and familiarity from the start. We shared some similar life experiences around divorce, infertility, and finding our voice as young women and now as older professional women in our sixties dealing with issues of aging and transition. In different ways, we both have the pull of competing priorities with husbands, children, grandchildren, friends, and work.

When we initially began talking, our focus was on developing a workbook that would help couples navigate retirement transition. But with our combined life experience and professional work with clients in midlife and beyond, as well as a plethora of ideas we generated, it soon became clear that we were actually envisioning a much broader concept. *The Couple's Retirement Puzzle: 10 Must-Have Conversations for Creating an Amazing New Life Together* developed a life of its own. Making the decision to collaborate put us on a steep learning curve.

Neither of us had written anything of this magnitude. Ignorance is bliss; we had no idea what would lie ahead.

Over the many months of working together, we have witnessed each other's meltdowns and celebrated moments of "brilliance." We made a decision to collaborate before really getting to know each other, but it felt right. A mutual friend commented that it was "a quick marriage." Not surprisingly, we have experienced many of the communication issues common to all "partnerships" and hopefully have become better listeners and better "partners" in the process.

A deep bond of friendship and mutual respect has developed as we worked together to accomplish our goal of creating a user-friendly book for couples who are on the continuum of retirement transition. We hope that the book will be a valuable resource to help you create your shared vision for the second half of life.

We welcome your feedback, stories, and comments. Contact Dori at dorian@dorianmintzer.com or Roberta at rkt@path making.com.

FROM ROBERTA TAYLOR

In my late fifties, I began to experience life from a different perspective. It wasn't just about getting older. I was transitioning into a new life stage, beginning to reflect on where I had been and thinking more about what was really important. After many years as a psychotherapist working in nonprofits and private practice, I was asking myself, "What's next?"

The message came on a beautiful spring day in 2004. I was

in a managers' meeting, and the team was discussing program changes for the following year. But my mind was not on the conversation. I was listening to an internal voice saying that it was time for me to leave the family service agency where I worked. For the past several months, I had been aware of a growing sense of detachment, but until that moment, I hadn't seriously thought about leaving my job. Hearing the message resonated with every part of my being, and it was a catalyst for change. I had no idea where it would lead me or "who" I would become in the process, but I knew that something more was out there for me to create.

The next few years would be a time of exploration, stepping out of my comfort zone and opening up to new possibilities. While I had always loved my work, I had a creative side that had not been fully expressed. It was time to let go and open the space, develop my strengths and interests, and learn new skills. Coaching was a natural segue, one that satisfied my desire to continue working with people in more proactive and creative ways, doing workshops, public speaking, and sharing some of the lessons from my own life to help others on their journey. I was networking with colleagues who were also in the midst of transition and becoming involved in the coaching world and the positive aging community. It was a relief to know I was not alone on the journey.

But in the spring of 2006, I was stopped in my tracks. Several years earlier, I had been diagnosed with mitral valve prolapse and told that, at some point, surgery would be necessary to repair the valve. When I began having symptoms of fatigue and shortness of breath, I knew the time had come. During the next three months, I had two open-heart operations, followed by months of recuperation. I had a lot of time to reflect on the past and think about how I wanted to live the next part of my life. I relied on my inner voice of wisdom to guide me on the journey. To continue to grow, I needed to embrace what it meant to age well and be all that I could be so I could help others do the same. That has become my personal mission.

While my professional life has always been satisfying, my personal life was challenging. With two divorces behind me, I thought I would never want to marry again. But sixteen years ago, Bruce, who was my first "real" boyfriend, came back into my life after thirty-four years. It was like coming home. We have a loving and thriving relationship that has brought contentment and peace to both of us. My children, Bari and Jonathan, have always been closest to my heart. They are both happily married to loving and supportive partners. Caitlyn, Jake, Lauren, and Genevieve, my four amazing grandchildren, light up my life and are often wise teachers. But my close women friends have been my most stabilizing force. Together we have witnessed all of the ups and downs of life's joys and disappointments, being there for each other during some of the most difficult times. Through my doubts and fears, my friends have supported and encouraged me to continue seeking what they knew was possible, sometimes even before I did.

The idea for writing a book grew out of both the desire for creative expression and the experience of transitioning into a different life stage. Bruce and I had been married just nine years, and here we were, facing retirement transition, with all the accompanying issues as well as opportunities. Making decisions as a couple was still new to us, but having had a few standoffs and differences of opinion, it was clear that being able to communicate more effectively was important for our relationship. And so ideas for the book began to formulate. Collaborating with Dori, who was on a similar path though in different circumstances, followed naturally. Our collaboration gave us the opportunity to support each other through the challenges and grow more into who we are each meant to be.

My plate is full—and sometimes overflowing—with competing priorities: What do I want to do? What "should" I do? What is my soul calling for? Finding balance is difficult, if not impossible. As I open to the potential of my own passion and creativity, Bruce is still in recovery from a lifetime in the corporate world. He was retired for a few years, then was unexpectedly offered a position where he could use his technology background and leadership skills to help others. This gives him a sense of purpose and satisfaction and brings balance to our relationship. At some point, however, in the next year or two, Bruce will want to retire, travel, and spend more time together. If you asked me now, I would say "no retirement for me." My work is so much a part of who I am. I get joy and satisfaction from the many things I do—writing, coaching, workshops, consulting, and speaking. But life changes, priorities shift, and what's true today may be different tomorrow.

The book has been a wonderful vehicle for Bruce and me to deepen our relationship and have our own important conversations as we look toward the next part of our life together. I've learned that we often teach what we most need to learn. In this case, that's meant being able to find balance, honor my priorities, and focus attention on what I love doing and on those I most love: my husband, children, grandchildren, and friends. That is what gives my life meaning and purpose. I hope that this book will help you find the path to your most fulfilling life.

Roberta

FROM DORIAN MINTZER

In my early twenties, strangers saved me from drowning. That experience shaped my approach to life as an adult. Realizing the fragility of life, I learned not to take it for granted and to make intentional choices about how I wanted to live. By age thirty-three, I had gotten married, moved to Boston, received my doctorate, and started a private practice. After deep reflection, I also realized that my marriage was not working, and I needed to end it before starting a family. The next several years were focused on my professional development and career. And then, in a new relationship, my focus again began to shift to wanting a family. In my early forties, with my new husband in his midfifties, we decided to do some individual soul-searching about how we wanted to live the next part of our life. During this time, I went on a trek with other women to Nepal. On the trek, I spent time reflecting on my life and realized how important it still was for me to be a mother. At home, David did his own soul-searching. When we were again together, we discovered we were in agreement: we wanted to revisit the issue of trying to have children, despite our age.

It took almost ten years. At age fifty, with my husband in his early sixties and when many of our friends were becoming grandparents, we became new parents for the first time. Now, in my late sixties, I have a teenage son, Louie. My life is an example that there is no "one-size-fits-all" retirement transition. There are some specific advantages of being older parents. We are in a more comfortable financial situation than earlier in our careers, and this enables us to have more flexibility with the experiences we can create together. Since we are healthy now, we go on active vacations together as often as possible. Louie has grown up sharing our love of hiking, biking, sailing, and skiing. He has told us that he loves his life and the adventures we share. It has been a joy to watch him grow and develop into a lovely young man.

There are also disadvantages that pose challenges. Older than most parents who experience an "empty nest," David and I want to continue part-time work as well as traveling and spending time with family and friends. My hope is that we will sustain our health and energy and enjoy the coming years, but we know there will be bumps along the way and, like everyone, we will have to deal with whatever happens.

We are "out of sync" as a family in our retirement transition. In some respects I am in the "prime" of my work life, while David, in contrast, is in a "winding down" mode, having given up his administrative responsibilities and now working part-time. We both want to keep working as long as we're capable, so no "total retirement" is in sight. In the future, I envision continuing to keep my actual therapy and coaching client group small, while increasing my speaking, writing, group and workshop facilitation, consulting, and teaching. In addition to my writing, I also want to explore other aspects of my creativity that have been put on the back burner. And we both look forward to watching Louie "bloom" in the years ahead as he discovers his passions in his work and life.

As I reflect on my life, these recent years have been my happiest and best. I am proud of my professional accomplishments, and I love my husband, son, and community of friends, family, and colleagues. Through some health scares and challenges, I have learned the importance of resilience and a positive attitude. David has opened my eyes to healthy and vital aging. Although older than I am, he is "young old." I also feel grateful that I have a supportive network of family and friends. I am particularly blessed with some special women friends who live near and far. We're there to listen to and support each other.

Having my own private practice over the years has enabled me to control the hours and amount of my work. My transition into coaching has allowed even more flexibility. I have welcomed connection with other professionals interested in positive aging through the creation of my Boomers and Beyond Special Interest Group and my involvement in the Life Planning Network. My "Revolutionize Your Retirement Interview with Experts Series to Help You Create a Fulfilling Second Half of Life" enables me to bring experts to both professionals and the public. My work enables me to use my professional holistic life planning expertise and understanding of adult development and positive psychology, combined with my life experiences, to work with people as they transition into their second half of life.

With Louie's increasing independence, I began wanting more creative opportunities for myself, and writing was one of them. I welcomed the opportunity to collaborate with Roberta on this book, and since then, I have also contributed to a number of other books, articles, radio shows, and blogs. Writing has seemed a natural outgrowth of my speaking and my personal and professional interest in the transitions people experience in the second half of life. Since we wrote this book, I've continued to learn about myself, my relationship with David, the varieties of the retirement transition, and the experience of aging. At times, I spend long hours writing or involved in my projects. Luckily, my family and friends, the people most important to me, are supportive and encouraging. Trying to find the right balance in life is a continual challenge for me.

My retirement transition is definitely a process, one that has involved self-reflection, conversations with David, Louie, and other friends and family, as well as writing this book with Roberta. Retirement, for me, is indeed a journey and not a destination. I feel blessed that I've been able to create a life that enables me to do so many things that I love as well as to help and give back to others. I hope you'll find help and inspiration to craft your own journey while reading this book.

Dori

On the Road to Transition: Getting Started

What Will You Retire To?

With twenty or more years ahead, have you thought about what you'll retire to? Several decades ago, you could have expected to live into your midseventies or eighties. Today, advances in medicine and technology—combined with living a healthy lifestyle and a little good luck—mean you can look forward to the possibility of living well into your eighties, nineties, or even longer. Centenarians, people who reach the age of one hundred years or more, are currently the fastest-growing segment of the population. Willard Scott, on *The Today Show*, may soon need to devote an entire show every week just to celebrating centenarians.

As Bob Dylan once said, "The times they are a-changin'." We are in the midst of what is being called a longevity revolution. Seventy-eight million baby boomers, and many more on the older fringe, are pioneering a new life stage characterized by living and working longer, developing encore careers, and taking advantage of opportunities for growth in the second half of life. The traditional notion of the "golden years," with Social Security and a condo in Florida, is becoming a thing of the past. In the twenty-first century, we are being challenged to redefine retirement and reinvent ourselves in order to live our version of "the good life"—having financial security, access to adequate health care, and enjoying a sense of meaning, purpose, and belonging as we get older. We are experiencing personal change and questioning how to continue to grow as individuals and as couples in this new life stage. The question for each of us is: "How do I want to live the next part of my life?"

If the notion of the "golden years" is no longer relevant, what do we need to be thinking about that will take its place, and how can couples plan for this together? "Retirement" is a concept that is in transition. It no longer reflects what people are experiencing or means what it used to, but it has yet to be redefined. The word "retirement" is used as a reference point in this book for the sake of common language, rather than as a description of what individuals and society are experiencing. Inherent in the book is our belief that, ultimately, what you are retiring to becomes more important than what you are retiring from. The term "retirement transition" is used in these pages to reflect a process of letting go of what is no longer necessary, while opening the space for creating what will come next.

The term "second half of life" comes from the notion that life is divided into two halves, and generally refers to people fifty and older. However, the terminology can be misleading. If you are sixty years old today, the chances of living another fifty years are slim. We use the term descriptively, rather than literally, to suggest that there are many possibilities and options for growth and renewal in this life stage, whether you are fifty, sixty, seventy-five, or older.

Although this time of life can be confusing, overwhelming, and scary, it can also be an opportunity for making choices about how you want to live the next part of your life. It does not necessarily mean not working. Many of us need to continue earning an income, and others choose to work because they love what they do. It is more about exploring the possibilities for living and working differently, whether that means full-time or part-time work or consulting, volunteering, developing an encore career, pursuing interests and hobbies, or something entirely different. The goal for many people at this life stage is being able to fit work into life, rather than continuing to squeeze life into work. Still others, finally having time for leisure after so many years of hard work, may decide they do not want to work at all and opt for a more traditional retirement. The why, what, when, where, and how are specific to you.

What does all of this mean for couples? How can couples continue to grow and redefine themselves and their relationships as they transition to the next part of life together? How do dual-career couples make decisions about when to retire, whether to retire together or separately, or if they can afford to retire at all? And how do individual needs, desires, and dreams fit in?

The Couple's Retirement Puzzle: 10 Must-Have Conversations for Creating an Amazing New Life Together was written to provide guidelines to help couples address some of these important questions, plan together, and set goals that support a shared vision. The word *puzzle* is both a verb and a noun. The conversations in this book will help you and your partner to "puzzle out" the pieces that are most important to you while you develop your vision for how they fit together.

LEARNING FROM EXPERIENCE

The development of *The Couple's Retirement Puzzle* was influenced by our clinical work with couples, retirement transition seminars, personal life experiences, conversations with friends and colleagues, and a series of focus groups, which added depth and richness to our understanding of the issues. Many couples said that even though they had a network of friends, issues related to retirement were rarely discussed. However, they all thought that being able to talk with other couples was helpful.

Several themes emerged from our many discussions with couples. Do we want to retire? Can we afford to retire? How will we spend our time? What is really important? What if one of us wants to move to Florida, but the other doesn't? What if we don't communicate and have trouble making decisions together? The "10 Must-Have Conversations" developed out of these themes. Although the conversations are not exhaustive, they do reflect the most prevalent concerns we encountered.

We found that some couples had been planning their retirement for several years, others had not gone beyond financial planning, and many had not done any planning at all. Several couples said they put off talking about the future because the issues seemed so overwhelming. Transition to a new phase of life is a process that requires time and patience. Decisions do not need to be made all at the same time. Having accurate information and planning together can help you make decisions you won't regret in the future.

WISE ELDERS

As our work with retirement transition progressed, we realized that we were missing a valuable voice in the conversation: the voice of "wise elders." We invited several couples ranging in age from sixty-eight to ninety-two years young to come together and reflect on their journey of retirement transition. With honesty, humility, and humor, they shared stories of joy and sorrow, vulnerability and resilience, success and disappointment, as well as the impact of illness, disability, and loss. Stereotypes of elders were challenged as we heard moving accounts of how hopes and dreams had been realized or reconciled. These "wise elders," reflecting on their lives and legacy, offered a rich and informative perspective on life transitions and aging. They are inspiring role models.

In this book, you'll hear some of their stories, as well as meet a variety of couples who have different relationship dynamics and are at varied points in their retirement transition. Although the baby boomer generation includes people who were born between 1946 and 1964, this eighteen-year age span can be thought of in three generational segments: younger boomers in their early to midfifties, middle boomers in their midfifties to sixty, and older boomers in their sixties. What couples are thinking about and planning for in their late forties or even fifty is very different than it is at age sixty or seventy. In addition to age, it is important to acknowledge that financial resources, education, health, and many other factors can make a big difference in the options people realistically have and how that may affect retirement planning.

HOW TO USE THIS BOOK

The Couple's Retirement Puzzle was written for couples who are interested in planning for the future, no matter what their age, ethnicity, religion, gender and sexual orientation, financial or marital status. The information and exercises in each section are intended to help you have conversations that can lead to mutual understanding and better decision making. Additional resources have been included at the end of the book (see pages 273–307).

Our hope is that, no matter where you are on the retirement continuum, whatever your age or circumstances, this book will be a useful resource and guide for planning the years ahead with more thought and intentionality. Approaching the second half of life is an opportunity to reassess outdated roles, let go of what no longer works, and open up to new possibilities. It takes courage, commitment, and compromise. Couples do best when they think ahead, communicate, and plan together. Remember, it doesn't matter how long you have been together: relationships are always a work in progress. Go at your own pace, allow for your differences, and be patient with each other. Most importantly, enjoy the book and the process of working together to create the life you both want to be living.

At one time or another, we all need direction and guidance to help us navigate transitions and make good decisions for the future. *The Couple's Retirement Puzzle* is a user-friendly guide that will help you learn how to communicate more effectively and make decisions together. It offers information, suggestions and exercises to help you deal with your retirement puzzle. Reading this book and working through the exercises will prepare you for

- having conversations that will help you plan together
- making decisions that respect each other's needs and goals
- developing your unique plan for the second half of life

This book is about transitioning to the next stage of your life. Transitions offer the potential for renewal, learning, and growth. Approach this process with an open mind, a positive attitude, honesty, and a willingness to listen from a different perspective, and you may discover things you never realized about yourself and your partner. Relationships are enhanced and even transformed when people agree on the guidelines for and importance of communication.

Not everyone is in the same place. You will read about couples to whom you may be able to relate. Some of the conversations may "speak" to you; others you may decide to skip or go back to later. You and your partner might not agree on what is important, or find that what you thought was important really isn't. Don't be discouraged if your partner is not interested in reading the book. You may be able to share what you're learn-ing and engage your partner in conversations. In the dance of relationships, when one partner initiates new steps, the other may resist at first but will eventually add twists and turns that create a new dance.

To help you get started, we suggest that each of you com-plete the Couple's Quiz: Are You Ready for Retirement? on page xxxi and then spend time talking about what you learned. Which questions did you agree on? Which answers surprised you? Where were your similarities and differences? What do you most need to talk about? You might want to begin with sub-jects that are easier to talk about, and then move on to more challenging topics. The more practice you have using the tips and tools in the following chapter, "Getting to Yes Together: The Importance of Communication," the better prepared you will be to have some of the conversations.

This book is designed so that each of the "10 Must-Have Conversations" will give you the opportunity to talk together about many of the important topics related to retirement transition. The questions and exercises at the end of each conversation will help you identify important pieces of your puzzle. For example, you may agree to explore living in a dif-ferent part of the country, turning off the TV and computer to spend a romantic evening together, or having a monthly pot-luck dinner with friends. In the "Creating Your Shared Vision" chapter on pages 257–266, write at least one to three items for each conversation.

Keep track of the things that you do not agree on and make time to explore those issues. Remember that creating a vision for what you both want in the next part of your life is a process that begins with small steps and evolves over time. The purpose of these conversations is to help you develop and realize your vision together. Maintaining the momentum is important.

You may decide that some of the exercises and homework, which we call "Funwork," will be more helpful than others. Experiment and see what works for you. The structure may help you avoid arguments and have more positive conversations. To get the most out of this book, keep a notebook or journal to record your responses to the questions and exercises as well as your thoughts, feelings, and ideas. The goal is to clarify what is important to each of you in developing a shared vision for the next part of your life together.

The following chapter, "Getting to Yes Together: The Importance of Communication," will help you develop or improve effective skills for talking with each other and making joint decisions. If you already have good communication skills, that's great. If not, or if you need help, we offer suggestions for sharing what is important, listening without being defensive, and learning how to compromise and problem solve so that you can get to "yes" together. Each conversation is an opportunity to practice skills that will reinforce productive and effective communication. Remember that it is not about "winning"; it is about being able to make decisions that will reflect how you both feel and what you want.

Ultimately, mutual decision making comes out of productive conversations that are based on good communication. This requires courage, commitment, and compromise as well as caring and respect. Have fun with it and be kind to yourself and each other. Every day is an opportunity to learn something new.

Couple's Quiz:
Are You Ready for Retirement?

Are you and your partner on the same page when it comes to retirement, or are you reading different books? This simple quiz will help you get a quick glimpse into how each of you views your communication.

Instructions: Put a T before any of the statements below you believe are true. Notice the areas that you may want to talk more about. Do the quiz separately, and then share your results.

___ We have talked about our timetable for retirement.

___ We make financial decisions together.

___ We know that our roles may change as we go through transition.

___ Having time together and time apart is important to both of us.

___ Intimacy and affection are an important part of our relationship.

___ We agree on our obligations and responsibilities to family.

___ We have planned for future medical and healthcare needs.

___ We talk about lifestyle and where we may want to live.

___ Social and community connections are a satisfying part of our lives.

___ We have shared values and know what's important to each other.

Where do you fall on the scale below? How many T's do you have in common? Remember, this is meant to be a helpful tool for opening up communication. It's not a measure of your relationship.

Scoring

10 Give each other a big hug. You're ready to write the "how-to" book for couples.

7–9 Sounds like you're in sync. Ongoing communication is important as you plan for "what's next."

4–6 You're on the right track. Practice listening to each other and sharing what's important to you.

1–3 You're not alone. Many couples need help being able to talk about important issues related to retirement and "what's next."

Getting to Yes Together:
The Importance of Communication

"Honey, We Need to Talk!"

Why is it that when men hear this, they often want to run the other way? It's not that they don't care what women have to say; they may just hear things differently. For their part, women often accuse men of not understanding, and they may be right—but not for the reasons they think.

It is not uncommon for couples to come away from a conversation with a completely different understanding of what was said. One reason may be related to differences in how men and women process information. Current brain research suggests that men process and use the logical, more rational left brain to solve problems and perform tasks. They tend to focus on solutions to "fix" the problem. Women, on the other hand, often approach problems more intuitively, from a relational and emotional perspective, using both the right and left sides of the brain. Of course, the reverse can also be true. Many women are "logical thinkers," and many men are more affectively oriented. It is easy to see why it may be frustrating when couples are trying to communicate.

Good communication is the key to a strong, healthy relationship. Understanding the similarities and differences in how you and your partner process information, approach problems, and make decisions can do a lot to help improve communication.

Starting a conversation by talking about your feelings with a partner who uses logic to understand and solve problems can be a setup for disappointment and frustration. Likewise, explaining things logically to someone who is more intuitive and emotional can be frustrating for both of you. Learning to bring up issues in a way that your partner can hear and understand will make a big difference in your communication.

In addition to brain function and processing differences, there are other obstacles to good communication. Cultural or societal expectations can play a role, as well as a couple's relationship issues, personality differences, and family dynamics. What often happens when couples are not in agreement is that one or the other, or both, will react rather than respond. If one or both partners come across as angry and defensive, it is easy for disagreements to erupt into arguments. With so many potential barriers, it is a wonder that couples find ways to talk together at all.

However, some couples do talk and do make decisions together. Others may have a great relationship but get stuck around particular issues. Still others need help in learning the basics of how to have a productive conversation. It can be easy to avoid difficult topics by being too busy, too tired, or too afraid to bring things up because of past experience. Trying to talk together may seem futile. Could the problem be that you keep having the same conversation in the same old way, while expecting a different outcome? If this sounds familiar, you may be thinking, "Why bother?" But maybe what needs to change is how you have the conversation. It does take a leap of faith to be open to learning a different way of communicating when you have been caught up in old patterns. Although we cannot guarantee the results, our experience tells us that trying a new approach can lead to a different outcome.

If people were required to go through basic training in communication, listening skills would be at the top of the list. We learn how to talk at a young age, but when and how do we learn to listen? Have you ever listened to your partner without really hearing what they were saying? How many times have you been tired, distracted, tuned out, or already thinking about your response before your partner was finished talking? Have you ever interrupted, jumped to conclusions, made assumptions, been defensive, or blamed your partner for something? Most of us would have to answer affirmatively to some or most of these questions. Being honest with yourself is an important first step to better communication.

Although we think of communication as a basic skill, it can be complex and frustrating. Communication involves both verbal and nonverbal aspects. It can be confusing if what you say conveys one message, while how it is said conveys another message. For instance, you may tell your partner that you are not angry about his or her being late for a dinner, but your tone of voice and body language send a very different message. The best way to develop positive communication patterns is to commit to the process, practice the skills, and be honest and authentic. Instead of giving a mixed message, you could own what you are really feeling by saying something like, "I feel hurt and angry when I've prepared a nice dinner and you come home late." You are letting your partner know how his or her behavior is affecting you without blaming or being critical.

Even with the best intentions, it can be hard to know how to start a conversation, especially if it concerns a difficult topic. It takes courage and commitment to work toward better communication and intimacy in your relationship. Family background, gender, and cultural and ethnic differences can also determine whether couples are comfortable discussing certain topics. It can be a relief for some couples to have things out on the table, but others cringe at the thought of bringing up issues they have been taught are taboo. You and your partner will have to determine what works best for you. It is helpful when couples are able to find acceptable ways to communicate about embarrassing or sensitive issues. Ultimately, building trust through good communication can lead to greater closeness and intimacy in your relationship.

This section is intended to facilitate communication by offering guidelines and tips for starting the retirement conversation, being a good listener, and communicating clearly and effectively. You need to be willing to practice even if it gets tough—and chances are it will. You can always agree to come back to the conversation after you have both had time to think more about an issue. You may also discover that you are ready to work on the relationship, but your partner isn't. If this is the case, don't despair. From our work with couples, we know that it is possible for one partner to be an agent of change. As we've already suggested, communication can begin to change when one partner alters the pattern by communicating in a different way.

Don't worry if you get stuck or begin to fall back into old patterns. In fact, you can probably anticipate that this will happen. After all, you have been practicing the old patterns for a long time. Progress can feel incremental when you are learning something new. If you come to an impasse, it is probably best to agree to disagree and come back to the conversation after you've both had a chance to think more about it. Agreeing to disagree leaves the door open rather than slamming it behind you and closing off communication. Most importantly, give yourselves permission to be imperfect, and appreciate the progress that you are making together.

COMPROMISE: MAKING COMMUNICATION WORK FOR BOTH OF YOU

When you do feel stuck or conversations begin to escalate into arguments, being able to compromise can be very helpful. In a marriage or partnership, it means that both partners may need to give up something they want in order to get something else they want more: reaching agreement for the sake of the relationship. The goal is to find a way to agree that is acceptable to both of you, even if neither of you gets all of what you want. For example, one evening you'd like to go out to your favorite Italian restaurant, where it's always crowded and noisy. However, your partner wants to have a quiet dinner in a nice seafood restaurant where you won't feel rushed. You compromise and decide to go to a quiet Italian restaurant that also serves seafood. In doing so, the situation becomes a "win-win" where you're both in agreement. Sometimes, compromise means taking turns: "This week I'll clean the bathrooms, and next week will be your turn." When there is a sense of balance in the arrangement, both partners feel valued and respected.

Compromise can feel like sacrifice if you are being asked to give up something that feels very important to you, especially if the stakes are high. There are major decisions to consider when planning your retirement transition, and you probably won't see eye to eye on all of them. Compromises often need to be negotiated, with offers and concessions going back and forth, until you meet somewhere in the middle. Each partner needs to determine how important an issue really is to them. A simple way to do this is by using a scale of one to ten to rate the importance of a given issue. For example, on a scale of one to ten, how important is it for you to live near the city? How would the level of importance change if you lived near public transportation and could easily get into the city? You may find that your perspective changes when you and your partner are able to talk together and consider possibilities that allow for compromise.

Relationships involve a certain amount of "give and take," which may not always be equal. It is a little like a ledger: the balance will not necessarily be one for one all the time. The key, however, is that there does need to be a basic balance. Compromise defines a relationship where both partners cooperate and try to reach agreement for the good of both.

COMMUNICATIONS 101

Tammy's husband, William, was rushed to the hospital with chest pain that turned out to be a mild heart attack. After the initial shock, fear, and finally relief, Tammy realized that if William had died, she would have been overwhelmed, not only by the grief of the loss but also by all the things they had not talked about. She did not know anything about their portfolio of stocks, bonds, and other assets, and had no idea where William kept their will and other important legal documents. Every time she tried to bring up the subject, William said that he was taking care of things. Tammy was angry that her husband wasn't responsive to her concerns. Meanwhile, William didn't understand why his wife was worried, and he tried to reassure her. Tammy wasn't satisfied, but she didn't know how to get William to understand her feelings.

Are you ready to start a conversation with your partner, but don't know how to bring it up? One of the best ways to engage your partner is to let them know how you feel about an issue and ask for help in working toward a solution together. It opens the space for joint problem solving and minimizes defensive reactions.

For Tammy, frustration mounted when she felt William wasn't listening to her concerns. If she started a conversation with him by saying, "You never listen to me when I talk," William would probably become defensive, possibly even patronizing. But if she said, "I need to learn more about our portfolio so that if something happens to you I won't be lost," it's more likely that William will be able to hear what Tammy is feeling and respond more positively to her request.

In the list below, we've compiled suggestions to start the conversation, learn how to communicate effectively, bring up difficult issues, and compromise and problem solve together.

THE 6-STEP PROCESS TO EFFECTIVE COMMUNICATION

1. Starting the Conversation

Even when both partners are committed to communicating, beginning a complex conversation can be difficult. Here are a few tips to help you navigate the process:

- Agree to a time and place to talk with the focus on listening to each other.
- Start with an agreed-upon topic.
- Agree to no blaming or shaming.
- Don't make assumptions.
- Appreciate what you are hearing, even if you don't agree.
- Agree to disagree.
- Remember that it's not about who's right or wrong—it's about being heard and understood.

2. Communicate Clearly

Clear communication starts with using "I" in your statements rather than "you," which can be interpreted as blaming. For example, you might say, "I feel hurt when you don't listen to what I have to say. It's important to me to be heard," rather than accusing your partner of not listening. Using "I" implies being honest and taking responsibility for your thoughts and feelings. It is a way of being assertive without putting your partner on the defensive. Here are a few tips to help you communicate more clearly:

- Express your thoughts and feelings clearly and honestly, and keep it simple.
- Avoid negativity in your speech and body language.
- Use "I" statements.
- Avoid words like "always" and "never."
- Be aware of your tone of voice and body language.
- Don't blame your partner for your feelings.

3. Be a Good Listener

Listening is an essential part of effective communication that takes skill, discipline, and practice. Being a good listener is more difficult than you may think, but it is one of the best ways to show your partner that you want to hear what he or she is saying. To improve your listening skills:

- Stay present; keep the focus on what your partner is saying.
- Make eye contact with your partner.
- Don't interrupt.
- Don't make assumptions about what your partner is saying before hearing them out completely.
- Listen while your partner is speaking rather than focusing on your next response.

- "Mirror back" what you heard your partner say to ensure accuracy.
- Avoid interpreting what you think your partner meant.
- Be aware of nonverbal clues to how your partner may be feeling.
- Avoid being judgmental or defensive.

4. How to Bring Up a Difficult Issue

Some issues are more difficult to bring up than others. When you have something on your mind, think about why it's important to you, what you're feeling, and the pros and cons of discussing it with your partner. It's usually better to get things out on the table instead of holding them inside. To bring up difficult issues:

- Let your partner know there is something important you want to talk about.
- Make a time to talk when you won't be interrupted.
- Turn off the computers, TV, phones, etc.
- Be clear and specific about your feelings.
- Be open to hearing your partner's perspective.
- Appreciate what you hear, even if you don't agree.

5. How to Compromise

Knowing how to compromise is an important communication skill. It's not unusual for couples to have different viewpoints or areas of disagreement. Compromise is not about "right" or "wrong." Instead of becoming polarized in a "win-lose" struggle, a "win-win" solution can be achieved when both partners are willing to make concessions for the good of the relationship. When reaching for compromise:

- Be open to making concessions.

- Approach the conversation with a positive attitude; be open to what you can agree on.
- Be clear about what is most important to you and why.
- Recognize that you and your partner have different points of view—compromise is not about right or wrong.
- Listen to what is really important to your partner.
- If you are disagreeing with your partner, don't shut down and dig your heels in; stay open to possibility.
- Look for "win-win" solutions that work for both of you.
- Don't give in just to make peace—it can lead to anger and resentment in the long run.
- Remember, compromising may lead to creative solutions.

6. Suggestions for Problem Solving Together

Creative problem solving can be an opportunity for growth and sharing responsibility. It's a way for couples to work together as a team to achieve positive outcomes and benefit the relationship. Here are a few tips for facilitating problem solving together:

- Based on your discussion, make a list of the areas that are most important to you individually.
- Take turns sharing one item at a time, alternating between you and your partner. When it is your turn to share, tell your partner what is important to you about the particular item.
- Don't waste time and energy on things you cannot control. Focus on what you can do.
- Make a list of the similarities and differences between your individual lists. Can you find a way to resolve the differences?
- Talk through the pros and cons together. Even if you do

not see eye to eye, you will each have a chance to see where your partner is coming from and how he or she is feeling.

- Start with the issue on which you most agree. Spend time brainstorming how you can work together to accomplish what you both would like. What are one or two action steps to move you toward your goal?
- Continue with other issues, brainstorming each time. Come up with one or two action steps for each issue.
- Remember that problem solving together is a way to share responsibility.
- Seek help if you need it. Talk with a therapist or coach, or find a support group.

SUMMARY

Communicating effectively is probably the single most important factor that predicts successful relationships. When couples can talk together without blaming and without being reactive and defensive, chances are they will have conversations that result in more positive outcomes. Good communication is the foundation for relationships that work. In addition, couples who communicate well, problem solve together, and make joint decisions have more satisfying relationships. There is always room for improvement and for deepening the conversation.

There is no magic wand for "getting to yes together." However, practicing the skills and guidelines suggested in this chapter will help you and your partner develop more effective communication skills and a better understanding of each other's needs and desires. When you each feel listened to and heard, there is greater possibility for honesty, authenticity, and closeness in your relationship.

Talking It Through: Creating Your Shared Vision

Spend some time thinking about the following issues. Use your journal to write down your thoughts and feelings, as well as anything you want to talk about with your partner. The following acronym, BLAST, will help you remember five tips for effective communication.

As you get started, remember, "Have a BLAST!"

- **B**laming gets in the way
- **L**isten without interrupting
- **A**gree to disagree and don't make assumptions
- **S**et a safe space for discussion
- **T**ake time to talk without distractions

Exercise 1

Go it solo: Things to think about on your own

1. What are my habits and patterns regarding communication with my partner?
2. What is working?
3. What is not working?
4. What would I need to change to communicate more effectively?

Exercise 2

Couple time: Things to talk about together

1. Take turns sharing your responses to each question in Exercise 1, one at a time.
2. After each question, make a list of steps you will take individually and together to improve your communication.

3. Discuss how you can support each other to communicate more effectively.
4. Share something positive that you learned about each other.
5. Take time to question anything that was not clear.
6. What's the most important thing you learned from this conversation?
7. Set a time for your next conversation.

Funwork
Do individually and share together

- Choose two or three items from the list you compiled that you will agree to work on immediately. For example, "I will work on not interrupting when you are talking," or "I will commit to putting the newspaper aside when we are having a conversation."
- Make a time to talk, at least once a week, about what is working and what is not working.
- Give each other positive feedback about what is working.
- Brainstorm suggestions that might help to resolve what is not working, and try them out one at a time. Remember that you are on the same team, with the goal of improving your communication and your relationship. Compromise is a great way to get unstuck and reach your goals together.

The 10 Must-Have Conversations

If, When, and How to Retire:
Twice the Husband, Half the Income

For years, Peter had commuted to work by train, traveling several hours a day back and forth. He was up at the crack of dawn and home after dark. Except for vacations and weekends, his time at home was limited. He was looking forward to retiring and being able to putter around the house, snowshoe in the woods, and be out in nature. Peter's wife, Sandy, an artist, worked at home and volunteered in the community. Peter and Sandy had talked about his retirement transition and how it would affect their day-to-day lives. When Sandy's friend Joan asked her how she felt about Peter being home all the time, she responded: "Twice the husband, half the income!"

RETIREMENT YOUR WAY: HAVE YOU TALKED ABOUT IF, WHEN, AND HOW TO RETIRE?

The timing of retirement is usually based on financial considerations, such as savings, assets, Social Security, health insurance, retirement packages, and pensions. But for some couples, money is not the only factor. As roles and responsibilities change, other issues may become equally or more important in mid- to later life. What you need and want in your fifties, sixties, or seventies may be different from what was true earlier in your life. For instance, you may have less tolerance for a work situation that is no longer fulfilling your needs or one that is inconsistent with your values. And priorities may need to shift if your health and well-being are undermined.

Carol and Steve first talked about retirement in their late fifties, focusing primarily on financial goals. They agreed to continue working and retire together when they were both sixty-five. In her early sixties, Carol's company reorganized, and she was transferred to a new division where she was doing work that was neither interesting nor satisfying. She felt like she had been demoted, and resented being supervised by someone younger and less experienced. Frustrated and unhappy, Carol began to dread going to work. Steve was aware of the situation, but he had no idea how close Carol was to quitting. At sixty-two, she could not imagine staying at her job another three years, even though leaving would mean losing health insurance coverage, which had been a big issue in their discussion about when to retire. Steve planned to sell his small but successful accounting business when he retired. He enjoyed his work and rarely complained. But Carol's job was draining her energy and giving her little more than a paycheck. Carol and Steve needed to revisit their timetable for retirement and decide how to resolve the dilemma.

Carol and Steve's situation is an example of how life can bring changes that affect decision making. Couples need to start talking about retirement well before they get there, and then reassess their decisions as circumstances change. Even the best plan may need to be revised. Carol was unhappy and disappointed. She wanted to leave her job but felt stuck, primarily because she depended on her health insurance benefit. Carol and Steve needed to talk about whether she had to "stick it out" until they were both eligible for Medicare, or whether it was possible for her to leave her job sooner. Perhaps there were also other options they had not yet considered.

Carol and Steve talked about their priorities and did some problem solving together, which helped Carol feel supported and more open to possibilities. Steve encouraged her to talk with her boss about how her experience and skills might be utilized in another part of the company. They agreed that if a transfer was not possible, they would find a way to pay for COBRA for eighteen months, which would give them time to figure out what to do. As it turned out, Carol's boss liked her creative thinking and offered her a part-time position that was new and interesting. Although health care benefits would not be fully covered, it was a good compromise and well worth Carol's peace of mind. She and Steve still planned to retire together at sixty-five, but with a somewhat different plan. Meanwhile, working part-time gave Carol the opportunity to begin taking courses and explore new interests.

Decisions, Decisions!

How do couples begin to prioritize and make decisions about whether to retire, when to retire, and how to retire? Is it better to retire separately or together? What if one of you does not want to continue working full-time? What if you both want to retire, but you can't afford to? Many couples who planned to retire early are finding that they need to work well into their seventies. You may not have a choice about whether to work, but there may be creative options for how to work and what you can do given your interests, experience, and skills.

In addition, how can you make decisions that will not jeopardize your financial security? This question is universal, but the solutions are particular to you and your situation. Making important decisions is an ongoing process. As we have seen with Carol and Steve, what you've planned for may change when circumstances change.

Information about health insurance, Social Security, and Medicare is constantly changing. It's important to stay current with the changes in order to have accurate information and facts. In addition, talking about how you feel will help you make decisions you're able to live with. Whether you are in your fifties, sixties, or seventies, you need to think carefully about how you want to use your assets and resources. Hopefully, you can still have fun and do the things that are important in your life, but be sure to consider the pros and cons so that you can make informed choices.

The most important part of decision making is communication. Some couples, like Sharon and Clarence, have based their relationship on good communication, planning ahead, and making decisions together. They may be more the exception than the rule.

Sharon and Clarence began planning their future after they had their first child forty years ago. Retiring together in their early sixties was the vision they are now living. They are both retired from full-time careers but work a few days a week in their respective fields. Part-time work allows them the time and extra income to visit their children, travel, and enjoy their lifestyle. Sharon continues to receive health insurance through the school department where she had worked for thirty-five years. Sharon and Clarence communicate well and make important decisions together. They share similar values and goals and are able to compromise and negotiate differences. For them, the decision about when and how to retire fit into the long-term plan they developed together.

Did You Know?

"Researchers at the Institute of Economic Affairs in the UK have recently identified 'negative and substantial effects on health from retirement.' Their study found retirement to be associated with a significant increase in clinical depression and a decline in self-assessed health, and that these effects grew larger as the number of years people spent in retirement increased." (Bloomberg, June 2013)

The Timing of Retirement

In the short span of twenty-plus years, the timing of retirement has changed. Many employers or organizations had a mandatory retirement age. In addition, retirement benefits were more secure and often more generous, but with a shorter life span, many people did not live long after they retired. Now the timing and concept of retirement has been changing. Decisions can feel complicated when, instead of a mandatory retirement age, the timing of retirement is up to you. You may be asking, how will retiring now affect our financial future? Am I bored, tired of what I'm doing, or just burned out? Am I supposed to retire because I'm sixty-five? It is interesting to note that many people in their sixties and seventies love what they do and have no plans to stop working in the foreseeable future. Others may have lost their jobs due to layoffs and downsizing but are not ready to retire. On the other hand, some younger boomers in their fifties still dream of an early retirement, while realizing it might not be possible. There are many variables and considerations in making the decision to retire, but it is important to be clear about two questions: "Why now?" and "What do I want to retire to?"

🧩 A Note from Dori

Prior to the birth of my son, I worked full-time as a therapist. When my son was born, I cut back my hours to part-time. Then, in my midfifties, I went through training to become a personal and executive coach. The coaching work, often phone based, gave me additional flexibility. I now combine therapy, coaching, teaching, speaking, consulting, and writing—all things that I love doing.

I envision continuing with these activities for many more years.

My husband, David, a physician, worked full-time in an administrative position until he was in his midseventies. After more than twenty-five years, he decided to give up the position, while retaining the clinical work and teaching he loves. He now works part-time and enjoys the combination of work and time off. He envisions working for as long as he is healthy and able to do so. Our retirement transition has included "cutting back" to part-time, using our strengths and skills, and feeling pride and satisfaction in our work. We also feel it is good role modeling for our son, who sees that we continue to be productive and inspired by our work even if we are technically old enough to retire.

Financial Considerations

It is naïve to think that decision making can be based solely on what you want. The realities of living expenses need to be taken into consideration, particularly in an economy where people often have not been able to save adequately for retirement or have lost a large part, if not all, of their savings. You may have been relying on a company pension or healthcare benefits that no longer exist, or maybe you've seen your 401(k)s, Keoghs, or IRAs drop significantly in value. With life expectancy extended twenty to thirty years or more, the dream of retiring leisurely at age sixty-five may no longer be realistic. Many people are working well into their seventies in order to have enough money to last them the rest of their lives. It is wonderful to think about living longer and healthier lives, but we still need to be able to support ourselves. Your ideal lifestyles may not be possible. We have all hopefully learned that get-rich schemes and using instant credit to support an unaffordable lifestyle is a recipe for disaster.

Financial considerations are often the bottom line when you are trying to decide when to retire. Does one of you have a higher salary, better benefits, or more perks? Is there an option to cut back or work part-time and continue benefits if they exist? There are many important factors to consider when you are making financial decisions.

Ultimately, your goal is to come up with a plan you both can agree to. But if you are trying to avoid conflict or appease your partner, you may be setting yourself up for anger and resentment down the road. Working things out may not be easy, but—in the long run—it is certainly worth the time and energy. Solutions do not necessarily come right away. Making these decisions is a process that takes time and exploration. Some people make decisions based on finances alone. But even if you have an unexpected inheritance, win the lottery, or have saved a sufficient amount of money, you will still need to make decisions together about what to do with your assets. Just because you can afford to retire does not necessarily mean that the timing is right for you or your relationship.

Should We Retire Together or Separately?
This is probably the question most frequently asked by dual-career couples. The simple answer is that "one size doesn't fit

all." There are pros and cons to both options and, of course, finances are usually a major factor in the timing of retirement.

Couples with solid relationships and good communication may experience less stress and a greater sense of companionship when they go through retirement transition at the same time. It can be an opportunity for renewal, strengthening, and enjoying time together. But retiring together doesn't work for everyone. Sometimes too much togetherness is just too much. It can foster dependence at a time when people may want the opportunity to work part-time, volunteer, or develop and pursue individual talents and interests. Whether to retire at the same time is an important choice that can have long-lasting effects. Honest and open conversations can help you share your needs and consider what would work best for each of you and for your relationship.

Fortunately, most decisions are not sealed in stone. You may decide to retire at the same time and later realize this was not a good idea. It's okay to go back to the drawing board and reassess. After all, retirement transition is a process, and there is always room for change.

Retire to What?

> *"Retirement is the extra time our generation has been given to dream new dreams, to discover all that we are meant to do and to explore all that we are meant to be."*
>
> —Carleen MacKay, director,
> Mature Workforce Initiatives

Retirement today is very different than it was a generation ago, when the norm for life expectancy was much shorter. With twenty to thirty "bonus" years, we have the opportunity to

Social Security

200K

65 - 69	300/m = 3,600/y	= $18,000
70 - 74	460/m = 5,520/y	= $27,600 45K for 10 yrs
	10 yr cost =	$ 45,600

consider questions such as: What do I want to retire to? What is it that will get me out of bed in the morning? What will give a sense of purpose and meaning to my life? How much do I need to earn so I don't outlive my money?

It is not unusual to be asking these questions at midlife. It is a time of exploration, possible reinvention, and redefining ourselves and our relationships. Many people look forward to fulfillment and satisfaction through the expression of creativity, developing encore careers, or seeing what emerges by exploring their interests and hobbies. Others want the freedom to redesign their current jobs or careers so that work is less stressful and more satisfying, with free time to enjoy other parts of life. Knowing what is not working can help you begin to figure out next steps. It is definitely worth thinking about how you would like to approach your retirement transition.

Not everyone retires to a life of fun and leisure. In fact, the majority of boomers cannot afford to retire and are choosing to continue to work in their field or look for income-producing work outside of their field. "Mature" workers who want to stay in the workforce will need to keep up to date with global trends and learn how to access the knowledge and skills necessary to be current and employable.

As the nature of retirement is changing, some people are choosing to work less or in different ways and slowly "phase" into their retirement, rather than totally retire from their work. As the population of older workers increases, we will continue to see the trend of more people retiring from full-time work but still working part-time or on projects, rather than full-time retirement.

Other options include encore careers and entrepreneurial ventures. An encore career starts after retirement and typically involves an entirely new field, which may mean that additional education or training is required. Many encore careers involve a greater focus on public service and work that is more meaningful or fulfilling. Entrepreneurship, which offers the opportunity for networking, learning, and creativity, is also growing in the fifty-and-over population. Many people in midlife who have worked for large companies and organizations are deciding that it is time to become their own boss.

> *"For many people, retirement from a long-held job is the start of the most satisfying part of their careers. Having built an expertise, a network of work associates, a file of exciting business ideas, and the financial stability to develop them, they become full- or part-time entrepreneurs—unleashing a creative rush that they haven't felt in years."*
> —Edward G. Rogoff, author of *The Second Chance Revolution: Becoming Your Own Boss After 50*

It is never too late to change your focus, to go back to something you loved, have dreamed about, or have not done before. If it is financially feasible, why not take the risk and try? Remember the old saying: "Life is not a dress rehearsal." For example, Maureen's life was transformed when she lost her best friend to cancer.

Maureen graduated from medical school and did a pediatric residency at an urban hospital that cared primarily for underprivileged immigrant families. As a young pediatrician, she had the fantasy of going to Africa to work with women and children. But she was not a risk taker, and her decisions tended to be well thought out and safe. She married Ray, an internist who fit her criteria for being a good husband. Maureen was content: she loved her work and had a trusted partner who was willing to equally share responsibilities for their home. Maureen and Ray decided together not to have children. They were both passionate about their careers, worked long hours, had good friends, and enjoyed their time together. They did not feel they had the time and energy a child required and deserved. At times, they had regrets, but they knew they had made the right decision for themselves.

When Maureen was in her midfifties, her best friend, Carol, was diagnosed with breast cancer. Maureen spent many hours with Carol in the months before her death. They talked about what women talk about: friendship, marriage, children, careers, and what their dreams had been when they were in their twenties. Carol knew about Maureen's dream of working in Africa. She also knew that fear was Maureen's greatest foe. With her own life slipping away, Carol did not want her friend's life to be cut short because of fear. She encouraged Maureen to live her dream, even though she was afraid. Carol's courage in facing her own life and impending death, along with her support and encouragement, inspired Maureen to do something she had never done before: she made a decision that involved change, knowing that her friend would be with her in spirit. Maureen shared her vision with Ray. He was surprised but supportive. In fact, Ray knew of a few other physicians who had worked in Africa, and he helped Maureen get connected. Maureen and Ray had never been apart for long periods of time; they knew they would miss each other. In the months before she left, they spent time talking about the separation and how Ray could arrange his schedule so that he could visit at least twice during the year she would be away.

Maureen left her group practice and took a sabbatical from her hospital position. By the following year, she was working in a small Ugandan village with HIV-positive women and children. Maureen loved the work and had never felt so alive and fulfilled. It had taken the death of her best friend for her to realize that playing it safe might have prevented her from doing what she was meant to do.

Witnessing Maureen's transformation prompted Ray to think about his life. He had always loved his work and had never had a burning desire to do anything else. But Carol's death reminded him that life was unpredictable. He also realized that his years of experience had given him a wealth of knowledge in the practice of medicine and caring for patients in a humanistic way. Although he had always taken his gifts for granted, he knew he had a lot to offer young doctors just going into the field.

During his second visit to Uganda, Ray and Maureen had lengthy conversations about the transitions in their lives and plans for the future. Ray shared his plan to cut back his clinical practice and submit an application to teach at the medical school. Maureen had begun thinking about how she could use her experience in Uganda when she returned home. Both Maureen and Ray felt a renewed sense of excitement and enthusiasm in discovering ways to grow by giving back. They also found that being able to share in each other's accomplishments brought new meaning and satisfaction to their lives and their relationship.

Transition for Maureen and Ray grew out of a significant loss, which evolved into a major change and opportunity in their lives and relationship. When we allow space to open up and face fears as just another part of growth, we can discover new meaning and purpose in life.

"Where talents and the needs of the world cross, therein lies your vocation."

—Aristotle

Encore Careers

Many people approaching retirement are considering the relatively new concept of an "encore career." The term was first made popular by Marc Freedman, CEO of Encore.org (formerly Civic Ventures). (See "Resources," page 275.)

The major characteristics of an encore career are:

1. It is a significant body of work that could entail several years of your life.
2. It takes place in the second half of life, after the end of a midlife career.
3. Ideally, it involves some type of pay or benefits.
4. At its core, it is about the search for new meaning and a deep desire to contribute to the greater good.
5. An encore career is a goal in and of itself. For many people, it is the opportunity to do what they have always wanted to do.
6. It is different from a retirement job, which is a way to make ends meet between the end of one's working life and the beginning of full retirement.

Ricardo is an example of someone who did not initially pursue a dream in his retirement, but then discovered a talent he never knew he had.

Ricardo had always loved cartoons. It did not matter whether they were in magazines, the newspaper, or the comic pages. He would make up humorous vignettes in his head and sometimes tell people about them. His wife, Connie, could see that he had talent, which she encouraged him to develop. One of Ricardo's soccer buddies asked him to sketch out some ideas for an upcoming flyer that he wanted to send out to customers. At first, Ricardo balked, saying he'd never drawn a thing in his life. But he soon became intrigued with the challenge. His friend was delighted with the cartoon and used it for advertising on the flyer. Ricardo began spending more time sketching and found that he loved the process of putting an idea together with a picture that could make people laugh. He signed up for an adult education class to learn the art of drawing cartoons. Before long, friends and relatives were asking Ricardo to do cartoons for birthdays, anniversaries, and other special occasions. When word spread, he began getting requests from people who had seen his work.

Connie was delighted that Ricardo had found something he loved doing and was good at. His prior career as an auditor had been mundane and boring. A funny, more playful part of her husband was emerging, and she loved watching the transformation. Connie believed in Ricardo's talent and ability and enjoyed helping him manage his new business as it took off.

Ricardo did not go looking for what to retire to. By following his interests and doing what he loved, the space opened up for a creative process that allowed his talent to emerge.

Adjusting to Retirement Transition

Surveys and articles related to retirement transition indicate that women generally tend to do better in retirement, in part because of their relationships. Women usually have support through their social systems and experience less loneliness and isolation when they retire. Women also tend to stay in contact with former friends and colleagues and develop connections through joining groups and organizations. As a result, they receive support from other women when they venture out on new paths.

In contrast, men tend to develop relationships with colleagues, which often end when they are no longer working together. Some men describe feeling lost and unfocused when their structure is disrupted and they have no place to go to every day. Men seem to do better with a context that keeps them in touch with others in a productive way. They usually make friends around common interests and activities. Several men in our focus groups talked about how difficult it was for them to make new friends when they retired.

Retirement can be challenging for both men and women who have relied on their jobs and careers as a major source of self-esteem, accomplishment, and identity. For example, Shelly, a real estate attorney, was ambivalent about leaving her practice. She wondered, "If I'm not an attorney, then who am I?" If your work role has become your identity, you may need to consider redefining who you are, who you want to be, and what you have to contribute. If one partner is dealing with issues of identity, chances are it affects both of you. Retirement transition issues can contribute to stress, loss of self-esteem, and depression. It is important to think about how your work fulfilled those needs and how those needs will be met when you are no longer working.

On the other hand, some people relish having more time.

In her early fifties, Evelyn retired from a stressful academic position. She says, "The days pass and I don't seem to accomplish half of what I want to get done. I now wonder how I did it all when I was working. The nice thing is that I now do things in a more mindful way, as opposed to always having to be several steps ahead of myself." Evelyn is busy with many creative projects and is devoted to her two Portuguese Water Dogs. She volunteers at the Dana Farber Cancer Center in Boston, and she loves feeling that she is helping others and giving back.

Still others are forced into retirement before they are ready.

Jim, a former executive, was laid off from a large engineering firm. Unable to find another job, he became depressed and bitter. "I feel like I'm struggling to remain relevant," he admitted. This is a common reaction to job loss, particularly when there has been prestige, acknowledgment, and success through work.

Women who have been at home raising children have to deal with similar issues when their children grow up. All of a sudden, their roles change. They are left to figure out, "Who am I now, and what am I supposed to be doing?" Whether you have worked for a large firm or worked in your home, who you are is more than what you've done. William J. Byron, author of *Finding Work Without Losing Heart: Bouncing Back from Mid-Career Job Loss*, says it well: "If you are what you do, when you don't, you aren't."

What If We're Out of Sync?

Many women put their careers on hold until their children are grown or off to college, then enter or reenter the work force to develop their professional identities. It may be that just as women are stepping into the world in a different way, their husbands are thinking about leaving their jobs, perhaps by transitioning into volunteer work or less demanding, less time-consuming encore careers. They may be thinking about travel and spending more time with their spouse. While husbands are winding down, their wives are revving up. They are both in transition—but the terrain can be very different.

Eduardo and Maria met through their church group and fell in love. Maria was in graduate school at the time, and Eduardo, who was five years older, had gone to trade school and worked for a large construction company as an electrician. They were married a year after Maria got her master's degree in education. She worked as a language teacher for five years but left teaching at the age of twenty-eight, when she became pregnant with their first child. Within the next several years, three more children were born. Maria was constantly busy taking care of the kids, chauffeuring them from place to place, going to doctor's appointments, and doing everything required of a "good mother." In her late forties, though, Maria began to feel like life was passing her by. She had no identity of her own. As much as she loved being a mother, she missed being out in the world as a professional and wanted to go back to teaching.

Eduardo had no idea what Maria was going through. When they finally talked, he was very supportive. Maria signed up for a refresher course at a local college and updated her teaching license. She had no problem getting a job in a system that needed Spanish-speaking teachers.

Maria loved working with the children and being back in the classroom. After three years, she was appointed department chair and then, a few years later, became the head of the regional speech and language division. At the age of fifty-eight, Maria was at the prime of her career and had no desire to retire.

Meanwhile, Eduardo was winding down. He was tired of the job he had been doing for over thirty years. He no longer enjoyed the work, and management was making more demands on employees. He thought about trying to get another job, but at the age of sixty-three, what he really wanted to do was retire. It was a difficult time for Eduardo. He wanted to buy a used camper and travel cross-country like they'd always talked about doing. But when Maria went back to work, everything had changed.

Neither of them had expected Maria to be at the pinnacle of her career in her late fifties. Eduardo loved his wife and was proud of her, but he was also angry that she wanted to continue working. His dream of traveling cross-country had to be put on hold, and he needed to figure out what to do. Eduardo knew that if he didn't leave his job, he would get very depressed. Maria saw how disappointed he was, but she knew that if she gave up her career, she would also be unhappy and resentful. Eduardo finally decided to see a career coach who was recommended by a friend. He began to explore what he might do next. In the interim, he consulted on small construction jobs, which he enjoyed. Eduardo and Maria were able to talk about how they were feeling. Eduardo requested that they create a timeline for retirement. Although he had to put his dream on hold, he wanted to know that at some point they would retire and be able to spend time together.

There are times in relationships when there are conflicting needs, where one partner might make concessions or compromises beyond what they really want. Resentments can build when couples aren't able to talk about and understand each other's needs and feelings. Eduardo's request for a timeline helped him move in a more positive direction, while providing reassurance that things would change in the future.

🧩 A Note from Roberta

My husband, Bruce, officially retired five years ago. It was his eighth and supposedly final foray into the world of "what's next." He was open to part-time consulting but had no interest in working full-time. With a background as a senior executive and experience in sales, marketing, and technology, consulting work had always come easily. But in his late sixties Bruce was confronted with ageism and the realization that being hired was going to be much more of a challenge than he expected. For a few years he enjoyed teaching basic computer and social networking skills to seniors at an Osher Lifelong Learning Institute and our local senior center. But with the recession, followed by some expenses that we didn't anticipate, Bruce made the decision to accept an opportunity that came up unexpectedly. He is again working full-time but looking forward to his next retirement transition.

Several years ago, I left the public sector after a long career in the mental health field. I wanted to continue working with people in ways that involved developing my more creative side. Transitioning into coaching, discovering a love of writing, and developing speaking skills has been part of my process of transition. I am energized and inspired to be doing what I love and loving what I do. Although Bruce is very supportive, he would like for us to have more time together to play. The challenge for us is creating a better balance that includes more time together for relaxation and fun.

Morris and Ruthie had been together for almost fifty years. They grew up in the same neighborhood, played together as kids, and dated in high school. Ruthie went off to college to become a teacher, while Morris went to community college for accounting, working part-time in his father's home-lighting business. Morris and Ruthie kept in touch and saw each other when Ruthie was home on breaks. When she graduated and returned home, Morris proposed, and they were married a year and a half later.

Morris had learned a lot about the business, where he'd been put in charge of managing the books and keeping track of inventory. Meanwhile, Ruthie taught in an elementary school and enjoyed her job. Three years after Morris and Ruthie married, their twins were born. Ruthie took a year off from teaching. When the twins were two years old, Morris's father died suddenly of a heart attack. Morris was grief-stricken and overwhelmed. He missed his father and did not feel that he could run the business on his own, but he didn't want to hire someone from outside the family. He and Ruthie decided that together they would run and eventually grow the business. Ruthie was a terrific saleswoman. She had a good sense of design and liked having control of the showroom. She and Morris made a great team, and for years the business thrived.

When Morris and Ruthie were in their late fifties, a competitor offered to buy them out. Given the economy and the fact that they were both ready to retire, they agreed to sell the business. With the profit from the sale and the money they had invested and saved over the years, Morris and Ruthie were looking at a comfortable retirement. But they had not worked out some important differences. Morris could no longer tolerate the winters and loved hot weather, golf, and boating. Ruthie could not stand the heat year-round and disliked a tropical lifestyle, which she found slow and boring. More importantly, she enjoyed spending time with their grandchildren. Ruthie had no intention of moving to a warmer area.

In all the years they had been together, this was the first time that Morris and Ruthie were deadlocked around a decision. Every time they tried to talk about it, they became polarized. They finally decided to see a couples' therapist, who helped them to work through their dilemma. Morris and Ruthie had never spent time apart, and it never occurred to them to consider this as part of the solution. The therapist helped them think about how it might work. The more they talked about it, the more logical it sounded. Together they decided that Morris would rent a condo for a few months during the winter, and Ruthie would fly down for at least a week during that time to spend time with him. They agreed to try the plan out as an experiment to see how it would work.

The experiment worked out well. Morris and Ruthie both discovered that being apart gave them each an opportunity to get to know themselves better as individuals and pursue their own interests. Ruthie joined a book club and learned how to play bridge. She took her grandchildren on excursions to the museum and introduced them to concerts and the theater. Morris found that he loved to cook and had fun creating new recipes. For the first time in his life, he developed friendships with other men who enjoyed similar interests and activities. When Ruthie visited Morris, they shared their new interests and had a lot to talk about. Not only were they rediscovering themselves, they were discovering a new way to be in a relationship with each other.

Morris and Ruthie's story is in some ways unique. Couples who have run a business together for many years may have some difficult challenges to face in retirement. Morris and Ruthie always found ways to work out business decisions. They each had strengths the other respected and relied on. For their business and their marriage to succeed and prosper, they'd had to be a team. Transitioning out of the business and being faced with decisions about how they were going to retire was a challenge. But it was also an opportunity to work out how their individual needs and desires could be met through a different kind of teamwork and through problem solving in a new way. Morris and Ruthie are a good example of how couples can grow individually and together through their willingness to be flexible and risk change.

WHAT IF THERE IS NO RETIREMENT IN SIGHT?

You may be feeling that none of this is relevant, that being able to retire is just a fantasy. Perhaps you have not saved enough for retirement, or your savings, along with your dreams, were decimated by an economic downturn or unforeseen business reversals. What if one of you has health issues that require unanticipated expenses, or your children have moved back home unexpectedly? Perhaps you have responsibilities for aging parents that need to be considered. Likewise, some people who are laid off take it as an opportunity to begin retirement. But others are not in the financial position to retire and need to look for a job in what can be a tough marketplace, one that can be even more difficult for "mature workers." Part-time or project work might be an alternative for people who need to work and can't find a full-time job.

Life is unpredictable, and there are things we do not have control over. The unexpected can challenge our resilience and resources, but does not have to do us in.

The Myth of Retirement

The postretirement years can be the best ones yet, but you also need to be prepared for a major life change. One of the biggest myths about retirement is that things will be fine and might even be great. After all, look at all that free time! In fact, depression is not uncommon when people are faced with too much free time or find themselves in a void.

Janine and her husband decided together that she would retire a few years before him. Money was not an issue, since Janine had taught in public school for many years and was eligible for a pension and health benefits. She was looking forward to spending more time at the gym, having lunch with friends, and taking an art class. But after a few months, she became bored and felt that she had no purpose. Feeling depressed and anxious, she began to realize that she needed more structure in her life. Janine decided to look for a volunteer position where she could use her teaching skills. She wanted to be doing something that made a difference.

Another myth about retirement is that as long as you're financially secure, everything else will fall into place. As we've seen over and over again, this belief can easily backfire. Money is an asset that can provide a certain amount of security and allows us to buy things we think will enhance our lives. But money, in and of itself, does not buy love, companionship, friendship, respect, self-esteem, joy, or a sense of being part of something greater than oneself. What brings fulfillment in life are usually things that can't be bought. This essential lesson, once learned, can bring a great deal of comfort and joy to the second half of life.

Tips to Help You Deal with Uncertainty

- Talk together about the issues you are facing.
- Clarify your goals.

- Meet with a financial adviser for creative planning.
- Consider cutting back your hours or negotiating ways to make your job more enjoyable.
- Study the trends in the global market so you can assess your transferable skills and consider new skills to develop.
- Brainstorm ways you and your partner can decrease or eliminate expenses.
- Talk with your partner about possibilities for improving the quality and enjoyment of your life.
- Talk with others: they may have additional ideas.

SUMMARY

Needless to say, there are many variables and no simple solutions to retirement decisions. Finances are an important part of the equation when planning for retirement, but there are many other factors to consider when thinking about if, when, and how to retire.

Talking together and being creative, resilient, and resourceful can help you discover options and possibilities you might not have thought about before. Most of us are not like Sharon and Clarence, the couple we met who began planning for retirement early in their marriage. If you have just started planning for retirement, don't be discouraged. You have taken the first step, and by reading this book, you're learning a great deal about what you need to consider. Although the many options and decisions can feel daunting, the beauty of it is being able to design a life that works for you.

Remember that this is just a beginning and only one part of your puzzle. You will not have all the answers right away, and there will probably be more questions. Important decisions take time, and you need to be able to express what you want and hear what your partner is thinking and feeling. Together, you are planning for how you want to live the next part of your life. Later in this book, you will have the opportunity to see how the various parts of your unique puzzle fit together.

Talking It Through: Creating Your Shared Vision

Spend some time thinking about the following issues. Use your journal to write down your thoughts and feelings, as well as anything you want to talk about with your partner. If you need a refresher on how to communicate effectively, go back to "Getting to Yes Together: The Importance of Communication," pages xxxiii–xlv.

As you get started, remember the five tips and "Have a BLAST!"

- Blaming gets in the way
- Listen without interrupting
- Agree to disagree and don't make assumptions
- Set a safe space for discussion
- Take time to talk without distractions

Exercise 1

Go it solo: Things to think about on your own

1. What does the word "retirement" mean to me?
2. What are my thoughts and feelings about if, when, and how to retire?
3. Who am I if I'm not who I used to be?
4. Am I financially and emotionally prepared for retirement transition?
5. Do I think we should retire separately or together?
6. What are my goals for the next stage of life?

7. What are my options if I decide to continue working?
8. What do I want to retire to?

Exercise 2
Couple time: Things to talk about together

1. Take turns sharing your responses to the questions in Exercise 1, one at a time.
2. Share something positive that you learned about each other.
3. Take time to question anything that was not clear.
4. Make a list of the things that you agree on.
5. Set a time for your next conversation.

It is important to remember these are big questions that take time to resolve. You are probably not going to agree on everything; most couples don't. But being able to communicate effectively can help you come to solutions, one conversation at a time.

Puzzle Piece: If, When, and How to Retire
What are one or more factors that you agree are important to consider regarding if, when, and how to retire? Write your discoveries in the Puzzle Piece section at the end of the "Creating Your Shared Vision" chapter, page 263.

Funwork
Do individually

- Imagine that it is five years from now. Write a description of a day well lived. Where are you living? How are you spending your time? Who are you spending time with? How are you having fun? What makes it a special day? Be as specific as possible—start with when you wake up, and imagine the entire day and evening until bedtime.

- Now share this with your partner.

CONVERSATION 2

....

Let's Talk about Money: Finances without Fighting

Paula and Stuart, currently in their midfifties, met on a blind date in their thirties. Sharing a love of movies, art, and ethnic foods, they had fun being together and got along well. They also shared a similar philosophy about money: work hard and spend freely. Paula and Stuart both had well-paying jobs in the pharmaceutical industry and could afford whatever they wanted. Money was not a concern, and neither was saving for the future. They got married in their midthirties, bought a house, and had two children within a few years. Paula's mother, who lived nearby, took care of the children so that Paula could continue to work.

Making money was a priority, and as their careers advanced, they were able to support a lifestyle where only the best would do. They bought top-of-the-line furniture, electronics, and appliances and used an expensive decorator when they remodeled. Stuart's cousin, who was a stockbroker, managed their investments, but saving was not on their radar screen. And they did not have to worry about college expenses, because Paula's parents had set up an education fund when the grandchildren were born.

Paula and Stuart assumed that they would retire in their early sixties and live "the good life." One day on the way home from work, Paula heard a radio commentator talking about boomers not adequately planning for retirement. At first, she thought, "We don't have to worry; we're fine." But as she listened to the commentator talk about the recent economic downturn and decline of the stock market, she began to worry. She remembered Stuart saying they had lost money on investments, but his cousin thought they would be okay in the long run. Paula began to wonder if this was true.

For the first time in her life, Paula began to worry about money and the fact that they had not talked about retirement planning. Stuart thought she was overreacting, but he finally agreed to make an appointment with a financial planner. Prior to the meeting, they filled out a questionnaire regarding their income, assets, investments, debts, and obligations, as well as their vision for retirement. At the meeting, the planner went over their financial assessment and readiness for retirement. Seeing the numbers in black and white was a shock: in order to continue their current lifestyle, they would need to work well into their late sixties or seventies.

Paula and Stuart were jolted into reality. Even though they lived in an expensive house and could pay for just about anything they wanted, they were in no way ready for retirement, at least not as they had envisioned their retirement lifestyle. They had some tough decisions to make in order to start planning for a secure future.

HAVE YOU TALKED ABOUT PLANNING FOR RETIREMENT?

Paula and Stuart did not worry about finances or planning for retirement until they saw the numbers in black and white. Because they made a lot of money, there was an illusion of wealth. They may seem like an extreme example of shortsightedness, but you would be surprised at the number of couples who live this way. The reality of getting older and having to think about retirement often does not hit until we are in our fifties and sixties. It is difficult to start playing "catch up" at a time when you may be overwhelmed with expenses such as mortgages, health insurance, and kids in college or out of school, living on their own and needing help financially. And how many of us have parents who can help with expenses? To the contrary, they, too, may need our support. And then there are couples with moderate incomes, spending money they don't have in order to "keep up with the Joneses." How do they save for retirement? Living in a society that advertises designer jeans when your income cannot stretch that far is a challenge. Those who have not planned well, and even many who have, are waking up to the fact that they will have to work longer than they expected to have enough to retire and not outlive their money.

Why Is It So Hard to Talk about Money?

> "Money is a primary cause of marital discontent and discord. But differences can be worked out if couples give each other the benefit of the doubt, communicate with respect, and listen before reacting."
> —Olivia Mellan, author of Money Harmony

Although money is one of the most important topics of conversation for couples, it tends to be taboo along with sex and death. Talking about money can bring up feelings of shame, guilt, and confusion. You may remember admonitions from your parents that it was impolite to talk about money, to ask what something cost or what someone earned. You may also recall fights or secrets in your family about money. Many of us did not have a clue about how much our parents earned because such topics were kept private.

It can be helpful to think about the impact of history on our views of money. "Leading edge" boomers (those who turned sixty-five in 2011) grew up with parents who were directly impacted by the Great Depression, and frugality framed their lives. They wanted their children to understand the importance of having financial security. Those in the younger boomer cohort may have grown up with more affluence until the bubble burst in the 1980s, or with a more recent economic downturn. Many younger boomers are facing some harsh realities they never expected, including unemployment or a decrease in the value of their assets.

Whether you are aware of the covert messages you have learned about money, the emotional residue can have a powerful impact on attitudes and beliefs. It is no wonder that talking about money is difficult. With all of the mixed messages, confusion, and fear, dealing with money tends to be a major stressor in relationships and a prime factor in divorce. It is distressing to think that many marriages fall apart because couples do not know how to talk about managing money. When couples are willing to talk about the issues and are open to understanding their own and each other's beliefs and opinions, they have a good chance of finding ways to work out their financial dilemmas. Sometimes, however, financial issues can be a distraction from more serious issues in the relationship.

Having accurate information and being well informed can take some of the emotion out of talking about money. Feelings do matter, but—bottom line—when it comes to managing money and planning for the future, it is hard to argue with facts. Conversations that include your feelings and beliefs about money as well as the realities of your unique situation can lead to productive outcomes as you plan for the future. Young couples may talk about their hopes and dreams for the future, but rarely talk about what money means to them or how they will afford their dreams. Meanwhile, older couples may advise newly married couples to talk about money and make decisions together, but it is often a case of "Do as I say, not as I do." Many couples try to avoid arguments by not talking about money, but financial issues inevitably come up. Some typical arguments that get played out over and over again include how to manage money, who pays the bills, levels of tolerance for debt and risk, what to spend money on, who manages the investments, and saving for retirement. Couples often get into blaming modes, with one accusing the other of spending too much or making bad financial decisions. When productive conversations do not happen, anger and resentment can build up. In addition, many couples avoid or are in denial about the need for financial planning because it raises issues they don't want to deal with, such as aging, long-term care, health, and mortality. But these issues eventually need to be dealt with, and sooner rather than later. As Benjamin Franklin said, "Nothing can be said to be certain, except death and taxes." Imagine how much better you and your partner would both feel if you could talk about finances without fighting, while making decisions now that will help you plan for your future together.

Together but Separate
What if you are in a long-term relationship but have not tied the knot? Many couples in midlife and beyond are choosing to live together full- or part-time; their lives and families may be intertwined, but their finances are separate. Sometimes they don't know anything about their partner's financial situation, which can become a sore spot when they are sharing expenses, making purchases together, or planning for the future.

Arlene and Mel, who were both widowed, have been together for over six years. They have their own homes but primarily live in Arlene's condo in the city. Arlene is a successful seventy-year-old businesswoman who has always loved her work and has only recently started to think about retiring. Mel, seventy-two, sold his accounting firm a few years ago and continues to work part-time, although he is ready to retire. They both have adult children and grandchildren who have become part of their life together. Although Arlene and Mel communicate about most things, they have never talked about money or what would happen if one of them becomes ill or dies. Periodically, the issue comes up, but they have both avoided the conversation.

Even in the most committed long-term relationships, money can be a difficult topic to discuss. When couples are in relatively new relationships or when their finances are totally separate, there can be a lot of sensitivity when issues of "who pays for what" come up. It is all the more important for couples to be able to have conversations about their finances and be clear about each other's intentions. If one partner is not able to pay for his or her share of the bills or cannot afford to go on vacation, the other partner deserves to know what is going on.

The Meaning of Money and Money Styles

"Money makes a huge difference in the happiness of poor people...but once you have a decent middle-class existence—food, shelter, and security...the incremental increases have little effect on your happiness."
    —Daniel Gilbert, author of *Stumbling on Happiness*

Although money is a resource and a tool for accomplishing hopes and dreams, it can symbolically represent issues such as self-worth, security, freedom, love, power, or control—issues that go way beyond dollars and cents. We have all heard it said that money does not buy happiness, but it can provide things that help us enjoy life. The question is often, "How much is enough?"

The answer is, "It depends." We all have different tipping points when it comes to money. This can be a huge issue for couples when they are trying to decide if and when they can afford to retire and envision what it will feel like to no longer have a paycheck. Issues about money are usually deeply rooted. It is not just about how much you have in the bank, but more often about your tolerance for discomfort and risk. You may be a saver or a spender, a worrier or an avoider, just to mention a few of the possibilities, while your partner may have a similar or different orientation to money.

If your partner is feeling insecure about finances, it is unlikely he or she will be reassured by a response such as, "Don't worry, honey, it will be fine." Your partner may have good reason to be concerned, and false reassurance not only doesn't help, but also can increase anxiety and fear. Rational or not, feelings about money are powerful and can undermine an otherwise trusting relationship. If the two of you have similar beliefs and values around money, security, and how much risk you are willing to take, planning may be easier. In general, however, there are so many contingencies that it is rare for couples to agree on everything. Talking about finances, even if you are not in agreement, does not have to be contentious. If you are willing to listen, you may learn something new that could change your point of view. Sometimes you have to agree to disagree, which can be good practice for dealing with the "what ifs" and unexpected events that come up in life.

It is normal for issues around money to stir up intense feelings, which may cloud objectivity. When you are considering a life-changing decision like retiring, you want to be as clear as possible and have all of the facts and information necessary to support your decisions. Consulting a knowledgeable and trusted financial adviser can be enormously helpful. A third party can share a more neutral perspective and provide facts without emotional attachment to the outcome.

How confident are you that if something happened to you, your partner would be able to handle the finances? How confident are you that you would be able to handle the finances? No matter your money style, it does not work to avoid talking about the realities of your finances when you are planning for retirement. In many relationships, there's an unspoken agreement about who handles the day-to-day finances, bills, and investments. Maybe one of you does it all, or the tasks are divided. There can be a lot of insecurity about what will happen if one partner becomes ill or dies. Not everyone feels competent to manage money or trusts that their partner can take over if something happens to them. And dealing with money issues is one of the last things a person feels ready to tackle during a time of crisis and grief. This is all the more reason for couples to talk about managing money and making decisions together.

🧩 A Note from Roberta

Going through a traumatic divorce in my late twenties taught me a painful lesson about trust, integrity, and how to take care of myself financially. By the time I married my second husband a few years later, I was managing my finances and starting to put some money away for the future. However, our "money styles" were polar opposites, and finances became a major issue in the relationship. When we tried to talk about how money was being spent, the conversation escalated into an argument. I was unaware of the mounting credit card debt. After eighteen years, some good and others very difficult, we divorced. Instead of hiring a lawyer, we agreed to work with a divorce mediator, which saved a great deal of emotional pain as well as money.

Although I was not interested in getting married a third time, when Bruce and I reconnected after thirty-four years—we had first met in high school—it was *bashert* (a Yiddish word meaning "meant to be"). By then, I had been managing my life and my finances independently for many years. From the beginning, it was clear that we each had a very different relationship to money which, admittedly, raised some red flags for me. Bruce is more of a spender, and I am more pragmatic. I can admire a beautiful piece of jewelry without reaching for my credit card. Growing up, the message was, "if it's not necessary, don't buy it," so spending money has always been associated with guilt. But Bruce and I have been good teachers for one another. He has taught me that some of my beliefs about money are no longer helpful or even valid. He is a believer in enjoying life while you are here. Although I agree, it's also important to know that your future is secure. I have taught him that planning is important. Although it's not easy to bring up some of the difficult issues, something positive usually comes out of the effort.

THE COMPLEXITIES OF FINANCIAL ISSUES

There are many issues affecting relationships that can take a huge financial and emotional toll. Addictions such as alcohol and substance abuse, gambling, and excessive spending are all too prevalent in our society and can go unnoticed or denied until there is a crisis.

Genevieve remarried when she was fifty-four, two years after her first husband died following a long illness. She met her second husband, Martin, when he hired her as an accountant for his contracting business. Genevieve knew that Martin liked to play the horses, but she didn't think it was a problem; he was "just having fun." Martin seemed to be financially stable: he had a successful business, a nice condominium, and he always dressed well. Financial security was important to Genevieve, who was left with very little money after her husband's death.

Genevieve and Martin got along well and enjoyed being with each other at work and at home. Four years into the marriage, Genevieve, who had taken over responsibility for the financial part of the business, began to notice some irregularities in spending. A lot of money was being paid out to companies she had never heard of. When she asked Martin about this, he gave her an explanation that seemed plausible, so for a while she didn't think much about it. But as time went by, Genevieve became suspicious and confronted Martin. At first he was angry and defensive, but finally confessed that he owed a lot of money on some bad bets. He seemed remorseful but denied that he had a gambling problem.

After some coaxing by Genevieve, Martin agreed to see a gambling addictions specialist, but only went once. After talking with her own therapist, Genevieve gave Martin an ultimatum: gambling or the marriage. Martin loved Genevieve and agreed to couples therapy. They have taken a step in the right direction, but if Martin is unable to deal with his gambling problem, he may sacrifice his marriage.

Financial Obligations and Emotions

In addition, previous marriages and blended families add to the complexities of finances. Issues of alimony, child support, college expenses, and other obligations can be financially and emotionally draining. Who pays for what when children from previous marriages are in college, get married, or need financial help? And what about the emotional residue that gets brought into a new relationship, especially when it's related to highly charged financial issues?

Both in their early sixties, Donna and Jerry have been married for eighteen years. They each have three adult children from prior marriages. From early on, they seemed to have an unspoken agreement that Jerry would manage the finances. Donna felt "taken care of" by Jerry, and she was relieved to not have to worry about money. As time went by and both she and Jerry began to have medical issues, Donna started worrying about what she would do if something happened to him. She did not know anything about their investments, what accounts they had, or how to access information and important documents. She feared, as many women do, that she would not be able to manage the finances if Jerry were to die.

Donna knew there were many complex issues they had never discussed. Jerry had been married twice before and had to pay alimony to his first wife, who had never remarried. She and Jerry had separate funds, which were to be left to their respective children. But Donna was not clear whether their joint assets were covered in their will or if their verbal agreement was binding. In fact, she did not know if their assets were held jointly or just in Jerry's name. Donna finally told Jerry that she wanted to make a time to talk about her concerns. She was taken aback when he reacted angrily, accusing her of wanting him to die. She had no idea where his reaction was coming from, didn't understand it, and was dismayed that he was unwilling to talk with her about it.

An intense reaction to a current situation may be related to what is happening in the present, as well as what is being retriggered from the past. Donna's request was totally appropriate, but Jerry wasn't able to hear it. If he had been able to talk with Donna, she might have understood that financial issues in both of his previous marriages felt lethal to him. He was paying a large amount of alimony to his first wife, and his second wife was awarded the house in the divorce settlement. Jerry had gotten seriously depressed after his second divorce and was not sure if life was worth living. When he met Donna, he felt renewed—but when she brought up concerns about money, all he could think about was the past. Donna had no idea what Jerry was reacting to, because he had never shared any of this with her. But Donna had her own issues related to money. Her ex-husband had used money as a weapon of control. When they divorced, she worried that the settlement would not be enough to adequately care for her and the children. Although Jerry knew the facts, he did not understand the underlying feelings Donna had about money.

For Donna and for many others, money brings up issues of power and control. But money is often related to security: "Will we be all right?" Older boomers with parents who grew up during the Great Depression may have gotten the message that no matter how much you had, it was never enough.

Whether you and your partner operate on the notion of abundance or scarcity, financial issues play out in relationships in many different ways. There is a lot of room for misinterpretation when it comes to the meaning of money, which can lead to fear, anger, and resentment when couples are not communicating well. The example of Jerry and Donna may seem extreme, but it is not uncommon. For various reasons, one or the other partner may not want to or know how to talk about the complex issues related to money. It is often less about dollars and cents and more about feelings and meaning.

In contrast to Donna and Jerry, Walt and Cathleen knew they needed outside help to talk about finances. This was a second marriage for both, and between them, they had four teenage children. Cathleen received child support for her two children, which would end when the youngest graduated from college. Meanwhile, Walt paid alimony and child support for his two daughters, who had remained with his ex-wife. Money was a source of anxiety and conflict for them. They felt they could barely keep themselves afloat, and Walt was concerned about upcoming college expenses for his children. They were grateful to have found each other and loved being together, but the financial stress was affecting their relationship. They decided to work with a financial planner to develop a strategy to pay for college expenses and begin to plan for their future. They knew from the beginning that they would be working for a long time. A couples' relationship coach helped them avoid blaming each other for the financial stress as they began to set goals for the future.

Life is filled with unexpected challenges that force us to make difficult decisions. Sometimes, no matter how well you plan or how careful you have been, you find yourself up against decisions you never thought you'd have to make. And there may be times when decisions are taken out of your hands, such as in a severe economic downturn. Many people lose their jobs, are on unemployment, or are working at much lower wages than they are used to. Having to foreclose on your home, claim bankruptcy, or live on your retirement savings is not the "American Dream." You may have bought a home that you counted on as "money in the bank" for retirement, but with a fluctuating housing market, and depending on where you live, your home may be worth less than it was when you bought it. And of course, no one could imagine being the victim of unethical financial schemes or even, in some cases, losing their life savings overnight.

If you have personally experienced any of these traumatic situations, you know how your life can be turned upside down without any warning. Having a supportive network of friends and family is critically important. It is unlikely that money will magically appear, but there are agencies that provide resources, support groups, and counseling to help you get back on your feet. (See "Resources," page 275, for more information.) Most importantly, this is a time when couples need each other's support and love. Unfortunately, a crisis can pull a marriage apart, especially if one partner takes to blaming the other. But adversity can also teach you to rely on each other, be resilient, and work together as a team. Going through a financial crisis is a difficult way to learn that you can live on less if there's no other choice, and it is a useful skill to have as you plan for the future.

Planning for the Future

If you are reasonably secure and comfortable, be grateful. It is harder to take things for granted when you see friends and family losing jobs and struggling to keep afloat. One thing is for certain: change is inevitable. Now, more than ever, it is important to talk with your partner about your financial situation, plan for the future, and make sure you both have whatever information you need to handle things on your own. If you have trusts set up, make sure that you both know where the information is and what needs to happen if one of you dies, even if you appoint someone else to manage the estate.

And make sure whomever you appoint is credible. There are many stories about a surviving spouse, often a widow, entrusting money to someone she or he did not know and eventually learning that the money was misappropriated.

> Donald's mother, Mary, was ninety-two years old when she died. Mary had always been independent and refused to allow her children to take over her finances after her husband died. For several years, her money had been managed by a relative of a friend. When Mary died, Donald, who was executor of the will, realized that his mother had signed over all of her assets to this person, whom nobody had ever met. The family was devastated to learn that Mary had been taken advantage of by a con artist who took off with her money.

Planning for the future does not protect you from adversity, but it certainly is a way to be as informed and on top of things as possible. It is hard enough to deal with an unexpected crisis, but the death of a partner or a divorce can be devastating. Financial issues can be the last thing on your mind when you are dealing with loss. Life does go on, and there are practical issues to deal with. Being prepared can relieve at least some of the stress in a time of grief and loss.

In addition, if you plan to leave money to children or grandchildren, it is helpful to talk with them so they can be prepared to handle their inheritance. Without discussion and preparation, the receiver of "sudden money" is often less able to handle it. (See "Resources," page 275, for more information.)

🧩 A Note from Dori

When I was growing up, there was a lot of fighting about money in my family, with the constant message that there was "never enough."

My parents grew up during the Great Depression. My father was frugal and controlling, while my mother liked to buy things she felt we needed. When I was a teenager, my mother started working and suddenly had her own money to spend. She would buy things and hide them from my father. When he discovered the purchases, there would be more fighting. Given the family dynamics, I learned that I did not want to be dependent on anyone for money and started working at an early age, which probably planted the seeds for my having my own business.

When my father became ill, his need to control intensified, though actually in a good way around money issues. Luckily for my brother and me, in his desire to control what he could in his life, he wanted us to know about their money situation before he died. We learned where he kept his legal documents, the names and numbers on many of the accounts, and how to contact his accountant and attorney. I got my name on checking accounts and access to the safe deposit box. My parents had set up a trust so the surviving spouse would be protected. They each set up healthcare proxies, living wills, and a durable power of attorney. In spite of this preparation, it was still a complicated process after my parents died. My father had numerous accounts in many different funds and, as he aged, he did not keep good records. In addition, my mother had no idea how to handle the finances and did not want to learn.

During our years together, David and I have been able to discuss money issues, which has deepened our relationship. We each maintain our own accounts, which we both think is important, but also have a shared account for our household expenses. We divide the financial tasks: he primarily handles the mortgage, taxes, and investment strategies, and I handle all of the other bills and spending issues. We have discussed our long-term goals with our financial planner and have set up the necessary legal documents to protect the surviving spouse and our son.

Money Offers Choices

Money does not ensure happiness, but not having enough to live on can lead to anxiety and insecurity. Developing financial intelligence and learning how to manage money, whether you have a lot or a little, will put you in a better position to make good decisions. Accumulating a lot of "things" may make you happy in the short run, but as we know, money does not buy happiness. We have met people like Paula and Stuart, who worked hard and didn't give a lot of thought to how much they spent. They were surprised to find they were not prepared for retirement and that, unless they began making other financial choices, they might end up outliving their money. Many boomers have found themselves in this situation, needing to confront the reality of their lifestyle choices. In contrast, saving and amassing great sums of money, but not connecting with people or enjoying life, can lead to isolation and unhappiness. The key is finding a good balance. As we said above, the question is: How much is enough? Some people can live on less and are satisfied, while others will never feel secure no matter how much money they have. Studies have shown that even wealthy people can have fears about becoming destitute. Women, in particular, fear becoming "bag ladies" as they age.

As we age, peer pressure as well as envy can be at work. It is helpful to realize that we do not have to do things exactly like our friends or neighbors. Maybe you have worked hard all of your life but still can't afford to take that dream trip to Hawaii. It's difficult not to be envious when friends are talking about their next big vacation. A certain amount of acceptance is important before being able to see what is possible. On the other hand, you probably know people who are always complaining about not having enough money but continue to employ housekeepers, go to expensive restaurants, and shop in high-end stores. Maybe the scenario sounds too close to home. If so, you would be amazed at how much can be saved over time by just putting aside the money from one expensive meal a week. Try cutting back on the number of coffees you buy and put the money saved into an account. Or put your credit card literally on ice: store it in the freezer for a week and only spend cash on what you really need. (Just make sure nobody eats it for dessert.) You might be surprised to find that, all of a sudden, you are the new role model, you have begun saving money, and your friends are joining you for potluck dinners instead of going out to eat.

WHAT WILL IT TAKE TO HAVE THE LIFESTYLE YOU WANT?

Choosing a lifestyle means making decisions that reflect your attitudes and values. Is it "How much money will I need for the retirement lifestyle I desire?" or "What lifestyle will I be able to have based on the money that is available?" Which comes first, the chicken or the egg?

It's a good question to ask when you are talking about how much money you need for retirement. Do you base your lifestyle on the amount of money you have, or do you decide together how you want to live and set goals around that? You probably need to think about it both ways. If you want to circumnavigate the globe for a year and stay in five-star hotels, you are going to need a lot of money. But if you want a simple lifestyle and don't need a lot of material things, that's a different story. Of course, you will need a certain amount of money to support any lifestyle you choose, but perhaps you have more options than you realize.

Many people expect to spend less when they are "retired." But what happens when you don't have a paycheck coming in? Will Social Security, pensions, or retirement savings be enough? Will you want more vacations and more dinners out than you have previously had? If so, you may need more money rather than less. Or do you think you will have fewer obligations and need less money? You may need money to renovate your home in order to stay in it, or decide to relocate, which can also be costly. There are a lot of issues to discuss. No matter what decisions you make, the challenge is to plan in advance so that you don't end up outliving your money.

Questions to Consider

- How much money is enough?
- Do our priorities reflect our values?
- What are our individual and joint responsibilities and obligations?
- Do we have enough money to support the lifestyle we want?
- Do we agree on what financial or other assets we want to leave to our children, grandchildren, or others?
- Do we share the same views and values about philanthropy?
- What is our strategy for continuing to build our nest egg for the future?

Money Anxiety, Fear, and Creative Solutions

In an economic downturn, fear and anxiety about the future can skyrocket. But couples often do not talk with each other, even if they're both feeling overwhelmed. Most people have had anxiety and fears about money at one time or another. What would it take for you to have a sense of security and stability? What is your tolerance for risk? It's important to be able to answer these questions for yourself and know how your partner feels. You may not be in agreement, but knowing each other's reality can help you find ways to talk and make decisions that you can both agree on. Some fears are realistic and give us warning about what we need to be paying attention to. Other fears may be related to lack of information or an overreaction based on past experience. Fear and anxiety can be paralyzing; information can help test your concerns and may provide a pathway to solutions. Rather than being overwhelmed by your money anxieties or fears, check out what is true and what is not true. If you think you don't have enough money to live on, sit down together and make a list of your income and expenses for at least three months, keeping a record of everything you spend. This will help you begin to track exactly what comes in and what goes out. Seeing numbers in black and white will either be reassuring or get you to take action. In either case, you will have hard facts rather than just fears.

We have seen creative problem solving from people who were not sure how they would manage in a difficult situation. For example:

Barbara, the owner of her own company, realized she could delegate some of the work she did at home to her assistant. This freed her up to bartend two nights a week, which she had enjoyed doing in college. She and her husband, Chuck, wanted to pay for their children's college education but realized they needed to swallow their pride and apply for financial aid.

Jim, a finance executive, discovered he could teach on the weekends at a community college and earn additional money. His wife, who had not worked for years, began looking for freelance editing jobs.

Tamika was good at organizing, and her friends often asked her for help. She started offering her services and charging for her time. Before she knew it, she had a small business growing. She liked earning the extra money and knowing she was helping people organize their lives. Her husband, Sam, was glad that they were able to have some extra money coming in each month.

When you are dealing with anxiety or fear, it can be helpful to think about other transitions or crises that you have faced, either individually or in your relationship. How did you handle it? What did you learn from the situation? You may actually know more about handling transition, fear, crisis, and money than you realize. It is possible to learn how to control fear rather than being controlled by it. No one wants bad things to happen, but that is not always in our control. What we can do is plan and prepare for the future as a way of trying to anticipate and deal with unexpected events, such as job loss, illness, death, declining retirement accounts and investments, or whatever else might come up. The better prepared you are, the easier it will be to go through potentially difficult times together.

Financial Planners, Advisers, and Retirement Specialists

There are many different kinds of financial planners and advisers with varying training and designations who may focus specifically on retirement planning. In addition, some planners and advisers focus primarily on financial issues, while others have a more holistic approach and consider the many aspects of your life, including your personal values and goals. It's important to ask about their level of experience, approach, and services so that you can find someone whom you both trust and can work well with.

Financial experts and retirement specialists encourage people to begin planning for retirement at least five years ahead of time, if possible. If you are reading this book and are already in your sixties, seventies, or eighties, do not panic. It is not too late to start the conversation, and there are usually steps you can take that will make a difference. By the same token, however, do not put it off any longer. The goal is to become conscious and intentional about your money—how you are spending it, saving it, investing it, or giving it away—and how you want to handle these things in the future. Talking with a financial planner can help bring an objective perspective to the discussion.

Tips for Finding a Financial Planner, Adviser, or Retirement Specialist

- Become familiar with the various kinds of financial special-ists and the services they offer. Although the certified financial planner (CFP) designation is the most highly regarded, many planners and advisers with other designations may also be well prepared. (See "Resources," page 275, to learn more.)
- Talk with your partner about what kind of planning services you need: overall retirement planning, investment strategies, or other services?
- Decide whether you want to work with a planner whose approach is more integrative and holistic, or more traditional.
- Get referrals from friends and family. You may want to interview

more than one person before making a decision about who to work with. It is important to find someone reputable who understands your needs and values.

- Before your first meeting, make a list of questions you want to ask. For example: What is their approach to planning? How will the planner help you establish and reach your goals? What services do they provide? How do they follow up with clients? What do they recommend to clients in an economic downturn? How do they make decisions about their own planning?
- Understand how the financial planner earns money: Are they fee-based or do they work on commission?

In addition to retirement planning, most financial professionals suggest saving a minimum of six months' of expenses to cover an unexpected emergency. Not everyone has this kind of solvency. Boomers are not a "one-size-fits-all" generation, and many have responsibilities for children and parents. What is your situation? Do you have children still at home or in college, or living on their own but still relying on you for support? Maybe you have "boomeranging" children who have returned home, children with special needs, grandchildren, or aging parents or other relatives with medical issues whom you help support. Perhaps one or both of you has health issues. There may come a time when you have to prioritize your values and responsibilities and acknowledge that there are limitations, financially and emotionally, to how much you are able to do for others.

Issues to Discuss with a Financial Planner, Adviser, or Retirement Specialist

- What are your hopes, dreams, and goals for the future?
- What kind of lifestyle do you want?
- What are your financial resources and assets?
- What are your financial debts?
- What are your current and future financial responsibilities and obligations?
- How much will you need to retire?
- What kind of financial and nonfinancial legacy do you want to leave?
- Do you have an emergency fund for some of the inevitabilities in life?
- If you're not already receiving Social Security, have you discussed the options of when to apply for Social Security benefits?
- Have you considered factors such as long-term care needs or medical premiums if you or your partner will not be receiving them through your employer and are not yet eligible for Medicare?
- If you are eligible for Medicare, have you learned what is covered and what your responsibilities are?
- Are you sure your will is up to date?
- Are you sure that all of your beneficiary designations on all of your policies are up to date? (See Conversation 7, "Health and Wellness," on page 159 for more information.)

As you read further in this book, it will become clear that the financial "puzzle piece" impacts many of the other conversations such as health and wellness, relationships, and family obligations, including lifestyle options and end-of-life wishes.

For this reason, in addition to talking with your financial adviser, it is also important to consult with a lawyer or an estate or elder attorney so that your financial and legal issues are in order. We will discuss this further in Conversation 7, "Health and Wellness."

SUMMARY

Hopefully, you now have a better understanding about why it is important to talk about finances and make decisions together. Perhaps you have been able to identify some of the things that might be getting in the way of having productive conversations. We encourage you to talk together about what you have learned from this conversation and how that can help you plan for the future. Good decision making starts with honest and open communication; listen to each other and have the flexibility and courage to let go of how you think things "should be" in order to open up to creative solutions. Being able to talk about money can be freeing. It can lead to having more options, reduce some of your financial anxieties and fears, and help you feel more emotionally connected. You may be thinking, "What planet are you on? Every time we talk about money, we end up arguing." The good news is that it is possible to talk about money without blaming, fighting, or going away angry. It is a step-by-step process that begins with understanding each other's "money madness" and eventually learning to solve your financial dilemmas together.

Anxiety and fear create the tension that leads to arguments. Having the necessary information, listening to each other without judgment, and agreeing to work together can be empowering and help the two of you feel that you are on the same page. Talking about your second half of life can be fun and exciting. It helps to know that you are working toward something that you both want, which may be very different from what you have had in the past. We have worked with couples who were able to transform their relationships once the power and symbolism of "the almighty dollar" was dispelled and they learned to share a more realistic understanding of money.

Don't expect immediate solutions. That is probably not going to happen. Money can be a highly charged topic that brings up all sorts of issues for couples, so be prepared and don't over-react. The exercises below will provide you with questions and tools to help you get the conversation started.

Talking It Through: Creating Your Shared Vision

Spend some time thinking about the following issues. Use your journal to write down your thoughts and feelings, as well as anything you want to talk about with your partner. If you need a refresher on how to communicate effectively, go back to "Getting to Yes Together: The Importance of Communication," pages xxxiii–xlv.

As you get started, remember the five tips, and "Have a BLAST!"

- **B**laming gets in the way
- **L**isten without interrupting
- **A**gree to disagree and don't make assumptions
- **S**et a safe space for discussion
- **T**ake time to talk without distractions

Exercise 1

Go it solo: Things to think about on your own

1. What did I learn about money growing up?
2. How has my background influenced the way I handle money now?

3. What meaning does money have for me now?
4. What is our strategy for continuing to build a nest egg?
5. How much of a risk taker am I regarding money?
6. How do financial decisions get made in our relationship? Do I want that to change?
7. What would help me talk more easily about money issues?

Exercise 2
Couple time: Things to talk about together

1. Take turns sharing your responses to the questions in Exercise 1, one at a time.
2. Share something positive that you learned about each other.
3. Take time to question anything that was not clear.
4. Make a list of the things that you agree on.
5. Talk together about steps that you need to take to be more financially secure.
6. Make a time for your next conversation.

It is important to remember that these are big questions that take time to resolve. You are probably not going to agree on everything; most couples don't. But being able to communicate effectively can help you come to solutions, one conversation at a time.

Puzzle Piece: Let's Talk about Money
What financial steps can you take that will give you options for your retirement transition? Write your steps in the Puzzle Piece section at the end of the "Creating Your Shared Vision" chapter, page 263.

Funwork

Before the next time you talk, spend time individually writing down your thoughts about the following:

- If money wasn't an issue, how would your retirement transition look?
- Now talk with your partner and share your thoughts and feelings.

Changing Roles and Identities: I Don't Do Windows

In her late sixties, Ruth decided it was time for reinvention. She had retired from a career as a social worker, working primarily with elders in a community agency. Although Ruth loved her job, she no longer wanted to deal with the politics and stress of cutbacks in public service. She began doing volunteer work in a local assisted-living community, where she was asked to run a small, informal discussion group for women who were interested in talking about their lives and legacies. Reflecting back, many of the women expressed regrets about not having taken more risks in their life. It made Ruth realize how she had always played it safe, not branching out on her own and doing something different with her skills and interests.

Growing up, Ruth had a special relationship with her maternal grandmother, who taught her to knit. Over the years, Ruth became a proficient knitter, making sweaters, scarves, gloves, and other handmade gifts for family and friends. She enjoyed the process of teaching and working with more advanced knitters to create their own patterns. Although knitting had always been a hobby, Ruth started to think about what it would be like to have a business where she could sell her work and offer knitting classes to women of all ages.

At the age of sixty-eight, with no prior business experience,

Ruth began to look for mentors who could support her plans. She talked with women who had started their own businesses and joined a small networking group for women, where she made contacts and got some terrific start-up tips. She applied for and was awarded a grant for women entrepreneurs who were developing new businesses. Ruth was in the process of reinventing herself by integrating her interest in knitting with her love of helping women to develop their creative skills.

Ruth's husband, Charlie, could see that his wife was reenergized and excited. He was supportive and helped her set up some of the systems she would need to run the business. But Charlie was struggling with his own postretirement identity. He had taken an early retirement package from the large company where he had been a senior manager for many years. Charlie had not thought much about what he would do after he retired. He looked forward to having time for projects around the house, catching up on reading, and getting back into a tennis league. For a while, Charlie enjoyed his new freedom, but as time passed, he began to feel like he was wasting time and not doing anything important. With his retirement, Charlie had lost an identity that had sustained him for many years. He had seen a few of his friends go through similar experiences. One became very depressed, and another had started drinking heavily. Charlie knew that he had to begin to redefine himself and decide what he really wanted to do.

HAVE YOU DISCUSSED YOUR CHANGING ROLES AND IDENTITIES?

One of the gifts of reaching the second half of life is being able to reflect on how you have become the person you are and how you might want to continue to grow and change. Midlife can be a time of questioning: "Who am I now that I'm no longer who

I used to be?" and "How can I use what I've learned in the first half of my life to create a fulfilling second half?" In addition, as we grow older, our priorities begin to shift, and we may question the choices that we made earlier in life: "Did I make the right decisions for myself and my family?" "Does what I'm doing now reflect my values and priorities?"

These questions are valid, but the answers may be in conflict with financial responsibilities and obligations to our partner, children, aging parents, or others. What if old dreams and goals are waiting to be revisited in the second half of life or new ones are emerging?

At the age of fifty-six, John was tired of his corporate job and wanted to do something more meaningful. His undergraduate degree was in education, and he had taught for a few years after graduating from college. His wife, Rhonda, had gotten pregnant early in the marriage and delivered twin girls on their second anniversary. When John was offered a job in the corporate world at twice his teaching salary, he decided to take it, although his heart was still in the classroom. John's measure of success had never been how much money he made, but salary was an important part of the equation once the twins were born.

Finally, in his fifties, John knew that he could no longer do work that felt empty. It was a relief to know that college expenses for the twins were covered by savings and student loans, and that it was time to move on. The shift was not easy for Rhonda, four years younger than John, who had difficulty adjusting to change and was concerned about financial security. John and Rhonda spent many hours talking about their differing priorities and how their lives would change with John's career transition.

In leaving the management position that had defined him for many years, John realized he no longer knew who he was supposed to be. In order to grow and feel satisfied, he would need to establish a new identity in the next part of his life. Meanwhile, John's transition forced Rhonda to think about the choices she had made. Being a wife and mother was a role she enjoyed and was good at. It had also given her a reason not to explore other parts of herself. Rhonda had excelled in writing in college and, in her junior year, was invited to be editor for the school newspaper. Because she lacked confidence and was afraid of failure, Rhonda declined the offer. It was a defining moment for her. By turning down the opportunity, her dream of a career in journalism also shut down. She continued to write but never showed her work to anyone. She convinced herself that getting married and having children would be the best path to take.

Now that the twins were in college and John was investing in his new career, it was time for Rhonda to face herself. She had "lost her job" and would need to figure out what to do next. Whether it involved reexploring life as a writer or something else, Rhonda knew that she was going to have to step out of her comfort zone and face some of her old challenges.

The midlife transition can be reminiscent of adolescence, when we're trying to figure out who we are and what we want to be doing, at the same time that we are adjusting to our changing bodies. Like wearing an old suit of clothes that we've outgrown, our jobs, careers, and lifestyles may no longer be a good fit. In midlife, finding what matters often involves letting go of the familiar and looking into the mirror to see who's there. John knew that being true to himself, as well as his values and goals, meant leaving the corporate world. Rhonda knew that moving on with her life would mean stepping out of her comfort zone and facing doubts that had essentially held her back in life.

We all have challenges that come up during times of transition, when roles are changing and identities are shifting. Leaving one career to start another, retiring, realizing that the role you had is obsolete, or, like a domino effect, questioning what's next for you when your partner is making changes: all are examples of identity transitions that are common to midlife.

Did You Know?

In our journey through life, we may have to take a step backward before we can move forward. If we see the step backward as "failure," we can never learn from our mistakes. This back step gives us the opportunity to reflect on decisions, refuel, and retool.

In their book *The Art of Possibility,* Rosamund Stone Zander and Benjamin Zander say, "Instead of getting so dejected by mistakes, we instead [should] exclaim: How fascinating! Another opportunity to learn...Only through mistakes can we see where we're lacking, where we need to work."

How Do You Feel about Getting Older?

When we were young, the popular mantra was "never trust anyone over thirty," which implied they were "old." But our perspective has changed with every passing decade. When you are in your sixties and looking back, "fifty-something" can seem youthful. How often have you heard people say that time passes more quickly as you get older? Wasn't it just yesterday that you turned forty? Is sixty the new fifty? We believe that sixty is really the new sixty! For the most part, our generation believes it is more youthful than previous generations. We are getting older but have a different perception of what it means to age.

You may be starting an encore career, becoming an entrepreneur, taking tennis lessons, or going back to school at an age when your parents were winding down. It is, however, important to be mindful of aging and make accommodations for body parts that no longer work the way they used to. No matter how youthful you may feel, the reality is that we all grow older, time is finite, and no one lives forever.

Tip: Evolving Role Models

Some adult children and grandchildren think that Grandma or Grandpa should "act their age." What does acting like an "old person" mean? As couples, we need to confront our own notions of aging and choose who we truly are. This may include doing things that our children consider outrageous, impractical, or silly. Growing older does not necessarily mean feeling and acting "old." We have the opportunity to be role models for our children and grandchildren, models of "successful aging." Maybe when they get there, they will understand.

A friend of ours tells the story of her nine-year-old grandson exclaiming, "Grandma, you have a lot of energy for an old person!"

The changing perception of aging is partially related to a growing consciousness about health and wellness. How we take care of ourselves impacts aging. We are getting the message that staying active and involved, exercising, and eating well can add years to life and keep us fit and more youthful. In addition, the benefits of a healthy lifestyle increase vitality and give us energy to do the things that create a more fulfilling life. But that is not possible for everyone. Many people suffer from chronic illness, poor nutrition, limited lifestyle options, and other issues. In addition, lack of motivation, resources, and access to adequate health care can be significant obstacles to aging well.

Think about people you know who are getting older. Are they aging with acceptance, vitality, and engagement, or do they struggle with negative perceptions of what it means to get old? Our society tends to marginalize elders with negative connotations about aging. And what you believe can have a powerful effect on how you age. If you think about aging as decline, lack of energy, disengagement, and loss of vitality, then you may be heading toward acting "old" and fulfilling the negative perception of aging in our society. Who do you know who is aging with optimism and vitality? There are, in fact, many role models who have a lot to teach us about aging well.

Ken is an extraordinary man in his seventies who lives life fully, still sharing his many gifts. As a former actor and speaker, he has lived with passion for his craft and the joy of helping others perfect their work. He continues to coach and mentor, and his expectations for his students are nothing less than his expectations for himself. In his presence, his passion for his work is contagious. It is a passion about living, learning, and embracing what is, and bringing your talents and gifts forward, while sometimes discovering ones you never realized you had. Ken lives with optimism and vitality: although "old" in years, he is young at heart. He is a true inspiration and a wonderful role model for aging with the spirit of giving back, sharing his many gifts with those fortunate enough to have crossed his path.

While the traditional concept of retirement conjures up the notion of withdrawing, declining, and deteriorating, renewal in retirement transition is an opportunity for new beginnings. Losses and gains, however, do come with change, and letting go is often bittersweet. When the focus is on "retiring to" rather than "retiring from," there is more opportunity to feel energized as you transition from one stage to the next.

> ### Did You Know?
> Are you planning for a landing or a takeoff? William A. Sadler, PhD, in his book *The Third Age: Six Principles for Growth and Renewal After Forty*, states: "We often think that after age fifty or sixty we should start to throttle down, to slow our approach so as to land safely in retirement...Experiencing midlife today is like reaching the top of a mountain, thinking we have finally achieved our goal, only to find on the horizon an enormous expanse of unknown terrain...Now, from the vantage point of increased longevity, we should see that there are more peaks for us to climb, if we choose to. This new third age frontier challenges us not only to go the full distance, but also to do so with style and a vital sense of purpose."

IDENTITY, PURPOSE, AND MEANING

As we mentioned earlier, one of the questions for couples at this stage is "Who are we now that we are no longer who we used to be?" Retirement transition is a time of letting go of old roles and taking on new ones. If children have been the focus of your life, you may be dealing with "empty nest syndrome." You may be asking, "What is my purpose if my children don't need me in the same way?" Couples who have not had children also experience unsettling changes at this time of life. The focus on achievement often shifts from outward to inward, to questioning the meaning of success and what is really important.

If your profession defined you and was a significant part of your confidence and self-esteem, the conflict can be: "Who am I now without my résumé or my paycheck?"

Jim, a former high school coach, retired at the end of his thirtieth year of coaching. He was not worried because, as he said, "I've practiced retirement every summer for the past thirty years." That summer, Jim and his wife took their dream vacation. But when September rolled around and Jim had no place to go, he felt lost.

Sometimes people find themselves becoming depressed after leaving a job that gave them a time structure, a paycheck, a sense of identity, connection with others, and a sense of purpose and meaning. If, all of a sudden, the job is gone, you may question your reason for getting out of bed in the morning.

🧩 A Note from Dori

David, my husband, had been chair of his medical department for over twenty-five years. He had always said that he would leave that position when the administrative responsibilities were no longer as much fun for him. Finally, he decided it was time to give up the administrative position, but he chose to continue his clinical work. He stayed in the position until a new chair was hired. He was not sure how it would feel to remain in the same department but in a different position. I watched the process unfold. He was able to shift his sense of identity from "chief" and was able to mentor the new chair as she moved into her role, while supporting her authority and position.

He has loved continuing his clinical work and being involved with the medical students and residents. He has no plans to fully retire from work and looks forward to continuing to work for as long as he is able to do so. He has a strong identity as a doctor and also likes to be a role model for our son and for the medical residents, who see him going to work three days a week, being vital and productive as he ages. He pursues other interests, such as golf, hiking, and reading, in his time off. In addition, he has taken on the role of preparing more breakfasts and dinners for us, which I love. He's an excellent chef, becoming even more creative each year!

Shifts and Changes: What If We Don't Want the Same Thing?

What happens if you are experiencing transition as an opportunity for transformation, but your partner wants to retire in a more traditional way? On the one hand, you don't want your partner to feel abandoned, and on the other hand, you need to follow your heart. A lot depends on how well you communicate with each other. If your partner is going full speed ahead on a new endeavor and you are feeling left in the dust, it is important to find a way to talk about it. Recognizing that you are in a life stage transition can help to put things in perspective.

All too often, the impact of retirement transition is underestimated. What gets focused on is the "retirement," but what you are experiencing is a transition that goes beyond the last day of work. When the retirement party is over, the tributes made and the good-byes said, a door closes, and it may feel like your identity is left behind. Everyone goes back to doing what they were doing, while you are left to figure out what's next. If you and your partner have been anticipating the change, then you may be ready to move on. If not, you might be in for a rocky road ahead as you redefine priorities and what you want to do individually and together in the years ahead.

Thomas, a seventy-year-old businessman, began a process of easing out of his high-powered position. He felt it was important to develop plans to transition by spending less time in the office and pursuing some of his interests. In addition to joining a community golf club, Thomas started taking drum lessons, something he had always wanted to do. He met interesting people who shared his love of music, and eventually they formed a group and began playing together once a week. Thomas still goes into his office a few days a week to stay connected but doesn't take on any big projects. In another year he will leave the company, but for now, he is enjoying the transition.

Thomas's wife, Wendy, had been worried about how he would deal with retirement, since so much of his identity was in his work. She was also concerned about the expectations Thomas might have of her. Wendy had not worked outside of the home, but her life was full with friendships and activities that she enjoyed and did not want to give up. She wasn't sure what effect Thomas's transition would have on them as a couple. Wendy was relieved that he was able to plan for transition and develop new interests and friendships. Playing music has revitalized him and given them another enjoyable form of entertainment. They also spend time together with family and friends who don't necessarily share Thomas's new passion. But Thomas welcomes this new part of his identity and feels happier now at age seventy than at many other times in his life.

Men and Women: Adjusting to Retirement Transition

Leaving a job often means losing a community of coworkers, people you had something in common with and who were part of your life. You may not have liked or gotten along well with everyone, but the group represented familiarity. They may have provided a primary support system and maybe even some good friends. You had an identity as part of the group. As much as we want to keep up with people, it takes time and energy to maintain connections, and when you are not a part of the day-to-day work operations, relationships tend to slip away unless there is an effort to stay connected.

Women get emotional support through mutual sharing and identification with each other. When they have a shared bond, it is not uncommon for a woman to know some of the most intimate details of another woman's life. Moreover, women often stay connected even when the common element, like work, is no longer there. To a large extent, a woman's identity is related to the groups she belongs to and the friends she chooses. Many women talk about having a number of different circles of friends, based on their association with community groups, book groups, religious organizations, or groups formed around common interests. Supportive relationships are probably one of the most important things to women, and they learn early on how to nurture those relationships.

Meanwhile, the majority of men tend to connect around activities such as sports and work, where the common interest is more external and their identities focus around doing things together. If most of their relationships have been work related, men may have a more difficult time in retirement transition. Talking with other men who are also in transition can be extremely helpful. There is a quietly growing trend toward groups of men coming together around common issues such as retirement. It helps to know there are other men in the same boat when you're feeling like a fish out of water.

🧩 A Note from Roberta

My husband is part of a men's group that grew out of "Discovering What's Next," an organization in Newton, Massachusetts. (See "Resources," page 275.) About a dozen men meet monthly in each other's homes to talk about issues such as finances, family relationships, health, spirituality, and other topics related to retirement transition. Together they have done community service projects, and some of the men and their wives serve Christmas dinner at a homeless shelter in Boston. The group offers the members an opportunity for connection, support, and learning. Once a year, the wives are invited to a potluck get-together with wonderful food, laughter, and stories. But the best part is seeing the camaraderie and connection shared by this terrific group of men who are supporting each other through their second half of life journey.

WITH ALL OF THIS GOING ON, WHO'S DOING THE WINDOWS?

What happens if you have been tending the "home fires" and decide to go back to work? Or your partner starts working from home, and you think the household responsibilities should be shared? Perhaps you've been doing double duty at work and home, and you want to change the equation. These scenarios tend to upset the balance of who does what, raising the question: "Who's going to do the windows?"

Lorraine and Colin are a couple who had to deal with changing roles when Lorraine, who had a small home-based business while the kids were growing up, jumped at the opportunity for a "real job" just as her husband was retiring.

When Lorraine was fifty-eight, she was offered an office manager position in a friend's medical practice. She loved getting up in the morning, going to work, talking with patients, and developing relationships with colleagues. Her husband, Colin, who was retiring from work, would now be spending a lot more time at home. He was looking forward to doing woodworking, a longtime hobby, and taking courses in furniture making.

Lorraine and Colin talked about their shifting roles, and Colin agreed to take on more of the household chores and responsibilities. He had not realized how much management and organization was involved in running a household and couldn't imagine how Lorraine had done it without help all these years. Finding shortcuts, Colin was able to get the day-to-day tasks done and still have time for woodworking, reading, visiting with friends, and playing golf.

Lorraine began to notice that the house seemed more disorganized and that laundry was not getting done on a regular basis. When she brought this up with Colin, he got annoyed. She was a perfectionist; he wasn't. He told her that if she wanted him to do things at home, she would have to accept that he would do it his way and not hers. Lorraine was upset but realized Colin was right. It was time for her to let go of the way she thought things should be. Like many couples, Colin and Lorraine needed to be flexible and adaptable as they negotiated their new roles and responsibilities.

When couples are going through changes that affect their roles and relationships, the division of labor and how things are done is up for renegotiation. Lorraine and Colin's dilemma is one that many couples share. She does it one way, he does it another, and they get backed in a corner about whose way is better or who is doing more. It is great when the division of labor is equitable, but that does not usually happen. Women often feel they have more than their share of housework, and men feel they have all the fix-it-up projects and yard work. Couples need to work these issues out so that resentment and anger don't build up. If you can afford to hire a housekeeper or someone who does the cleaning or yard work, it can relieve a lot of the burden. But for many couples, that is not possible. They are left with deciding, "Who gets to wash the windows?"

A Note from Roberta

My husband loves shopping for groceries. He clips coupons every week and can spend hours meandering down one aisle and up the next in the supermarket. Because he always checks out the sales, we have a garage full of paper towels, toilet paper, and tissues that could last us for at least a year. But I'm not complaining. I dislike going into supermarkets, which always seem too cold and overwhelming. When Bruce was still working, we often had dinner out or picked up something on the way home. Neither of us had the time or energy to cook. When he retired he did more of the household chores and prepared dinner if I was working late. Now that he's back at work, I do more of the cooking. In general, though, we share the chores and neither of us feels like we are doing more than the other.

Somehow we were able to fall into a routine, which can be difficult for many couples. I am fortunate to have a husband who shares in household responsibilities and, in fact, often does more than his share because he wants it done his way (like loading the dishwasher). But what seems to work best for us is that we each do the chores we enjoy, that we do not mind doing, or know just need to get done. Neither of us really wanted to clean the cat box when our beloved cat, Ballou, was still alive, but someone had to do it. By the way, neither of us has volunteered to do the windows. Maybe we'll just splurge and have them cleaned.

Old Familiar Arguments

If you and your partner are having disagreements about who should be doing what, make sure an underlying "culprit" isn't to blame. You may think you are fighting over household chores, but there may be something more important that needs to be addressed. In addition, anger can surface when an underlying issue gets triggered. One popular example is "How come I always have to be in charge of the social calendar?" It is not uncommon for women to get angry about having to be the one responsible for initiating social plans. It can feel like another job. When the same argument comes up over and over again, it becomes an "old familiar argument" and most likely needs to be put on the list for renegotiating.

Tip: Plan and Experiment Together

Experiment with planning for social activities together. For instance, make a list of movies you both want to see or friends you would like to spend an evening with. Or take turns planning for other activities, such as going to the theater, finding free events in your community, or organizing a potluck dinner. Decide together who will be responsible for different parts of the plan. Be willing to experiment to see what works best. And have fun! A social life doesn't have to be another chore.

Was it really that simple in "Dick and Jane's" time, when fathers went to work and mothers stayed home cleaning and baking cookies? The roles may have been more clearly defined, but that does not mean there was more harmony and satisfaction in relationships. One of the major differences today is that many of us are multitasking and have too much on our plates. Retirement may seem like an ending, but it can also be a beginning of a new phase, with couples figuring out together how all the "to do's" will get done.

SUMMARY

The process of changing roles and identities in midlife and retirement transition is complex and multifaceted. Couples are in it together, but at times, it can feel like a solitary journey, especially when you're trying to reinvent yourself and your relationship. Many people in their fifties and older are looking at what they have done in their lives, who they have been, and "what's next."

As we age, we have the opportunity to grow whole, reintegrating parts that may have been rejected, neglected, put on the back burner, or left behind for any number of reasons. Ideally, we grow in wisdom and experience. The bonus years can be a time of redefinition, but they also can be a challenging time for couples as roles and identities shift. When couples can talk about transition and adapt to change, they are better able to support each other and grow together.

It is important to add that there is a societal shift beginning to reach a tipping point. More and more, we hear of ordinary people doing extraordinary things later in life. Just as boomers have redefined each life phase, the second half of life is undergoing redefinition. We have more teachers to guide us and role models who are paving the way for changing roles and identities in the second half of life. And we are becoming role models of positive aging for our children, grandchildren, and society.

Hopefully, the wisdom and experience of elders will be valued and utilized for the betterment of our society.

Talking It Through: Creating Your Shared Vision

Spend some time thinking about the following issues. Use your journal to write down your thoughts and feelings, as well as anything you want to talk about with your partner. If you need a refresher on how to communicate effectively, go back to "Getting to Yes Together: The Importance of Communication," pages xxxiii–xlv.

As you get started, remember the five tips and "Have a BLAST!"

- **B**laming gets in the way
- **L**isten without interrupting
- **A**gree to disagree and don't make assumptions
- **S**et a safe space for discussion
- **T**ake time to talk without distractions

Exercise 1

Go it solo: Things to think about on your own

1. How do I feel about getting older?
2. What have been my primary roles and how are they changing?
3. What are my values and priorities now?
4. How can I integrate what is important to me into my life now?
5. How can we work together to share household chores?
6. Make a list of the chores you are willing to do and the ones you want to negotiate.

Exercise 2

Couple time: Things to talk about together

1. Take turns sharing your responses to the five questions in Exercise 1, one at a time.
2. Share something positive that you learned about each other.
3. Take time to question anything that was not clear.
4. From your list in Question 5, choose two or three things that each of you can agree to do differently.
5. Make a time for your next conversation.

It is important to remember that these are big questions that take time to resolve. You are probably not going to agree on everything; most couples don't. But being able to communicate effectively can help you come to solutions, one conversation at a time.

Puzzle Piece: Changing Roles and Identities

What have you each discovered about roles you want to let go of and those you want to hold onto or create? Write your discoveries in the Puzzle Piece section at the end of the "Creating Your Shared Vision" chapter, page 263.

Funwork

Before the next time you talk, spend time individually writing down your thoughts about the following:

- Imagine walking on a long and winding road reflecting on who you were as an adolescent and who you are now. What were your dreams then? Are any still on the back burner waiting to be rekindled? Or are there other dreams that you might want to pursue?

- Write a brief description of a dream you would like to be living in the next chapter of your life.
- Now share your responses with your partner!

Time Together, Time Apart:
I Love You and I Need My Space

Sue and Jack have been married for forty years. Their close relationship, the envy of many friends, has been a balance of time spent together and apart from each other. They both traveled for work, but neither was gone for long periods at a time. Weekends were sacred, devoted to spending time with each other and their adopted son, now grown and living abroad. Sue and Jack agreed that traditional retirement was not for them, but they had not talked very much about what they might want to retire to. Their work schedules had always helped them maintain the balance in their relationship, which added to the success of their marriage, and although they loved each other and thoroughly enjoyed their time together, full-time togetherness would not have worked for them.

Sue began to think about what she might want to do well before leaving her job. She thrived on having structure, doing work that was purposeful, and feeling a sense of accomplishment at the end of the day. When she finally left her job, there would be several areas she planned to explore. Jack wanted to work for another few years before doing something more low-key. He looked forward to a different kind of balance, including creative projects like building a shed and rock garden in their backyard. Although Sue loved Jack's ideas, she worried that being together at home "full-time" might drive both of them crazy. It was time to have a conversation about how they were going to manage time together and time apart.

HAVE YOU TALKED ABOUT THE RIGHT BALANCE FOR TIME TOGETHER AND TIME APART?

"Because retirement is no longer 'one size fits all,' it's important for each to be clear about what you want in the next stage, communicate openly with your partner, negotiate the differences—and remember you don't have to be attached at the hip 24/7."
—Lin Schreiber, Encore Career coach and speaker

Sue and Jack had not thought much about how retirement transition would affect their relationship and the balance that had worked so well for them. But when Jack talked about some of the projects he wanted to do, Sue realized this meant that they would be spending a lot more time at home together. They needed to talk about how to prepare for and manage the change.

Women, more often than men, can have difficulty thinking about 24/7 with a partner, particularly if home is their domain. Balancing independence and intimacy can be challenging in retirement transition, especially if one partner wants more time together and the other needs more space. There is a continuum on which couples go from looking forward to being together all the time to having fairly separate lives. Most couples fall somewhere in the middle, but regardless of the particular way you divide your time, communication is key to finding balance in your relationship.

You may know couples who are inseparable and do everything together. What could be wrong with wanting to spend all your time with the person you love? Of course it is not wrong, but not having a sense of separateness and individual identity can foster overdependence in a relationship. When something happens to one partner, the other may be totally lost. It can also feel suffocating to the partner who needs some time apart. The most successful relationships seem to be when both partners enjoy their time together as well as their time apart. We all have our own sense of boundaries and what feels comfortable.

Sometimes couples look back on the early stages of their relationship and wonder what happened to the passion and unending hours together. Being in love is a wonderful place to be, but real-life responsibilities eventually take over, and the demands of work and family often take priority over the relationship. As time goes by and responsibilities grow, many couples find that they don't have much time to spend with each other except for weekends and vacations, and even then, there may be limits. Having dinner together just a few nights a week may be a challenge for some couples. In fact, feeling disconnected because of not having enough time together is one of the reasons couples seek marital counseling.

Tip: Planning a Date Night

Coaches and therapists frequently recommend that couples plan a "date night" at least once a week to have time to connect. If it's hard to make time in your schedules, maybe twice or even once a month would work, just to get the process started. Most couples find they enjoy this time together and want to do it more often. A word of advice: if you allow other things to get in the way of a date night, you will end up back where you started.

Issues arise when partners have different needs and desires for spending time together. You may begin to feel hurt and angry if your husband starts going to the gym three nights a week and there you are, home alone. Similarly, for husbands, you may resent the time your wife spends with her friends or working on projects that don't involve you. Sometimes one partner is involved in a religious or spiritual community even though the other has no interest. It is not uncommon for couples to have individual interests and spend time involved in activities that they enjoy; however, problems arise when one partner feels left out, neglected, or abandoned. Then it's time to talk about how things can change so both your needs get met.

What Will It Really Be Like When You Retire?

People often approach retirement with thoughts of leisurely days, maybe puttering around the house, reading a book, going for a walk, or visiting with family or friends. But you need to remember that even though you may be sitting home "retired," the world still goes on. Relaxation and leisure are wonderful, but too much of a good thing can lead to boredom and leave you wondering, "What am I supposed to do now?" This is exactly why planning is so important. Being too dependent on your partner is not a good idea. Although it is important to plan together, you both need to figure out your own path as well.

🧩 A Note from Roberta

Bruce and I dated on and off for seven years in high school and college before going our separate ways. Thirty-some years later, we reconnected and got married. One of the things I remembered from our early "on and off" years together was that Bruce had an underdeveloped sense of boundaries. When we reconnected and talked about it, he said, somewhat bewildered,

"Boundaries—what's that?" He thought boundaries were something drawn on a map between two countries. He didn't get it. After it came up several times, we talked again, and I became more specific. In fact, I went to extremes, like refusing to allow him to open the car door for me. (I was trying to make a point about not crossing the boundary of my autonomy, but it didn't take long before I realized how silly that was.) Now, fourteen years later, we have a better understanding of each other's needs (and I love when he opens the car door for me). Bruce wants more together time, and I need a certain amount of time and space alone. We are more conscious of each other's needs and respect our differences. When boundary issues come up, we talk them through and try to work out a compromise. We're both getting better at sharing our feelings and listening to each other. It makes for greater harmony and joy in our marriage.

Does this sound familiar?

SHE: Honey, I made plans to have dinner with the Smiths on Saturday night.

HE: You know I don't like Bob—he is always talking about himself. I would rather stay home and watch the game.

Sometimes the roles are reversed and it's the man who pushes for more connection. Either way, this is one of those arguments that can become a theme in your relationship. For example, as soon as one partner starts talking, old and familiar arguments may get triggered and old scripts reappear. A compromise is certainly possible, but each of you would first have to acknowledge and agree to talk about your differences. Maybe you make plans one weekend night with another couple whom your partner enjoys being with, or perhaps you stay home together every other

Saturday night. There are many ways to negotiate the dilemma, but it takes both of you to decide how that will happen. What are other issues in your relationship that come up over and over again and never get resolved? Maybe it is time to talk.

ASSUMPTIONS AND EXPECTATIONS: NEGOTIATING A NEW BALANCE

When Ginny and Doug were in their early fifties, their lives began to change. They both enjoyed their jobs, but they had busy schedules and worked long hours. Ginny finally decided to cut back on overtime and began looking forward to going home early, having a glass of wine, and cooking dinner.

But Doug continued going out for drinks with colleagues a few nights a week and getting home late. The nights he was out, Ginny ate dinner by herself and either read or watched TV. She felt hurt and angry. Although they hadn't discussed it, she assumed that when her schedule changed, Doug would come home in time for dinner. She didn't understand why he was choosing to be with colleagues instead of being with her. A few of Doug's colleagues were attractive younger women, and although she trusted him, she started to feel jealous and insecure. Ginny began to question Doug about who he was with and why he was still going out if she was home. Doug felt that she was being unreasonable. Just because her schedule had changed didn't mean he had to give up something he enjoyed. They began to argue, and most nights, Doug ended up sleeping in the guest room.

Doug began to feel suffocated. He hated the arguments and started staying out later, hoping that Ginny would be asleep by the time he got home. They had always respected each other's time and interests and had rarely felt that their marriage was in trouble. It finally came to a head when Doug left the house after a particularly painful argument. They realized that their marriage was falling apart, and neither wanted that to happen. Ginny and Doug decided to work with a couples' therapist, who helped them to see that their unspoken agreement was disrupted when Ginny's work schedule changed. When they both got home late, they either went out for dinner or brought food in. But when Ginny started getting home earlier, she assumed Doug would come home early, too.

Although they had talked about Ginny working fewer hours, they had not talked about how the change would affect their relationship. With the therapist's help, they worked out a compromise. Doug agreed to scale back his time out with colleagues to once a week. The other evenings they could either have dinner at home or go out. They also talked about looking into an adult education course that they would enjoy taking together. In retirement transition, Ginny and Doug learned to understand and respect each other's needs and create a balance for time together and time apart.

A key issue for couples is clarifying assumptions and expectations, especially when it comes to time together and time apart. Assuming that you know what your partner is thinking or feeling may be a setup for disappointment. Couples who have been together a long time often think that they can "read" each other's mind. Although you may be right, you really can't be sure unless you check it out with your partner. Part of negotiating is accepting how your partner feels, even if you feel differently. Nobody gets to be "wrong." Dealing with time together and time apart is not meant to be rigid or overly structured. It is a dynamic, ongoing process of being open to what you both need and recognizing how things change over time.

For years, Ricardo's schedule was the same: visiting various work sites, overseeing projects, and writing reports. He had been looking forward to retiring from his job as foreman in a construction company. He envisioned himself relaxing, playing golf, and taking day trips with his wife, Tina, a freelance writer who worked from home. Ricardo enjoyed his newfound freedom, waking up early, going to the gym or out for a walk. He found things to do around the house or visited some of the local sights and had coffee with former colleagues. But after several months, Ricardo began to feel restless and bored. He had hoped that Tina and he would spend more time together, but that didn't seem to be happening.

Tina was used to getting up at dawn and having time to do yoga or meditate and have breakfast before she started work. She sometimes met a friend for lunch, went shopping, or visited her mother in the nursing home. Before Ricardo retired, Tina's routine had gone well, but now Ricardo wanted her to do things with him during the day. Tina loved spending time with Ricardo but began to resent feeling responsible for filling his time.

Ricardo realized that the retirement "honeymoon" was over: he needed to decide what to do. Although he did want to spend more time with Tina, he knew that he was unfairly looking to her for a solution. On the other hand, Tina realized that she needed to compromise, which meant freeing up time at least a few days a week to spend with Ricardo. After many years of being used to their routines, things had shifted when Ricardo retired. Although initially disruptive, it led to some positive changes. Ricardo began looking into part-time teaching at a technical school. Tina continued her morning routine, but a few days a week she and Ricardo went out to lunch and planned something for the afternoon. As they spent more time together, they discovered mutual interests they enjoyed pursuing as a couple. With some concessions, Ricardo and Tina adjusted to a new routine, which enhanced their relationship and gave them the opportunity to spend time together in a different way.

Ricardo and Tina had not anticipated what would happen when Ricardo retired. Tina assumed he would find things to occupy his time and her routine would be the same. But when one partner is going through a transition, it inevitably has an effect on the other. When Ricardo was working full-time, there had been a natural flow in their time together and apart. When he retired, they needed to talk about creating a different balance, one that would work for both of them.

🧩 A Note from Dori

Unlike other couples our age, David and I have an adolescent son. Although we traveled a lot together before Louie's birth, we now primarily opt to travel together as a family during school vacations, but have more time together as a couple when Louie is involved in his own programs.

David and I also respect each other's need for individual time and space. Since David is now semiretired and works part-time, every six weeks or so, especially during the winter, he takes a long weekend to play golf with friends. I enjoy the time when he is away and also like the time I am away for talks, conferences, and/or time with friends.

We are a little "out of sync" regarding time together and time apart on a day-to-day basis. Although I work part-time with clients, I am involved with our son's school, professional organizations, and taking various courses, as well as writing, speaking, teaching, and facilitating workshops, so I am often busy during times when David would like me around. He is very supportive of my projects and has activities of his own, but I know it is difficult for him when I get wrapped up in my work for long stretches of time. I work hard to try to balance time apart and time together so it works for both of us.

Negotiation is key to successfully balancing individual and combined interests in times of transition. In the following sections, we explore a number of issues couples in retirement transition face as they work to balance time, interests, and intimacy.

When Home Is the Shared Office

More and more people are working from home, and many are couples. They may each have an office, or share space with separate desks and computer setups. Some plan lunches together, while others work until dinner before closing up shop. Type A personalities may have a hard time relaxing, and it is all too easy to "go back to the office" after dinner. Some couples who work at home like to connect over an intercom during the day just to say hi, to take a coffee break together, or to make other plans. Even when couples have a good relationship and respect each other's boundaries, being in the same house all day with your partner can lead to tension, especially if you have different work styles. As with other issues, honest and open conversations can prevent conflicts down the road. Make sure you understand each other's needs, expectations, and boundaries. It can save you a lot of grief in the long run.

When Things Change with Age

As youthful as you may feel, over time there are changes that impact your physical resilience and energy. We do not all age at the same pace or in the same way, and you or your partner may begin to have less energy for the things you used to do together.

Rosalie and Joe are in their early seventies. They have been married almost fifty years and have two sons and eight grandchildren. For many years, Joe owned a successful travel business, which his sons now run. Joe continued to go into the office three days a week to plan special excursions for some of his long-term clients.

Rosalie had been a real estate broker and started doing sales training for new agents, which she loved. Rosalie and Joe always had a lot of energy and they enjoyed their active lifestyle and being able to travel all over the world together. They particularly loved adventure travel involving physical activities, such as hiking in the Himalayas, biking in Europe, or white-water rafting in the Grand Canyon. Once a year, Joe and his sons went on a "guys'" fishing trip, while Rosalie either stayed home or spent time with friends.

When Joe started having physical problems and limited mobility, he knew it was time to cut back on travel. He was looking forward to doing research on an adventure travel book he was planning to write. Rosalie was also experiencing a shift in energy, but she was not ready to give up travel. She had renewed her interest in photography and went on a photo trip out West with her instructor and several other students. Although Rosalie and Joe had traveled extensively together over the years, they respected each other's individuality and interests. They had agreed that as they got older and things changed, at some point one of them might continue to travel without the other.

As time went by, Rosalie traveled less, but she continued to take pictures and became quite a good photographer. In fact, Joe used many of Rosalie's nature pictures in the book, which ended up being a collaborative effort.

What If Finances Don't Support the Dream?

Ron and Becky met while training in the police academy and got married a few years later. Ron went on to work in the drug enforcement unit and, when their first child was born, Becky took a part-time desk job. She returned to work full-time when all four of their children were in school.

Money was always tight, and vacations were limited to renting a cottage on a lake for a few weeks in the summer or camping in the mountains. But the family enjoyed their time together and looked forward to going back to the same spots and seeing old friends and familiar faces. Becky dreamed about going to Europe, and in her early fifties, she started saving a small amount of money each month in her "Paris Fund."

Ron also had a dream. He had fallen in love with the ocean at the age of thirteen, when he was invited to go sailing with his best friend's family. From then on, he dreamed about buying a boat and sailing to the Caribbean. He often talked about this with Becky, who did not feel safe in the water and could not imagine living on a boat. She also knew that they could never afford a boat. Their discussions had always ended in an impasse, but it didn't matter because retirement seemed so far off.

In their late fifties, Ron and Becky began talking about retirement. At that point, having worked in public service for many years, both were eligible for pensions. But their funds were limited, and their dilemma had not been resolved: Becky had no interest in sailing, and Ron hated to fly. If Becky wanted to go to Paris and Ron wanted to sail, they would have to go about problem solving in a different way. After many conversations, they agreed that although they could not afford for Ron to buy a boat, he could talk with friends who might be interested in sharing expenses for a charter. Becky began to explore reasonably priced tours that she and her sister could do together.

Ron and Becky had never gone on separate vacations, but they appreciated the importance of each other's dreams. They also knew that their dreams needed to fit into the reality of their finances. Together they figured out how they could afford for each of them to have their once-in-a-lifetime experience, and in the process, they opened the space for growth and renewal in their relationship.

No matter how well you have planned, you may finally reach "that age" and realize that you just cannot afford to retire. Whether you want to spend more time together doesn't matter, because one or both of you still has to work. If that's the case, as it is for many couples, having a balance of work, play, and relaxation, separately and together, is extremely important.

Some couples find that if they both work part-time, they are able to save and the burden is shared. Others go back to the books to see how much is really needed and how much is "enough." If you have not already done so, consulting with a financial planner can be an important and useful step. You may find that time is more precious than money and you do not really need as much as you thought you did. Perhaps you are considering a lifestyle change, or your values have shifted. (For more about finances in retirement transition, see Conversation 2, "Let's Talk about Money: Finances without Fighting," pages 31–58.)

Out of Balance

It is not uncommon in midlife to discover a passion or interest that becomes all-consuming. It is like falling in love. You may think about your passion constantly and want to spend all of your time with it. It wouldn't be a surprise if your partner became jealous, angry, or resentful.

In her midsixties, Karen discovered that she had a gift for sculpting. She always looked through the museum school catalogue to see what classes were being offered, but she didn't have the time to "play with clay" while she was still working. When she finally took her first class, she was elated. She loved the process of using her hands to create something unique. Karen signed up for classes two nights a week and often went to the open studio a third night. She stopped playing tennis with her husband, Todd, because it interfered with her studio time.

Todd was angry and felt left out of Karen's new world. Although he was consulting part-time, he thought that when she left her job they would have more time together, but instead it seemed to be the reverse. It was not that Todd didn't have his own interests, but he was missing time with his wife. Being so absorbed in her new passion, Karen had not realized how her behavior was affecting him. She was willing to readjust her schedule so that she and Todd could have more time to do things together, while still making time for her sculpting.

When Health Issues Play a Role

Together, you have gone through negotiating time together and time apart, adjusted to an affordable lifestyle, and are looking forward to the years ahead. Of course, you're not expecting a health crisis just when you get to the good part. But, occasionally, things happen that you have no control over, and you will need to respond.

No matter how well you have planned or worked out your

dream life, the reality of getting older often means dealing with health issues that may eventually lead to one partner taking care of the other. If you have witnessed friends or relatives going through this or been there yourself, then you know how stressful caregiving can be. If there has been a long illness, you may see it coming and have time to prepare. But illness can be sudden, and you may be left trying to figure out what to do and how to cope.

Caregivers may feel responsible, guilty, angry, or a confusing combination of feelings, which can interfere with deciding how much is enough. It is always helpful if you and your partner have talked about the eventuality of one of you becoming ill and the other being a caregiver. Then, at least, you have some expectations to guide you. But the truth is, when something happens, it may feel like you are on your own. This is a time to be able to ask for support. Caregivers need time apart to take care of themselves.

At age fifty-five, Jim was in a serious accident that left him a paraplegic. In spite of his disabilities, Jim and his wife, Carmella, both had positive attitudes and were able to move on and develop a remarkable life for themselves. They renovated their home, making changes to accommodate Jim's physical needs. They traveled together and spent time with family and friends.

But after a few years, Carmella realized she was feeling burned out and needed to take some time for herself. Initially, she felt guilty going on a vacation without Jim, but she realized that her own physical and mental health were important. She knew that taking a break to refuel was part of self-care that would benefit both of them. Carmella now travels with friends a few times a year and comes back feeling renewed.

She also started taking a memoir-writing class with thoughts about possibly putting her experience into words that might benefit others.

When Couples Choose to Stay Together

You probably know couples who have had long-standing resentments or issues that seem to come up frequently. Many couples don't enjoy spending time together, or avoid it because they can't agree on anything. Others have an unspoken agreement about staying together without trying to resolve their issues. We are creatures of habit, and we sometimes choose the familiar, even when it's painful.

Belinda and Clive have been together for thirty-five years. The circumstances of their marriage had more to do with convenience than love. Clive was the primary caretaker of their two children, both of whom had difficulty during adolescence. Although Belinda and Clive argued a great deal when the children were growing up, there seemed to be nothing more to fight about when the kids left home. Over the years the disconnection grew, both physically and emotionally. Although Belinda and Clive continue to live under the same roof, their lives are separate and they rarely spend time together. They have agreed to a lifestyle where security is more important than love.

It's sad but true: some couples argue as a way to stay engaged with each other. When the "source" of the disagreement is no longer there, they either have to find a different way to be connected or the relationship falls apart. Or, like Belinda and Clive, they may stay together but become more disengaged.

ONE THING YOU CAN
COUNT ON: THINGS CHANGE

You and your partner are finally on the same page; you have talked about your needs, discussed assumptions and expectations, and have come to an understanding about how much time you need together as well as separately. Then, all of a sudden, life throws you a curve ball. Something else comes up that you didn't expect: your mother breaks her hip, you need to babysit for your grandchildren, one of you gets sick, or the water pipe bursts. Whatever it is, your plan goes out the window temporarily or, sometimes, permanently, and you have to adjust all over again. Flexibility and resilience are important life skills, no matter how old you are. Having to prioritize your dreams and goals, whether or not you want to, comes with the territory, and often what you thought you wanted most is no longer the top priority.

Things to Consider: Intimacy, Space, and Togetherness

- How will you plan for the adjustment to your changing situation?
- What about privacy needs?
- How will you negotiate space and boundaries if there is too much togetherness?
- How will your roles and responsibilities change?
- How will you each spend your time?

Negotiating space and boundaries can be a huge issue for couples, particularly when they haven't spent a lot of time together on a daily basis. At a retirement seminar, participants were asked what concerns they had about retiring at the same time as their partner. One woman shouted out, "24/7 with my husband!" Although not everyone feels that way, it's not an uncommon response.

SUMMARY

When patterns of time together and time apart begin to shift, paying attention to the balance in your relationship is important. Having the time to finally explore some of the interests that have been put off for years can be an exciting opportunity. But change can stir things up like nothing else, and your relationship needs to be nurtured and supported in the process. Open and honest communication is particularly important during times of change, when you are creating new pathways for the future. The more we grow as individuals, the more we have to bring back to our relationships. A healthy life is a life in balance. The healthiest relationships are usually ones where there is a balance in time together and time apart, recognizing individuality as well as mutuality, and independence as well as togetherness.

Talking It Through: Creating Your Shared Vision

Spend some time thinking about the following issues. Use your journal to write down your thoughts and feelings, as well as anything you want to talk about with your partner. If you need a refresher on how to communicate effectively, go back to "Getting to Yes Together: The Importance of Communication," pages xxxiii–xlv.

As you get started, remember the five tips and "Have a BLAST!"

- **B**laming gets in the way
- **L**isten without interrupting
- **A**gree to disagree and don't make assumptions
- **S**et a safe space for discussion
- **T**ake time to talk without distractions

Exercise 1
Go it solo: Things to think about on your own

1. What makes us a couple?
2. How much "my time" do I need for the things that are important to me?
3. How would I like us to spend time together?
4. What, if anything, would I change if I could?
5. What are my expectations of my partner for time together and time alone?
6. What are my concerns about the time and space issue when one or both of us no longer has the structure of work?

Exercise 2
Couple time: Things to talk about together

1. Take turns sharing your responses to each question in Exercise 1, one at a time.
2. Share something positive you learned about each other.
3. Take time to question anything that was not clear.
4. Make a list of the things that you agree on.
5. Set a time for your next conversation.

It is important to remember that these are big questions that take time to resolve. You are probably not going to agree on everything; most couples don't. But being able to communicate effectively can help you come to solutions, one conversation at a time.

Puzzle Piece: Time Together, Time Apart

What are two or three ways we could compromise so that our needs for time together and time apart are satisfied? Write your discoveries in the Puzzle Piece section at the end of the "Creating Your Shared Vision" chapter, page 263.)

Funwork

Do individually and share together

- Plan an ideal weekend, including your version of time together and time apart, doing things that you would enjoy. We're not talking expensive, we're talking fun!
- Share your responses with each other.
- Take turns telling your partner about your ideal weekend. Can you find a way to incorporate each of your plans into an experience you both enjoy? As an alternative, you may decide to do each of your plans on separate weekends. Get out your calendars, schedule the dates, and make it happen.

CONVERSATION 5

....

Intimacy and Romance:
Love Birds

Patricia and Kevin met their first year in college and fell in love. As time passed, their relationship deepened, and they became inseparable. They were best friends and first-time lovers for each other. They talked about getting married after college and saving for a home and their future. Although they were careful about birth control, in the middle of her junior year, Patricia became pregnant. They married at the end of the academic year, and their first child, Katie, was born four months later. Although it was stressful at times, they loved being parents and continued to enjoy a close and intimate physical relationship. Kevin graduated with a degree in journalism and got an entry-level position as a reporter for a local newspaper. Patricia thought about taking courses to finish her degree but wasn't ready to return to school.

When they moved into a larger apartment, Patricia took a part-time evening job to help out with the budget. A few months later, Patricia found out she was pregnant again, and delivered Devon just before Katie's second birthday. Things changed significantly after Devon's birth. Caring for an infant and a toddler was stressful, especially after Patricia returned to work when Devon was three months old. Patricia and Kevin had started putting a small amount of money away for the down payment on a house. When they had to use the money for living expenses, it seemed like their dream would never come true. They lived from paycheck to paycheck, needing all of their earnings to make ends meet, and continued to work different shifts so they wouldn't have to pay a babysitter. Patricia and Kevin were both exhausted and rarely had time for themselves or each other.

What had begun as a close and passionate relationship shifted to a "task-oriented partnership." Over the next several years, Patricia and Kevin had two more children and continued to work hard to support the family. After several years of sacrifice and saving, they were finally able to move into their own home. They were excited to have accomplished this milestone together. When Patricia and Kevin were able to find time to talk, they shared their feelings and concerns about the distance that had grown between them. The conversations would often rekindle their intimacy and led to the kind of lovemaking they had enjoyed early in their relationship. The glow would last for a few days until life took over again.

Patricia and Kevin loved their children and parented well together, but family responsibilities took priority over their relationship. They both looked forward to having an "empty nest." Even though they would both need to work for several more years, at least they would have time for themselves and for their relationship.

Patricia and Kevin's story is not unusual. A passion that once burned in a couple's relationship often dims with the realities and obligations of life. Having four children, working long hours, and feeling stressed is not conducive to having the time and energy for romantic interludes. But Patricia and Kevin were committed to each other and knew the importance of staying emotionally and physically connected. They never blamed each other for their circumstances and took equal responsibility for the family. When couples value the same things and are able to talk about what is going on, even during difficult times, it bodes well for the relationship.

CAN WE TALK? MAKING EACH OTHER A PRIORITY

Couples in their child-rearing and career-building years often describe themselves as being on "automatic pilot" or feeling like "ships passing in the night." Taking care of themselves and the relationship often gets put on the back burner, with last night's leftovers, while other things take priority. There is often too much to do and too little time to do it. When partners finally fall into bed exhausted and set the alarm clock for 6:00 a.m., making love is probably the last thing on their minds. Some couples make their relationship a priority by reserving time to enjoy each other and spend time together, even if it's not always as often as they might like. They are usually couples who have good communication and a strong relationship.

Tip: Schedule Time for One Another

People schedule appointments, meetings, activities for children, and so on. In a similar way, it is helpful to schedule in "dates" with each other on your calendar. Once a time is written down and blocked out, there is more chance that you'll follow through.

As time goes by and children leave home, there is more time, space, and privacy for intimacy. When couples have paid attention over the years to each other and to the relationship, their fifties, sixties, seventies, and beyond can be a time of renewal, enjoying more time together and deepening their physical and emotional connection. But if the relationship has been neglected, there may be a sense of disconnection or disappointment. Sometimes one or the other partner questions their commitment to the marriage.

🧩 A Note from Dori

Notions about my body, sex, and sexuality were confusing to me as I was growing up. I benefited from the "consciousness-raising" focus of the 1970s, when I began to learn about myself and my sexuality. This awakening also helped me fully appreciate the importance of the interplay of sexuality and intimacy. My own relationship with David has gone through the ebb and flow of our years together. We have experienced issues of infertility, medical problems, body changes, and an increased intimacy as we've aged. Throughout the years our relationship has deepened, and we continue to value, appreciate, and love each other.

INTIMACY AS A BAROMETER

Intimacy can be defined differently depending on the couple, the relationship, and the circumstances. Sometimes intimacy is more physical and less emotional. Other times couples experience both a physical and a more deeply felt emotional connection. For some couples, just being close can be as emotionally satisfying as having a more physical connection. Intimacy can be simple or complex. It is one aspect of a relationship that communicates without words and with meanings that can be overt or covert. A couple's romantic relationship, good or bad, satisfying or not, can be a barometer for other issues. What's important is being able to share your needs and desires with your partner in a loving way. Often what isn't talked about gets acted out.

John and Theresa had an erratic sexual relationship throughout their thirty-year marriage. John liked being physically intimate at least three or four times a week. When things went well, Theresa was more available, but if they had a fight, she disconnected physically and emotionally. At those times, John felt like he was being punished, which made him angry. Not knowing how to talk about the issues, it often took days before the anger passed and they were back to their usual pattern. However, the issues were never really resolved, and things just continued to build up.

A pattern like John and Theresa's erodes trust and safety in a relationship and can eventually lead to a crisis or breakup. Lack of physical intimacy may be experienced as punitive when one or the other partner is feeling emotionally disconnected. This is where being able to talk about what's going on is so important. It is easy to make assumptions about your partner's behavior, but unless you ask, you don't really know what he or she is thinking or feeling.

Disappointments, old arguments, and lingering resentments can get played out in the bedroom and, unfortunately, never get resolved if they are not talked about.

There are couples who stay together but live very separate lives, and others who separate and are still good friends. Some couples continue living together but have an open agreement in terms of relationships. And of course, many couples are committed to each other and their marriage and work very hard to find ways to change and grow within the relationship. We are a generation that is creating our own norms.

Romance Is More than Intercourse
The physical expression between partners goes through changes as the individuals and the relationship change over time. Some

men and women believe that physical satisfaction is the goal of intimacy. Others, and women in particular, talk about the importance of emotional connection, intimacy, and even spirituality in lovemaking. Mutual satisfaction is more likely when couples are able to talk together about their preferences.

> *"The core power of sexual connection is its ability to transform our lives, at any age."*
>
> —Gina Ogden, PhD, author of
> *The Heart and Soul of Sex*

Studies have shown that many older adults enjoy lovemaking more as they age. Emotional maturity, a renewed sense of freedom, feeling less inhibited, decreased pressure of time, and being freed up from earlier responsibilities seem to have a positive effect on the sexual lives of older adults. Couples report having more fun and enjoying giving and receiving pleasure in many ways, not just with intercourse.

No matter whether you continue to have intercourse as you age, the needs for intimacy, warmth, sharing, and feeling loved and cared about are ageless. Taking comfort in the familiar, accepting yourself and your partner, and finally being able to let go of issues and concerns about body image can be an enormous relief and open the space for renewed pleasure and satisfaction. The lovemaking between two people can feel relaxed and mutual, reflecting emotional closeness as well as physical satisfaction.

LOVE, PHYSICAL INTIMACY, AND AGING

Beginning a new relationship in the second half of life, meeting someone after having been divorced or widowed, or never having married—none of these experiences are easy, but they can be a life-affirming experience. We all love to hear stories of high school sweethearts reconnecting after many years, couples who meet and fall in love after a chance encounter, or who perhaps develop a relationship after meeting over the Internet. Whether within your existing partnership or in a new one, the possibilities for renewed love and intimacy in midlife or later abound.

Melinda was forty-five years old when she and her husband divorced after twenty-three years of marriage. At the time, she had no desire to begin dating, and instead focused her life on working part-time as an editor and taking care of her three high-school-aged children. Even when her children were off on their own, Melinda was content to pursue some of her many interests, including art and nature. She dated casually and thought she was in love once or twice, but the relationships didn't work out.

Then, at the age of seventy, Melinda met the love of her life. Andrew was sixty-four, his wife had died a few years earlier, and he was just stepping back into life. Melinda and Andrew had an immediate connection; they both enjoyed physical activity and being in nature, and they loved going to the movies together and sharing their passion for good food. They began spending a lot of time getting to know each other.

As their attraction grew and the relationship became more romantic, Melinda started to get nervous. Since meeting Andrew, she had become more aware of the changes in her aging body. Looking in the mirror was difficult. Not only was Andrew six years younger, but he was very good-looking and had been dating women in their fifties. Melinda hadn't had an intimate relationship in quite a while, and she wasn't sure her body would "still work." Although she knew that Andrew was attracted to her and admired her youthful attitude and zest for life, she wasn't sure how he would react to her aging body. Melinda's fears dissipated as their physical and emotional relationship deepened and they were able to share openly with each other.

It's Never Too Late to Find Love and Companionship

"Love, intimacy, sex, and meaningful relationships are not the exclusive domain of the young."
—Connie Goldman, author of *Late-Life Love: Romance and New Relationships in Later Years*

Sam and Lila, eighty-eight and seventy-seven, respectively, were both widowed and living in an assisted-living community. They were introduced through other residents and found they had many interests in common. They loved talking about current events, taking walks, doing crossword puzzles and playing Scrabble, and visiting with each other's children and grandchildren.

Although they had separate apartments, sometimes Lila would stay overnight with Sam. They also traveled together. Everyone could see the deep fondness they had for each other and how enlivening the relationship was for both of them. Lila and Sam made a point of enjoying each day and looking forward to the next.

When Sam died, five years after their relationship had begun, it was sad and difficult for Lila. She said, "It was like becoming a widow a second time." She talked about the wonderful relationship they had, how enriching it was for both of them, and how thankful she was for their time together. Lila and Sam's family still stay in touch with each other.

Finding Love through the Internet

Carmen and Joe met online. They were both in their sixties, divorced, and neither had children. Social and outgoing, they both had been playing the dating game for a few years and were somewhat jaded. Meeting when they did was a once-in-a-lifetime experience. Their story may seem like a fairy tale. Most couples "don't get it all," but for Carmen and Joe, it happened.

Joe was initially put off by Carmen's attitude when they talked on the phone. She had dated a lot of men and was discouraged about whether she would ever meet someone who was honest and sincere. She wasn't interested in casual relationships or men who were looking to be taken care of. Carmen wanted a committed relationship, an equal partner, and someone she could have fun with. Marriage was not necessarily in the picture. As they got into the conversation, however, Carmen became more receptive. She was attracted to Joe's ease and sense of humor. They talked for quite a while, learning about each other's lives and their mutual love of dancing. By the end of the conversation, they decided to meet at a local restaurant. Joe suggested a caveat. If they liked each other, they would go dancing after dinner. If one or the other didn't want to take the next step, the evening would be over. They both agreed they were too old to play games and wanted to be up front and honest.

When Carmen and Joe met in person, there was an immediate attraction. They had a wonderful time over dinner, with no question that they would go dancing. A year and a half later, they are together in a monogamous relationship with no immediate plans. They both like having the privacy of their own homes, but stay with each other on weekends. They seem to have just enough of the right ingredients for a close and satisfying relationship. They both agree that not living together keeps their relationship alive and exciting.

The Body Plays a Role

It is easy to joke about hot flashes, menopause, and the decrease of desire as we age, but physical intimacy can be impacted by hormonal changes. Psychological and emotional factors also play a role. In our later years, physical arousal can become a "chicken and egg" phenomenon: hormonal changes can have an impact on our emotions and how we feel about our bodies, and conversely, our emotions and feelings about our body can affect hormonal levels. When you feel good about yourself, you have more resilience to cope with your changing body and often rediscover a more accepting sense of yourself.

Eric and Charlotte were in their early sixties and had been married for sixteen years. Together they had seven adult children from previous marriages. For the first several years they were together, their physical relationship was mutually satisfying. But this changed when Charlotte went through menopause at the age of fifty-four and gained a lot of weight in a short time. She was unhappy with herself and less interested in intimacy. Eric felt confused and upset about Charlotte's lack of interest in physical intimacy and his own decreasing libido, which he thought might be related to her weight gain.

Eric and Charlotte avoided talking about these issues, which they found painful and humiliating. Charlotte went on periodic yo-yo diets, losing weight and then gaining it back. She finally decided to talk with a therapist and get some help with the issue. The therapist suggested that Eric be involved in the process as well, since the issue related in part to both of them.

It can be difficult for couples when there is a change from intimacy and closeness to a distance that affects their physical relationship. It is hard to know how to address these sensitive issues without anger, blaming, or hurting each other's feelings. Talking together and getting support is important. It makes sense to check out the possibility of there being a physical explanation, which is sometimes the case. If so, help may be available.

The Impact of Medical Issues

Medical issues at any age can affect physical desire and drive. People with heart conditions may experience a decrease in desire, as well as physical symptoms such as shortness of breath, decreased energy, stamina, and endurance. Diabetes can cause poor blood flow, fatigue resulting from fluctuations in blood sugar, and difficulty reaching orgasm. Depression, stress, and fatigue not only drain energy, but also cause a lack of interest in pleasurable experiences, including lovemaking. In addition, medications taken for high blood pressure, depression, and other conditions can play a part when it comes to interest, arousal, and performance.

Andre developed prostate cancer when he was in his sixties. His wife, Antonia, was in her fifties. Andre was afraid the cancer would kill him, as it did his father. As a result, he opted for the removal of his prostate, which, at the time, didn't include nerve-sparing procedures. Andre didn't realize the impact the surgery would have on his marriage. He recovered well physically, but emotionally he was depressed and frustrated that he was unable to "perform" in the bedroom. Feeling ashamed and humiliated, Andre threw himself into work, where he could still feel powerful and in control. He began avoiding Antonia by going to the gym early in the morning and working late. Antonia felt abandoned and angry. She missed her husband, who seemed less and less available. She also missed their intimate physical relationship and felt that she was too young to be going through this. Antonia finally confronted Andre and asked him to make an appointment to talk with his doctor. She wondered whether her husband's problem was more psychological than physical. Andre, fearing that Antonia was thinking about leaving him, agreed to make the appointment. It was a stressful time in their marriage, but with medical intervention and the help of an excellent therapist, Andre and Antonia were eventually able to reconnect emotionally and physically. Sometimes things do get to the breaking point before couples are able to seek help.

There are many reasons for a decline in interest or ability to enjoy physical intimacy. One of the first steps may be a thorough exam to make sure there is no underlying medical issue or adverse effects of medication. Once the medical issues are addressed, there are therapists and coaches specifically trained in helping couples deal with issues of physical intimacy in their relationship. (See "Resources," page 275.)

IS IT OKAY TO TALK ABOUT AND ENJOY MAKING LOVE?

Many of us grew up at a time when anything related to our bodies and pleasure was a taboo topic. The message for girls, in particular, was often "good girls don't do it" or "good girls don't like it." The pendulum swung in the seventies with the advent of the women's movement, which encouraged women to embrace their bodies in positive ways. Many women of that era "reclaimed" their bodies and a sense of pleasure. Others struggled with persistent conflicting messages and did not feel comfortable embracing what they had been told was "bad." Likewise, men have experienced conflicting messages about being macho versus being warm, considerate, and gentle.

🧩 A Note from Roberta

I first learned about sex when my Girl Scout leader handed us a book titled *Becoming a Young Woman*—in other words, getting your period. I showed it to my mother, who had little to say. When I finally did start menstruating, her response was to slap me on my face (a warning that I could now get pregnant) and tell me to ask my older sister what to do. I figured it out on my own, which was pretty much my story growing up. That was my introduction to "womanhood": the message that talking about sex was taboo and potentially dangerous. This was the fifties, when "good" girls didn't—and those who did were "sluts." This attitude shaped a lot of my early experience and took time to overcome. Learning to appreciate my body and to honor the role of sexuality and intimacy in my life has been a gift.

Today we get messages from movies, television, and the Internet that making love is supposed to be spontaneous, easy, and fun. But where is the message about the importance of couples talking about their relationships? Without communicating, how can you know what feels good to your partner and what doesn't? How does your partner know what turns you on or what turns you off? Making love is not necessarily intuitive. Lack of communication can and does lead to false assumptions, blaming, anger, hurt feelings, and disconnection. It's often not easy to have a conversation about your physical relationship, even in a loving and trusting relationship. Old belief systems and inhibitions can get in the way, making you feel uncomfortable and embarrassed. Yet taking the risk to talk can be worth it. Just being able to start the conversation can help you feel more connected and begin to approach the issues together.

WHEN THE INTERNET REPLACES ROMANCE

The Internet has become a complicated double-edged sword when it comes to physical intimacy. In some respects, the Internet provides an incredible resource for almost anything. However, it has also been a "third party" in many relationships, with partners often finding themselves in competition with their spouse's computer. Although it can be a big issue, it is often a harmless one unless it progresses to addiction, something far more serious. If online relationships begin to take the place of your partner, that's a red flag: a sign of a potentially serious threat to your health, well-being, and marriage. Another red flag is spending more virtual time with your partner than real time. If virtual food was all that you had to eat, you would starve.

Did You Know?

Older adults are one of the fastest-growing groups being infected with sexually transmitted disease, including HIV/AIDS, according to the Center for Disease Control and Prevention. Reasons for this include:

1. Many people over age sixty are dating and are physically intimate with their partner(s).
2. Many older people don't know how to prevent the spread of diseases transmitted through intimate

contact and aren't comfortable talking with their doctors and asking questions.

3. Many doctors, healthcare workers, and educators are
   not comfortable talking with middle-age and older
   people about their intimate physical relationships,
   drug use, and other risky behavior.

The best protection against diseases transmitted by
physical intimacy is to have just one partner at a time
and to talk with that partner about risk prevention.

SUMMARY

Intimacy and romance are more than just intercourse; they involve the interplay of body, mind, and spirit. The paradox of intimacy and aging is that although sexual desire may decrease, or even come to a screeching halt, as we get older the potential for greater intimacy and satisfaction can deepen. Intimacy can fuel the heart and soul of a relationship. The premise of this book is that one of the greatest obstacles for couples is lack of communication, and this is especially true when it comes to physical intimacy. Being able to talk about the most intimate parts of your relationship with love and respect can lead to a deeper connection and often a more satisfying physical relationship.

The second half of life holds the opportunity for rediscovering yourself and your partner. As we age, not only do our bodies change, but also our perspectives on life. Hopefully, we have learned well from our life experiences and come to our fifties, sixties, and seventies with wisdom and maturity. How well do you really know who you are now, and who your partner is now? Getting to know each other as you are at this time of life can be interesting and exciting and lead to a more fulfilling relationship. Although renewal of intimacy in the second half of life can feel like a risk, the rewards are usually well worth it.

If you are feeling stuck, talking with a therapist or coach trained in emotional and physical intimacy issues can be extremely helpful. (See "Resources," page 275.)

Talking It Through: Creating Your Shared Vision

Spend some time thinking about the following issues. Use your journal to write down your thoughts and feelings, as well as anything you want to talk about with your partner. If you need a refresher on how to communicate effectively, go back to "Getting to Yes Together: The Importance of Communication," pages xxxiii–xlv.

As you get started, remember the five tips and "Have a BLAST!"

- **B**laming gets in the way
- **L**isten without interrupting
- **A**gree to disagree and don't make assumptions
- **S**et a safe space for discussion
- **T**ake time to talk without distractions

Exercise 1
Go it solo: Things to think about on your own

1. What messages did I get as a child about my body and physical intimacy?
2. What is my definition of intimacy?
3. What role does physical intimacy play in my life?
4. What do I enjoy about our intimate relationship?
5. What changes, if any, would be more satisfying for me?

Exercise 2

Couple time: Things to talk about together

1. Take turns sharing your responses to Exercise 1, one at a time.
2. Share something positive you learned about your partner.
3. Take time to question anything that was not clear.
4. Make a list of the things that you agree on.
5. Set a time for your next conversation.

Puzzle Piece: Intimacy and Romance

What are two or three things that could add to your enjoyment of romance and physical intimacy? Write in the Puzzle Piece section at the end of the "Creating Your Shared Vision" chapter, page 263.

Funwork

Do individually and then share with your partner

- Think about what would help you feel more intimate with your partner.
- Share this with your partner.
- Surprise your partner by doing one or more of the following, or come up with your own ideas:
  - Based on your partner's response, find something that would help him or her to feel more intimate.
  - Send your partner a love letter by snail mail.
  - Set the ambience for a romantic evening: light the candles, turn on music, warm up the oil or choose your favorite lotion, and offer to give your partner a massage.

- Plan an evening or weekend together in which each of you contributes one or more romantic elements. (Or each of you can plan a romantic time with your partner.)

Relationships with Family: The Theory of Relativity

For most of his working life, Monty was a foreman and then a manager in a steel plant, and his wife, Belinda, taught in a preschool. Neither of them was good at managing money, and they accumulated several thousand dollars in credit card debt over the years. When their children, Andy and Michelle, started middle school, Monty and Belinda decided it was time to get some help with finances. They realized they had not planned well for the future, and they needed to start saving money so that Andy and Michelle could go to college. With the help of a good financial adviser, they were finally able to consolidate their debt with a lower interest rate and start to put money away for the kids' college education and for retirement. While they were eventually able to accumulate enough for college expenses, retirement would still be a stretch.

Monty wanted to teach Andy and Michelle to be responsible about money. He did not want them to be in the predicament he and Belinda had been in. When they were teenagers, Andy and Michelle were each given a monthly allowance to budget. If they ran out of money, they would be out of luck. Belinda did not agree with Monty's approach. She thought that children could learn responsibility over time and did not need to feel so burdened. She felt badly when Andy ran out of money before the month was up and always gave him a few dollars. Michelle was good at managing her money and rarely asked Belinda for extra cash.

Andy and Michelle were able to go to college on savings, scholarships, and loans. They paid for day-to-day expenses with money they had saved working during summers. Monty was proud that he had taught his children well.

Several years went by, and Andy and Michelle both married and had families. But when Andy's eldest son, Mike, was a senior in high school, Andy asked his parents for help to pay for college. Monty blew up! He was furious that Andy had not planned for Mike's college education and had missed the application deadline for loans. Monty could not believe that Andy was asking them for money. Andy knew how tight things had been and that Monty could not afford to retire. In addition to being angry, Monty was hurt. He felt that Andy was taking advantage of them.

Although Monty wanted his grandson to be able to go to college, he was adamant that it was Andy's responsibility. Monty was also worried about what it would mean financially for himself and Belinda. The couple had differing opinions about what to do. Belinda had always thought Monty had been too hard on Andy. She felt that it was their responsibility as parents to help him. Whatever money they had would be left to their children and grandchildren anyway, she thought, so why not help them when they needed it? She was brought up to believe that you do not say no if someone you love is in need.

Monty and Belinda went back and forth, becoming more polarized in their positions. They finally decided to compromise and make their decision based on the reality of their finances. After going over the numbers and talking with their financial planner, Monty and Belinda finally agreed to pay room and board for Mike's first year at school, with the caveat that Andy meet with their financial planner and fill out a loan application for the following year. The immediate issue of money was taken care of, but the incident had an effect on family relationships. Monty and Belinda need to find ways to talk about their differences regarding family obligations. Hopefully, at some point, Monty and Andy will also be able to talk about their relationship.

HAVE YOU TALKED ABOUT FAMILY OBLIGATIONS AND RESPONSIBILITIES?

Monty and Belinda's dilemma was complex, but not uncommon. Money is a particularly difficult issue, one that inevitably brings up relationship issues or feelings from the past. (See Conversation 2, "Let's Talk about Money: Finances without Fighting," page 31.) For Monty, there was the reality of their financial situation and how much, if anything, they could afford to contribute to their grandson's college education, complicated by the relationship issues with his son. For Belinda, the decision was clear: you have a responsibility to your family when they are in need.

Have you and your partner discussed your responsibility to your adult children and grandchildren? What if someone you love needs a place to live? Or your elderly parents become ill and need care? What if your heart says one thing, your head says another, and your gut has a totally different opinion? Whether you are talking about children, parents, other relatives, or maybe even friends, you and your partner may not agree on where your obligations begin and end. This can be difficult for couples who do not share the same values. Being clear about your own feelings and knowing where your partner stands is a good place to start the conversation.

We live in a society with cultural, ethnic, and religious intermarriage, traditional and nontraditional relationships, and many couples are part of a blended family. Each partner may bring different beliefs, values, and sense of family responsibilities to the relationship —and it can be complicated, to say the least. The following sections explore some of the many complex issues that can arise in relationships with parents, children, and grandchildren as we age.

RELATIONSHIPS WITH CHILDREN

Sally and Frank had been married for fifty years. Having grown up in single-parent homes, they wanted to convey the importance of family to their children, Carrie and Todd. When the kids were young, Sally was involved in their school activities, always being the first to volunteer in the classroom or go on school trips. Her life as a mother and wife was fulfilling and gratifying. When grandchildren came along, she and Frank were delighted. They often babysat on weekends or had the kids sleep over. Sally's priority was being a good mother and grandmother.

Things began to change when Todd was offered a job in his father-in-law's San Francisco–based company. Sally was devastated when Todd and his family moved away and started spending holidays with his wife's parents.

Carrie, who was divorced, still visited Sally and Frank, but not as frequently, as her kids were involved with their own activities and spending time with friends. The past seemed like a distant memory, and Sally no longer felt needed. Frank tried to cheer her up, but she was inconsolable. She finally talked with a close friend, who helped her understand that her children had to adapt to the changing needs and priorities in their own lives. Sally eventually began to see that she had been holding on to an idealized vision of how families were supposed to be and trying to protect herself from the reality of how things were.

Sally and Frank were going through a major life transition. Their lives, especially Sally's, had been focused on the needs of their children and grandchildren. It was now time to let go and begin to refocus. This realization helped Sally see that she and Frank had accomplished an important goal in raising and supporting their children, but that they now needed to talk about their relationship and how they wanted to live the next part of their life. Since they had never had time for travel, they thought maybe San Francisco would be their first stop. Sally and Frank had fun planning their itinerary. They would stay in San Francisco exploring the city, going to museums and cultural events, and then spend time with Todd and his family.

"Together parents and emerging adults need to craft a way of finding a balance between losing touch and smothering each other. It is a journey into unknown territory and will remain so for the rest of our lives."
—Dr. Ruth Nemzoff, author of *Don't Bite Your Tongue: How to Foster Rewarding Relationships with your Adult Children*

Have you experienced that defining moment when, all of a sudden, you realize that your children are grown up and they don't need you in the same way? Maybe it happened when they left home for college, landed their first job, or got married. One day you're telling them they have to be home by midnight, and the next day you have no idea where they are, whether they are home, or how they are living their lives. You discover you have very little say in what your children do in life or who they choose to be with. Children grow up and have lives of their own. You have done the best job possible to raise them and, at some point, it is time to let go. The challenge can be how to let go and stay connected at the same time.

You may now be "empty nesters" with fewer responsibilities, and although it can be a huge financial and emotional relief, it can also be hard to let go of "what was," adapt to "what is," and consider "what's next." Some couples struggle with this change, while others find they welcome it and love their newfound freedom. In either case, you are facing decisions and life stage challenges, redefining your roles, and planning for retirement or whatever is next. What is unique about this life stage is that both you and your children are in transition, which can be an exciting as well as a difficult time for everyone.

Did You Know?

"The sooner you begin to prepare for the empty nest (even if it never empties!), the smoother the transition you will make to this new and challenging stage of life." —David and Claudia Arp, coauthors of *Fighting for Your Empty Nest Marriage*

Not every couple has the freedom to experience an "empty nest." Whether or not they have children, some couples may be responsible for the care of aging, dependent parents who may be living with them and require a lot of attention. This can be a burden emotionally and financially, with couples finding that they have very little privacy and time for each other. If you do have children, relationships with them change as they grow up, become adults, and have careers and families of their own. One of the most interesting challenges for parents is "What kind of relationship will we have with our children now that they are adults?" Most people do not think much about it, but as time passes, life happens and roles shift and change. There may be a lot of adapting to the "what ifs." Perhaps you have very different political views, or your son has a finance degree but wants to be an artist. You and your daughter-in-law may not get along, or your children move cross-country and you don't get to see your grandchildren very often. Any number of scenarios is possible. When relationships have been close, we come to trust that they will continue, but there is no guarantee.

Lillian and her son-in-law, Herb, can't seem to see eye to eye on anything, from how to cook a turkey to how to raise the kids. Because Lillian doesn't want to put her daughter in the middle, she usually bites her tongue. But there are times when she feels like she will explode. Lillian would like to have a conversation with Herb but doubts he would be open to it.

When our children bring their partners into the family, the dynamics become more complex. If you're lucky, everyone gets along and the son- or daughter-in-law becomes a part of the family. But it doesn't always happen that way, and there can be painful divisions and bitter feelings that are difficult to heal. Lillian made an assumption that Herb would not be open to getting through some of the obstacles in their relationship. If she approaches him with that attitude, she'll probably prove herself right. But if she can be honest and sincere, and not put blame on Herb, she may be pleasantly surprised. A gesture of goodwill may be just what's needed to open the door for a more positive relationship. It doesn't hurt to try, especially if you can value the trying and not get too attached to the outcome.

For couples who have had conflicts with or about their

children during the parenting years, this time of transition may be an opportunity to resolve past issues and heal old wounds. It sometimes takes years for healing to happen. Sadly, however, there are times when reconciliation either does not happen or isn't possible because it is too late.

Yours, Mine, and Ours

For better or worse, divorce and remarriage are common in our society, affecting the lives of adults, children, and extended families. Common patterns include

- Split families, in which your children may still be living with you, your ex-partner, or on their own.
- Blended families, or "yours, mine, and ours." These are families that may be like the Brady Bunch, but there are different versions in which you both have children from previous relationships and perhaps have one or more children together. In fact, if you first had kids when you were very young, it is possible that your most recent children are the same age as your grandchildren. On the other hand, if you did not have children until later in life, your children may be the same age as your friends' grandchildren.

Family structures can be very complex with a multitude of dynamics, especially in large families. Jim and Grace's story illustrates some of the complications that can arise.

> Jim and Grace were both divorced when they met and fell in love. Being in their sixties, they felt that time was passing, and they wanted to get married and start their lives together. They had both gone through difficult divorces, and relationships with their adult children were strained. Jim had paid child

support for years while his kids were growing up and continued to help support his son, who was irresponsible and had
difficulty holding a job. One of Grace's daughters had never
forgiven her for leaving the marriage, and their relationship
went through cycles of acceptance and rejection.

Although Grace constantly tried to make things better, she
always felt like she was walking on eggshells around her daughter. Despite the ongoing issues, Jim and Grace loved spending
time with the grandchildren they had between them, going to
the kids' sports events or taking them out for day trips. But as
the kids got older, it was harder to schedule which games and
events to attend, since they didn't want to disappoint anyone.

Jim and Grace were also challenged by the ongoing issues
they had with their children: Jim's son had lost another job
and asked him for help, while Grace's ex-husband remarried,
which was difficult for her daughter. The stress they were
experiencing with their children began to cause tension in
their own relationship.

Jim and Grace knew that if they did not start resolving some
of these issues, they could end up divorced, which neither
of them wanted. They both needed to step back, set some
limits with their children, and begin to make their relationship a priority. Jim and Grace found things that they enjoyed
doing together and began to let go of some of the relationship
"debts" that had been paid long ago. They had done their jobs
as best as they could, and it was time for their children to take
responsibility and accept the reality of their lives.

Whether you have been with the same person for years or
have had more than one marriage, chances are there are conversations you and your partner need to have about relationships with your children. You may not agree with each other on

everything—you probably will not—but it is important to talk about how you both feel and begin to find solutions you can all live with.

Issues like "yours, mine, and ours" can become extremely problematic later in life if you have not planned together. For instance, wills, material legacies, and end-of-life decisions can be fertile ground for family feuds. Talking with an estate attorney who has had experience with complex family situations can help you make some of the important decisions that affect everyone. There are also family and elder-care mediators who work with families in dispute about assets, resources, and other issues. (See "Resources," page 275, for more information.) In addition, it's helpful if your children know what your wishes are should you get sick, disabled, or die.

The Boomerang Child

Guess what? Your kids are back!

More than twenty-two million adult children are living at home with their parents, per the U.S. Census Bureau in May 2013. This phenomenon, known as the "boomerang child," refers to adult children moving back in with their parents. Adult children may return to the nest for a variety of reasons, including financial problems, job loss, or relationship issues. Often, they come with their children.

Stephen and Marla's daughter, Alison, married and began having children in her early twenties. Stephen and Marla worried that the couple was too young to take on the responsibilities of marriage and a family, but they liked their son-in-law, Jake, even though the relationship between him and Alison seemed tense at times. Stephen and Marla loved being with their grandchildren and always had a hard time saying good-bye. They returned home savoring the memories, yet happy to be in their own space.

But life changed drastically when Alison found out that Jake was having an affair. She called Stephen and Marla, who agreed that she and the children could stay with them until things stabilized and she decided what to do. For the next couple of months, life was chaotic for everyone. The children were upset, and when bedtime came, there were tantrums and crying. Marla began preparing meals, but they refused to eat what she made. Mealtimes were erratic and stressful.

Before Alison moved in, Stephen and Marla had just begun to enjoy life after retiring. They had started pursuing individual interests and spending more time together, doing things they both enjoyed. They often went out to a movie during the week or got together with friends. They liked the simplicity of their lives and the peace and quiet of their home.

All this changed when Alison and the children arrived. The kids were upset; they missed their dad and were having a hard time at school. Things were out of control, the house was a mess, and much of the burden fell on Stephen and Marla, who began to feel resentful. As a result, the tension between Stephen and Marla grew, and they began snapping at each other and having frequent spats.

After an argument over something irrelevant, Stephen and Marla finally talked about how they were feeling and decided they needed to include Alison in the conversation. They explained to Alison that the stress was impacting their relationship and things needed to change. They encouraged her to get help in order to figure out whether she wanted to reconcile with Jake. They were willing to continue to provide financial and emotional support, but they had to establish a timeline and some boundaries.

Alison saw an individual therapist, who recommended that she and Jake go for couple's counseling. Alison and Jake had a lot of issues to deal with, but they still loved each other and were willing to work together to save their marriage. After several sessions with the couple's therapist, Alison and the children moved back home. She and Jake continued seeing the therapist, who was helping them work on their relationship. Stephen and Marla were glad to see that Alison and Jake were doing better, and were relieved to return to their own lives.

The return of adult children can be stressful when space is limited and there is no privacy. You may have already downsized or converted that extra bedroom into a lovely office, study, or TV room. Having more mouths to feed can be an additional burden for couples who are already concerned about draining money from their retirement savings. What are your responsibilities to adult children who should be on their own? If you do have an adult child moving in, expectations need to be clear. How will they contribute to the household? What about chores and responsibilities? For how long will they be there? If you want to have a relationship with your adult child after they move out, try to have the conversation before they move in. It is a different conversation if things begin to fall apart.

Conversations When Adult Children Are Moving Back Home

- What are your expectations?
- What are their expectations?
- Will the situation be temporary or permanent?
- Will you set a time frame?

- How will they contribute to the household—via rent, chores, or some other means?
- What are the expectations for child care and limit setting?
- Will the grandchildren have any age-appropriate responsibilities in your household?
- Who gets to make the rules: the grandparents, since it is their house, or the parents, since the children are theirs?

When Relationships with Children Are Strained

If you are a parent, you have probably experienced many ups and downs in relationships with your children. When they were young, they may have adored you and thought you knew everything there was to know about the world. Then they became adolescents and thought that you probably didn't know anything. And finally, they matured and realized that we all know a lot, but nobody knows everything. In most families, people learn what to expect and who they can count on. Relationships tend to find a comfortable level of closeness and distance. But there are an infinite number of variables involved in situations with adult children or their partners, some of which may cause relationships to be strained or cut off completely. For instance, sometimes an adult child gets along well with one parent and not the other. Such situations can cause a great deal of tension for everyone.

Some adult children feel so estranged from their parents that they want nothing to do with them and may even refuse to allow contact with grandchildren. John and Judy found themselves in this situation with their daughter, Sara.

Sara, an only child, blamed her parents for her unhappiness. When she was growing up, John had a drinking problem and sometimes became belligerent and verbally abusive. He didn't go for help until Sara was a teenager, and by then, the damage had already been done. Sara was angry and ashamed to have an alcoholic father and a mother who stayed with him and did not protect her. When John got sober and he and Judy went for help, Sara refused to go with them. It was their problem, and she did not want any part of it.

Sara was relieved to finally leave for college and rarely went home for holidays and breaks. John and Judy were heartbroken when they found out she had married and had a child without letting them know. They desperately wanted to see Sara and meet their grandchild, but she refused to respond to letters and phone calls. Because of old wounds and trauma, Sara saw no other way but to leave her parents out of her life. She thought she was protecting herself and her child and was unable to see that something good might come out of taking an emotional risk.

Sometimes, later in life, we are able to be more forgiving. We may find ourselves missing those from whom we have been estranged, and realize that time is passing. Leaving the door open without expectations is often more reasonable than slamming it behind you.

When You Don't See Eye to Eye

Conflicts with children can develop if your upbringing was more traditional, but your children were brought up in a culture with very different societal values and expectations. This is especially true for immigrants who come to the United States with values from their homeland, only to find that their children are totally immersed in American society. For example, interfaith and intercultural marriage is certainly more prevalent now than when our parents were growing up. And that is also true for our children's generation. If we want to have relationships with our adult children, we need to respect and be open to their choices. It is no longer uncommon for individuals of different cultural, racial, ethnic, and religious backgrounds to choose to be together.

Leila and Natan came to the United States with their two young children five years after they were married. They were both steeped in the values of their native country and expected that would also be true for their children. But as the children adapted to their new culture, they wanted to be like everyone else. Although Leila and Natan understood this, they were worried about the future of their heritage should their children want to marry out of their culture and religion. When their son brought home his American fiancée, they were devastated. Although they liked the young woman and were happy for their son, they also felt a deep sense of loss. However, they knew that trying to change things would not be the wise thing to do. They accepted their American daughter-in-law and grew to love her and her family. Through their acceptance, their relationship with their son deepened. They knew that someday they would be able to offer their grandchildren a rich and diverse heritage.

Another common scenario is having an adult child come out as gay, lesbian, or transsexual. Although this may be against your particular moral or religious code, if you cannot find a place of acceptance in your heart, you probably will not have a relationship with that child.

Catherine and George had been married for thirty-five years. They grew up in religious families with strict guidelines about marriage, children, and the importance of family values. Their two older sons married partners of the same religion and had children whom they raised according to their family's beliefs. When Frank, their youngest son, was twenty-five, he announced to his parents that he was moving in with his gay lover. Catherine and George could not believe this was happening, and they urged Frank to "get help." In response, he cut off communication with them, feeling they would never accept or understand him. Catherine and George were both saddened and relieved—they did not want any of their friends or relatives to know about Frank, and they certainly could not explain it.

For several years, Catherine and George silently refused to accept the fact that their son was gay. They never mentioned his name and did not talk about their feelings. But when George was diagnosed with cancer, Catherine convinced him it was time to reconcile with Frank. Catherine and George found it helpful to talk with other parents who had similar issues. They felt less alone and were able to ask themselves what was really most important. Although they had not approved of Frank's lifestyle, they loved him and wanted him back with the family. Together, they wrote Frank a letter asking for forgiveness and inviting him and his partner to come for the holidays. Although this was a stretch for them, they discovered what they most wanted was reconnection with the son they loved. Luckily for them, Frank and his partner welcomed this connection.

Childless by Choice

For couples who do not have children, either by choice or circumstance, being around people who do have children and grandchildren can be difficult. We live in a society where the typical family structure includes parents, children, grandchildren, and extended family. But what is typical is not necessarily the norm. Maybe you wanted children but were not able to have them, and decided that adoption or surrogacy was not an option for you. You might have found other ways to have children in your life, such as being a special aunt or uncle or a substitute grandma or grandpa, but you still may feel a twinge of regret or sadness in your heart. Or you and your partner may have decided that focusing on each other and your life together was more important than having children. Parenting is not for everyone. It's important for couples without children to have friends who share similar interests and values. Childless couples usually do not want to be surrounded by people who have little to talk about but their children and grandchildren.

RELATIONSHIPS WITH GRANDCHILDREN

Many younger boomers equate the idea of becoming a grandparent with being "old." They have difficulty relating to a role that will make them feel old but, of course, it is not their choice. You may have heard of grandparents who want to be called by nicknames or even their first names. Imagine your kids calling your mother Sally when you call her Mom.

For others, becoming a grandparent can be the most exciting event since the birth of your own children. You fall in love all over again, but it's even better because you don't have to lose sleep and wake up for midnight feedings. Embracing the role of grandparenting has many dimensions. Not only do you get to witness your children becoming parents, but you also experience the emergence of a new generation. When you meet a new grandparent, you can usually hear the excitement and pride in their voice.

Alice, a high-level executive, was phasing out of work when her first grandchild was born. The timing was perfect: she took care of her granddaughter two days a week, had a day for herself, and consulted the other two days of the week.

For Bill, a retired engineer, his greatest joy in retirement was being able to spend time with his grandchildren. When his own children were young, he worked all the time and always felt he was missing out on something important. Now he had the opportunity to make up for at least part of what he had missed.

Grandparents can be wonderful role models for what we call positive aging—that is, aging with energy, vitality, and spirit. We have the opportunity to begin to shift the perception of what it means to grow older. When your grandchildren see you doing things that you enjoy—playing tennis, hiking and skiing, singing in a chorus, taking an art class, or learning a language—they may begin to think about aging in a very different way. It can also be fun to share in some of the things they like doing, in whatever way is possible for you.

🧩 A Note from Dori

The grandparent role does not have to come with being a biological grandparent. My husband and I had both lost our parents before our son, Louie, was born. On occasion, he would see friends with a grandparent, ask about our parents, and comment that "it wasn't fair" he did not have grandparents. When Louie was around four years old, he realized that dear friends of ours did not have children or grandchildren. He asked if they could be his grandparents. We told him it was a great idea, if they were willing. After this discussion, with some support from us, he asked them if they would become his grandparents. They were delighted and immediately accepted his invitation. The resulting relationship was wonderful for all of them. Our close friends became his Omi and Opa. Omi sent him a picture of each of them that said "Grandma" and "Grandpa." During one of their visits, Louie and Opa went to a pool together with children who were with their grandparents. Opa saw how proud Louie was to introduce him as his grandfather. He realized how important it was to our son to have grandparents, as the other children had, and they talked about our son as their grandchild. When Omi was sick and dying, we all went to say good-bye to her, tell her how much we loved her, and thank her for her special role.

Several years later, at Louie's bar mitzvah, Opa was publicly recognized as Louie's grandfather, and we saw how important it was for each of them to be "family." Although we didn't get to see Opa as much as we would wish, it was special whenever we did, and we welcomed Joan, his special friend, into our family, too. Ultimately, when Opa died, we gathered together as a large and extended family, celebrating Opa's life and our love and special relationship with him. We have also maintained our friendship with Joan.

What Is Your Grandparenting Style?

We all have our own style of grandparenting. If your grandchildren live nearby, you may want to be with them as much as possible when they are young. Maybe you take care of them during the week or babysit on weekends, or both. Some grandparents would never miss a sports event or concert; their grandchildren are the center of their lives.

But you may be one of the many grandparents who have

limited time and busy schedules devoted to work and an active social life. You love your grandchildren and enjoy spending time with them, but not to the exclusion of other things. You have a different way of being with your grandchildren that works for you. You might take them to a movie, do something special on a weekend, or have a sleepover. Some grandparents have special time with each grandchild, taking them on mini vacations, adventure trips, or other things they would not ordinarily have the opportunity to do.

There is no right or wrong way to be a grandparent. What is important is the quality of the relationship—who you are with them, and how you spend time together—not necessarily how much time you spend. Do you plop them in front of the TV, or do you interact through games, reading, or talking about things that are important to them? Are you a teacher, role model, or loving presence who makes sure they feel safe? In past generations, children were often seen and not heard. We know differently now. Our grandchildren have the right to be heard and, in fact, they can be our greatest teachers.

Talking about Expectations with Your Partner

You and your partner may need to work out your own grandparenting styles. Perhaps your partner has different expectations regarding the role and responsibilities of being a grandparent. Once again, you may not agree with each other on a common role for the two of you, but you need to understand each other's feelings about what is important. It may be as simple a matter as time availability. Maybe your partner has more time during the day and wants to see the kids, but you are busy with meetings or made plans with friends for lunch. He or she doesn't want to go without you, but you can't go—or vice versa! The two of you need to work out availability so that no one feels "wrong." It is easy to feel guilty if you choose to do other things, so perhaps you go sometimes and other times you don't. It can be difficult to reconcile time you need for yourself and time to be with your grandchildren. If this sounds familiar, it may have something to do with expectations or unresolved issues with your children.

Talking about Expectations with Your Children

Talking about expectations with your children can stir up feelings from the past, on both sides. Your children may expect you to show up for every game like you did when they were young. Or maybe they get jealous when you do things with your grandchildren that you didn't do with them, or get angry if you spend more time with their sibling's children. If these things are not talked about, they can come up over and over again, along with feelings of anger, guilt, and disappointment. It is a courageous conversation to initiate because relationships with our children can sometimes feel fragile, especially if there are unresolved feelings from the past.

Long-Distance Grandparenting

It used to be that families lived closer and spent more time together. Many older boomers grew up with grandparents in the same household. But our society today is more mobile, with our children living in different parts of the country or the world. It is not uncommon to hear one grandparent say to another, "You're so lucky to have your grandchildren close by."

When grandchildren live far away, there may be a great deal of planning and negotiating that takes place, sometimes with your partner as well as with your kids, prior to visits. When will you visit? Will you stay with your kids or in a hotel? How long will you be there? It can get more complicated if you and your partner have grandchildren from previous marriages or if there are rifts in the relationships.

As grandchildren get older, traveling cross-country to see them can be disappointing. Teenagers often want to spend time with their friends rather than hanging out with Grandma and Grandpa. Some grandparents remember this stage with their own children and accept it as a part of life. Others may feel hurt and rejected. Or the converse can also be true, and your grandchildren may want to do things with you that you don't have the energy or interest to do.

Even when grandchildren live nearby, there are logistics to work out. Most kids today are involved in so many activities that spending time with them means having to fit time in between events like soccer games and gymnastics practice. This can be fun, but what if there is more than one grandchild? How do you decide which game to attend? These decisions may not be earth-shattering, but they are important. It can help to talk with your grandchildren and find out what is most important to them. Your children can also help you figure out the details; they know their children's schedules, and they usually know what is important to their children and what they like to do.

Sue and Tom moved from New York to California to start a jewelry business with their son, Larry, and his wife, Joanne. Their daughter, Karen, stayed in New York to be with her partner, Julie, and go to graduate school. Larry and Joanne have three children, whom Sue and Tom have been close to since their birth. Karen and her partner have two young children. Sue and Tom visit Karen, Julie, and their children twice a year and love spending time with their "New York" grandchildren. But Karen is disappointed that they don't visit more often. She worries that her children aren't going to know their grandparents.

During their last visit, Sue talked with Karen about the tension she feels exists between the two of them. Karen was able to open up and share her concern and disappointment. Together, they thought about ways to stay more connected, and Sue decided to email pictures, notes, and short stories that Karen could share with the kids. They also set up ways to talk via videoconferencing calls, which was fun for all of them. Now that she was more stable financially, Karen and Julie decided to plan a "first annual trip" to California so that the cousins could also get to know each other. Sue and Karen's conversation helped them to feel closer and resulted in a way for the whole family to be more connected.

If you have a great relationship with your children and grandchildren, you may decide you want to live closer to them. But think again: be careful and do your homework. It is important to do research, spend time in the area, and maybe even rent a place for a few months. See if it is the kind of lifestyle you would enjoy, and then decide if you would want to live there no matter whether the kids are nearby. You may be there a year or less, only to find that your kids are moving to the other coast because of a job change, or because they are not comfortable with the close proximity and need boundaries and more distance. You could be stuck living somewhere for the wrong reasons.

You and your partner may have very different ideas about how much time to spend with grandchildren. Some men complain that their wives spend more time with their grandchildren than they do with them. This is not always the case, and it could be reversed as well; however, many men see it as a "maternal instinct to nurture," one that takes away from their relationship with their wives.

What If There Are Multiple Grandparents?

Given the divorce rate, second, third, or more marriages, and blended families, there may be multiple people vying for the grandparent position, which can be confusing and stressful for everyone. Even something as simple as what the kids call you can become very complex. The hope is that the grown-ups will be "grown-up" and work things out so the children do not have to be caught in the middle. Just like in divorce, decisions should be made on the basis of what is best for the kids.

Step-Grandparenting

Step-grandparenting can also be a slippery slope. It is not easy to have another person come into the life of your children and grandchildren and remain neutral about it. It is particularly difficult when there has been an unwanted divorce and relationships are already strained. Or perhaps the previous partner has died, and the children are not yet comfortable with a new person in their lives. On the other hand, it is hard being the "intruder" and not knowing what your role should be.

These are complicated situations couples need to talk about and be prepared for. Being a stepparent or step-grandparent can be very stressful if you don't feel supported by your partner, who is bringing you into the family. It's your partner's job to pave the way by preparing you and helping you feel comfortable. Depending on the circumstances of your partner's previous marriage, whether it ended in divorce or the death of a spouse, you may be welcomed with open arms or polite indifference, or made to feel unwelcome. It takes time to establish who you will be to the family and who they will be to you. Be patient and allow relationships to develop on their own terms. That way no one feels pressured and you can get to know each other over time.

When Grandparents Become the Parents

Some of the most difficult and unexpected situations occur when your children, for one reason or another, are not able to adequately take care of their children, and you need to step in and be the parent. Whatever the reason, this situation is usually painful, challenging, and difficult for everyone.

When Jeremy and Ruth were in their early fifties, their daughter Gretchen turned fourteen. It was like she changed overnight. One day she was a clean-cut kid who had good friends and excelled in school, and the next day, she was drinking and smoking pot. Within a few months, Gretchen's grades began to plummet, and she became totally disinterested in school and her old group of friends. Jeremy and Ruth felt overwhelmed and powerless. They tried to get help for their daughter and suggested family counseling, but she refused. The next few years were a nightmare. By the time Gretchen turned sixteen, she had dropped out of school and was pregnant.

Gabriela was born a few months before her mother's seventeenth birthday. Ruth had agreed to help Gretchen with the baby, and for a while, this seemed to work. But Gretchen began spending less and less time at home, forcing Ruth to leave her part-time job to care for Gabriela. Jeremy and Ruth finally had Gretchen admitted to a detox center, where she was able to get sober and start going to AA meetings. She found a part-time job and talked about getting her GED. But within a few months, Gretchen had relapsed and was readmitted to rehab. When Gabriela was four years old, her mother died from an overdose. Jeremy and Ruth were devastated. As parents tend to do, they blamed themselves for Gretchen's death, even though they had done everything they could to help her.

Jeremy and Ruth felt they had no choice but to adopt Gabriela, whom they loved. With the chaos in the family and their constant worry about Gretchen, they had not talked about planning for retirement. They now had a long-term obligation to raise their granddaughter. Jeremy and Ruth never expected to be parenting a young child at this stage of life.

Not every grandparent is willing or able to take over parenting responsibilities for a grandchild. Although releasing the child for adoption is one option, it can be a difficult and painful decision. There are qualified agencies and therapists who can help grandparents sort out what is best for the child and for them. But whatever decisions are made, the ramifications last for a lifetime.

What If You Don't Have Grandchildren?

You may not have grandchildren because you did not have children, or your children may have decided not to have children. Many young people today are focusing on careers, getting married later, or putting off having children. Some decide not to become parents, while others may have difficulty conceiving. Fertility declines with age, and it can become increasingly difficult to have a child at thirty-five, forty, or older than it was at twenty-five or thirty.

Not having the experience of being a parent or grandparent can be painful when peers are spending time with their adult children and visiting with grandchildren. Even after many years, it can hurt when someone asks, "How many children or grandchildren do you have?" Couples find that talking with others who share similar experiences and feelings can be helpful.

Vivian and Matthew decided years ago not to have children. They were both career-driven, worked long hours, and felt it would be unfair to have a child they could not really be there for. Periodically, when they were still able to have children, they revisited their decision, but they always felt the choice they made had been right for them. Most of their friends had children, although some did not. Vivian could recall many uncomfortable situations being with a group of friends who talked continually about their children. She felt like an outsider, having nothing to contribute to the conversation.

Now in their late fifties, Vivian and Matthew have friends who are proud grandparents and talk about their grandchildren all the time. Again it brings up old feelings about their choices, even though they agree they would make the same decision all over again. They have enjoyed a very close and intimate relationship that probably would not have been the same with children. Vivian and Matthew adore the "children" they do have, two special dogs and a beautiful cat, but few of their friends share an interest in hearing about them.

If, like Vivian and Matthew, you do not have children, you may be wondering, "Who will take care of us when we're old?" Although it is not a given that adult children will be willing or able to take care of their aging parents, when there are no children, it is not even a possibility. If there is no one to fill the gap, this is all the more reason for couples who do not have children to think ahead and have financial and health plans for their later years. Vivian and Matthew are aware of the issues and have developed a network of other childless couples who share similar concerns. It helps them all to feel supported and less alone as they age.

RELATIONSHIPS WITH SIBLINGS

Having close siblings can be one of the greatest gifts in life, or it can produce rivalries that haunt you throughout life. In many families, sibling relationships are somewhere in between. But sibling issues can come up in different ways at different times. An imbalance in education, wealth, or a number of other things can trigger issues of resentment and jealousy between siblings.

Lyle and Claudia grew up in the South and met in graduate school, where they were both studying architecture. They got married in their midtwenties and had four children. Balancing work, family, and finances was an ongoing challenge. In their early thirties, they started their own architectural firm, which did well over the years.

Lyle, an only child, grew up in a blue-collar family and worked his way through college and grad school. He was proud of his accomplishments and finally felt that he had made it. Claudia, the oldest of four children, was the only one to go to college in her family and received a full academic scholarship. Her two sisters went to community college and her youngest sibling, Devon, dropped out of high school in his senior year. They all looked up to Claudia, who had a graduate degree in her chosen profession. Claudia's sisters were both married and had good jobs and close families. Devon had two children from his first marriage and was divorced from his second wife. He had gone from one job to the next, never seeming satisfied with what he had. His dream was to start a music business, but he knew very little about the industry or how to start a business.

Over the years, Devon had called Claudia many times asking to borrow money. She never refused and did not expect him to pay her back. She had always felt sorry for him because their father died when he was young, so he had never had a male role model to guide him. Claudia knew that Lyle would be furious if he found out about the money. Lyle was constantly berating Devon for being a "loser."

One day, Devon called Claudia asking to borrow $5,000 for a down payment on a business. She knew she had to talk with Lyle. Predictably, he blew up. Devon had already lost a business after defaulting on a bank loan, and his track record for follow-through was poor. Lyle could not understand why his wife felt like she had to take responsibility for her brother even though he was a grown man. Although Claudia did not want to disappoint her brother, in a way, Lyle's response was a relief. She knew he was right; Devon had to start taking responsibility for his own life.

Relationships with siblings can be extremely complicated, especially when money is involved. If not addressed, the issues can create ongoing tension in the marriage and between family members. One fairly common scenario occurs when one or more siblings refuse to be involved with planning for the care or placement of a parent, and another sibling is left with the burden. It is easy for anger and resentment to build up.

🧩 A Note from Roberta

I was the middle child, with five and a half years' difference between myself and each of my two sisters. The lack of any real communication in the family, as well as our age span, created a sense of emotional disconnection. My parents grew up during the Depression and were preoccupied with concerns about money and family issues. In retrospect, they were probably both depressed, and they didn't have much emotional energy for us. After my father's first heart attack (he was forty-five and I was fourteen), the tension in the house grew palpable. I did my best to stay out of the way as much as possible.

The family spent little time together except at dinner, and even then things were strained.

Growing up, my sisters and I were always at different stages with issues and problems that were never shared. I realize now how alone we all must have felt. We have always stayed in contact by phone, with conversations often going back to our parents and childhood experiences. Talking about our lives can be difficult. I have a wonderful husband, a career I love, and children with whom I am close. Neither of my sisters seems content with their lives and there is always disappointment and searching. We have all had challenges, but some are more difficult to overcome than others. The last time the three of us spent time together was when we moved Mom from Florida to New York, where she lived with my younger sister before going into a nursing home. That was over twenty years ago. Despite efforts to make it different, I've learned to accept and appreciate the relationships we have rather than the ones I wish we could have.

It's a huge loss when siblings who could be close are distant and disconnected. The opportunity may be there, but the willingness to take the risk, reach out, and try to have a deeper relationship may just be too difficult. Everybody loses, and no one understands why.

In addition, old sibling rivalries may develop when grandchildren come into the picture. There may be competition around whose grandchildren are smarter, more attractive, or better at sports. Siblings can be your best friend or your worst enemy. But as mature adults, we can take the opportunity to "right" the relationship and maybe even find a loving sister or brother you never knew you had. Life is too short to stay in an embittered place. It does not always work out, but it may be worth a try.

RELATIONSHIP WITH PARENTS: WHEN ROLES ARE REVERSED

"Parental relationships are hard for almost everyone. They are, by definition, challenging, and not just because they are weighted with baggage from when you were young, but because they continue to evolve, to become even more complicated as you gain experience, marry, have children (or not), grow older yourself."

—Dale Atkins, author of *I'm OK, You're My Parents: How to Overcome Guilt, Let Go of Anger, and Create a Relationship That Works*

Regardless of your cultural, ethnic, or religious background, watching parents age and become more disabled is a very painful process. At some point, it becomes clear that the roles have been reversed and your parents need to be taken care of. But, no matter what, they are still your parents. The best-laid plans may change when a parent or in-law needs care. Suddenly, you are facing a job you are not trained for. On top of that, you may already have a full-time job, a family, and many other responsibilities. When a family member, most often an elderly parent, becomes incapacitated, our worlds can be turned upside down. One woman described feeling like she was being literally and figuratively pulled in different directions. We think about our parents growing older and know that, at some point, they may no longer be able to live independently. But when the time comes, it can be a shock.

Gail is a sixty-five-year-old woman who says, "I'm living my mother's life; I've lost my identity. I have no time for myself or my spouse." Gail is managing the care of her eighty-eight-year-old diabetic mother, Elizabeth, who insisted on staying in her home after her husband died. As Elizabeth's physical and mental capacity began to deteriorate and she was diagnosed with Alzheimer's, Gail began to stop by during her work day to do a few household chores, help her mother bathe, and make sure she was eating and taking her medication.

Thomas, Gail's husband, was primarily supportive but at times felt lonely and exasperated. When Gail started paying the bills, she discovered that Elizabeth had been writing monthly checks to various charities. She had become the victim of a very costly phone scam. (Elderly people can be easily taken advantage of by predators looking to make a fast buck.) Gail began to feel resentful, exhausted, and burned out. She realized that instead of doing everything herself, she could be the "project manager"—still an overwhelming job—and hire people to do the day-to-day care. Although this was a costly decision, it helped Gail with the emotional and physical burden of having to do it all alone.

Gail's story is not uncommon, and it shows the bind that adult children find themselves in when parent-child roles are reversed later in life.

Considering a Parent's Long-Term Care

Whether to consider placement or care for a parent at home should be a well-thought-out decision made prior to taking action. Although we cannot predict the future, we do know that our parents are aging and will eventually need care.

Harry, the oldest of three brothers, was the caretaker in the family. During summers and school vacations, Harry worked with his father in the family-owned gas station. When his father died of a heart attack at age sixty-four, Harry took over the station, which he owned with his brothers. Harry's mother, Edith, was devastated by her husband's death and disliked being alone. She started spending a lot of time with Harry and his wife, Elise. At the age of seventy-eight, Edith had a stroke, which left her partially paralyzed. Everyone except Harry thought she should go to a nursing home, but Harry refused.

Elise had watched the scenario unfold and was worried. The relationship with her mother-in-law had never been easy. From the time they were married, Edith was constantly in their lives, calling Harry to come over and fix things, complaining to him about his father, and demanding attention even when he was busy and overworked. The pattern had always been a source of tension between Harry and Elise.

Elise knew that Harry wanted his mother to live with them, but she was adamantly opposed. She could not imagine being with Edith all the time and allowing her to rule their lives. But Harry felt an obligation to take care of his mother. He knew she was not easy to have around, but she was frail and frightened and he could not bear the thought of putting her in "one of those places." Elise held her ground, agreeing with her brothers-in-law that they needed to find a nursing care facility for Edith.

Harry and Elise had both avoided what they knew was a difficult topic, so when the time came to make a decision, they felt pressured. In the best of circumstances, conversations about long-term care for a parent should include siblings and other family members. The decision to have Grandma move in can certainly have an impact on children still living at home. There may be disagreement among the siblings, which can lead to a deadlock, with family members getting polarized and stuck in their position. These are highly charged situations that sometimes require a third party, such as a family or elder mediator, who can help family members get unstuck and come to a resolution.

Tips for Family Caregivers

- The first—and most important—tip is to take care of yourself.
- Ask for help! A small favor can go a long way.
- Locate resources for support and respite care.
- Talk about your feelings with someone who can listen.
- Make time for yourself and your family.

Harry and Elise's dilemma is not uncommon. When one partner feels obligated to care for a sick relative, especially a parent, and the other is opposed, it causes a lot of stress in the relationship. Being in the midst of emotionally charged issues like this one is difficult. But, having read this far, you know by now that in order to work out solutions, you need to be able to talk with each other, as well as be willing to listen and try to understand your partner's feelings. Compromise becomes more likely when feelings are better understood. (See "Getting to Yes Together: The Importance of Communication," pages xxxiii–xlv, if you need a refresher.)

Harry and Elise realized that they had to find another solution. Elise was close to saying she would leave if Edith moved in. Harry explained that putting his mother in a nursing facility would feel like abandoning her. Elise admired her husband's loyalty and devotion, but was afraid of having to shoulder the burden of her mother-in-law's physical care. Elise was also concerned that their privacy and time together would be sacrificed if Edith moved in. Harry was not good at setting limits with his mother.

Understanding each other's feelings helped Harry and Elise work out a temporary solution. They agreed that Edith could live with them on a trial basis to see how it worked out. She was eligible for in-home services, and they could hire a housekeeper to help out. They would also ask his brothers to share the cost of care. Harry and Elise made sure to plan time together to continue talking about how things were going. It was not ideal, but at least they were communicating. They had a temporary solution, and in the interim, they could begin to visit facilities in preparation for the possibility of long-term care.

For some adult children, like Harry, caring for an elderly parent is "the right thing to do." After all, haven't they taken care of you? But it is not for everyone, and your beliefs and sense of obligation may be different from how your partner feels. Caregiving can be overwhelming, exhausting, and bring up underlying family issues and old resentments. Being a caregiver is a stressful job, ideally shared with others but often left to one family member. It can be especially burdensome for women, who in our culture usually end up providing more of the care, no matter whether the person being cared for is her own parent. The stress of caregiving is cumulative, and without adequate support, it can lead to physical and emotional burnout. No matter how devoted you are, you cannot do it alone.

Undoubtedly, we can all empathize with Harry or Elise, or both of them. Some couples cannot imagine putting their parents in a nursing home or other facility and, instead, make the choice to care for them at home. It may also be that the parent is opposed to going to a nursing home and wants to be cared for at home. It is difficult to deny their wishes for the final stage of life. But caring for a parent at home is not only physically, emotionally, and financially stressful, but it also impinges on a couple's privacy and time together. Some couples plan ahead and add an in-law apartment or other separate space to accommodate elderly parents. But before parents move in, whether they are healthy or more debilitated, talking together about feelings, expectations, and roles is essential. Ongoing communication is important. Most communities have for-profit and nonprofit organizations that provide resources, support, respite, home services, and referrals. There are also agencies and organizations that offer support groups for adults who are caretakers for their parents. Senior centers have day programs that have activities and meals and can be a wonderful way for people to connect and enjoy companionship. Isolation can lead to depression, illness, and even premature death.

It is important to research what is available in your community for elders as well as caregivers. (See "Resources," page 275, for more information.)

🧩 A Note from Dori

I learned through personal experience how difficult and stressful long-distance caretaking can be. My parents lived on the West Coast and I lived on the East Coast. Six months after my father died, my mother was visiting my brother in Virginia and had a stroke. She stayed in the Washington, DC, area while she was recovering, but she eventually wanted to move back to California, where she had family and friends.

I coordinated her social life and care, while my brother managed the financial issues. After many phone calls and a trip to

California, I found an assisted-living facility in the location she wanted that met many of her criteria. We were able to rent an apartment for her, and when the unit became available, I helped her move in. She was happy to be back in California and adapted fairly well to her new home.

Given her medical and emotional issues, I realized over time that it was impossible to effectively coordinate her care from so far away. After consulting with the facility, I got names of geriatric care managers, had phone interviews, and found one whom I felt my mother would like.

Although my mother didn't like the idea of having help, I felt confident she would like the person I had found. I "fudged it a little" and told her that I wanted her to meet a friend of a friend who lived nearby and whom I thought might become a new friend. As I predicted, after meeting, the two women developed a friendship. My mother accepted her help to get her to appointments, visit with her, and introduce her to other "friends" who were hired as companions when needed.

But there were still a few things that needed to happen for this to work. I arranged for my mother to give written permission to all of her healthcare providers so they would communicate with the geriatric care manager. I maintained regular phone contact with my mother and the geriatric care manager, as well as with the health providers as needed. I felt supported to have this extra help and "extra set of eyes" and relieved not to have to do as much crisis management from far away. My mother admitted she was appreciative of this help, even after I eventually told her that we were paying for it.

The decision to hire a geriatric care manager enabled me to reclaim some of my own life and my relationship with my husband. We had been going through a difficult ten-year period dealing with all four of our parents' deteriorating health and deaths. During my mother's final months, she was in and out of the hospital. When the time came, I arranged for hospice care in her apartment. My brother and I were there during her final few days and were able to be with her when she died.

It is difficult enough to manage the care of parents when you are close by, but what if you are an only child, have siblings who refuse to be involved, or have parents who live far away? Trying to make long-distance arrangements for in-home care or finding an appropriate facility can feel like a full-time job. You may have to do a lot of traveling back and forth to visit facilities and make decisions about providers, and then make numerous phone calls and handle inevitable complications. It is heartbreaking to go through all of this, especially if you cannot even have a conversation with your parent because they no longer remember who you are, such as the case with dementia.

Tip: Accepting Help

We hear from many families that "white lies" often help a parent accept some help. Pride can get in the way, and some people feel it is a weakness to need help. The purpose is not to be deceitful, but to creatively frame a situation in a way that may enable the person to accept help.

At some point, we all have to face our own mortality. No matter whether we were involved in planning the care of our parents, when they are gone, it is a reminder that life does not go on forever. Our children or others will be doing the same for us in time. It has been said that it is our parents who bring us into the world, and it is our job to help them leave.

Bev and Dave were in their early fifties and had three children. Bev's parents and two married sisters lived in neighboring towns. The families were close and got together for holidays and other events. When Bev's parents were in their early eighties and becoming more infirm, they told their daughters they had put money away to pay for whatever was necessary to keep them in their home as they aged.

They wanted to have the support of their own doctors, friends, and religious community. Bev's father became ill and died at home with the whole family around him. Bev's mother developed a debilitating muscular disorder and needed help with bathing, dressing, and going to the bathroom. Although she would have gotten more intensive care in a facility, everyone knew how important it was for her to be at home, and they all helped out, taking shifts during the day and hiring a nurse at night. Her death was bittersweet. She died quietly in her sleep, having her last wish fulfilled and knowing that the family had been with her until the end. The sisters and their husbands had worked together to make it happen. When it was stressful, they eased the tension with comic relief and a good laugh, a nice meal or a quiet conversation. In the end, they were able to laugh and cry together, feeling more connected through the love and support they had shared.

SUMMARY

Family relationships are incredibly complex. The bottom line is that we all basically want the same thing: to be loved, respected, and cared about, and to be part of a clan we call family. If we all want the same thing, then you would think it would be easy, but of course, it is not. We often don't know how to get what we most want. We come out of families who have their own issues and find that our partner's family has other issues. There is a Yiddish word, *mishegas*, which means craziness—and every family has their own brand. The better you communicate, the more likely you will be able to keep *mishegas* out of your relationship.

The importance for couples to be able to communicate is foundational to this book. And when it comes to family issues, communication is critical. Couples rarely talk together about their expectations for relationships with their children, grandchildren, parents, siblings, or even each other. We make assumptions based on what we learned in our own families and then act on them. But your partner had different teachers and may have different assumptions. When disagreements come up, you are probably both playing out your version of how things are "supposed" to be. It is important to understand your partner's beliefs and assumptions so that you can work together in making some of the decisions related to family. What are your boundaries? What are your responsibilities and obligations? What are your expectations? How do you want to spend time with family? What are your values and priorities? When it comes to family, the more you know about how your partner thinks and feels, the better prepared you will both be to make decisions about your relationships.

Talking It Through: Creating Your Shared Vision

Spend some time thinking about the following issues. Use your journal to write down your thoughts and feelings, as well as anything you want to talk about with your partner. If you need a refresher on how to communicate effectively, go back to "Getting to Yes Together: The Importance of Communication," pages xxxiii-xlv.

As you get started, remember the five tips and "Have a BLAST!"

- Blaming gets in the way
- Listen without interrupting
- Agree to disagree and don't make assumptions
- Set a safe space for discussion
- Take time to talk without distractions

Exercise 1
Go it solo: Things to think about on your own

1. How do I feel about my relationships with family members?
2. What obligations and responsibilities do I currently have for family members? How might this change in the future?
3. How do my family relationships and current or anticipated obligations and responsibilities impact my partner and our relationship?
4. How can I continue to honor my family obligations and responsibilities in a way that also supports our relationship?

Exercise 2
Couple time: Things to talk about together

1. Take turns sharing your responses to Exercise 1, one at a time.
2. Share something positive that you learned about each other.
3. Take time to question anything that was not clear.
4. Make a list of the things that you agree on.
5. Set a time for your next conversation.

It is important to remember that these are big questions that take time to resolve. You are probably not going to agree on everything; most couples don't. But being able to communicate and compromise effectively can help you come to solutions, one conversation at a time.

Puzzle Piece: Relationships with Family

What are two or three ways you can fulfill your family obligations and responsibilities, while still honoring your partner's feelings and protecting your relationship? Write in the Puzzle Piece section at the end of the "Creating Your Shared Vision" chapter, page 263.

Funwork

Do individually or together

- What family member(s) do you feel most ambivalent about? Do something nice and unexpected for them: plan a family dinner, send them a card or email greeting, or call them on the phone.
- If you did this individually, share with your partner what you did and how it felt.

······························

Health and Wellness:
Will Medicare Pay for the Spa?

Brian and Deena decided they needed to start exercising and get back into shape. Brian's blood pressure was higher than it had ever been, and Deena realized she had put on a lot of weight. They used to enjoy hiking, running, and playing tennis, but in recent years, they had become less physical and more sedentary. They knew they needed some structure to get started, so they joined a health club that offered classes and personal training. Their primary care physician gave them the go-ahead and suggested they call their health plan to ask about coverage for the club. They were pleased to find that insurance would partially cover the joining fee—although, unfortunately, it didn't pay for the spa.

How we take care of ourselves throughout life has a huge impact on our health and wellness as we age. We expect a lot from our bodies, but we don't always treat them very well. As we get older, some of the parts wear down: we feel an ache here, a pain there, or maybe something that just doesn't seem to be working well. The voice of intuition can be powerful; if yours is giving you a message, pay attention. Annual physical exams are a must, and if your body is telling you something's not right, be sure to see your doctor.

Taking care of your physical body is important, but it is just one part of the equation. What about emotional and spiritual health? Later life presents us with challenges that call on our deepest resources and coping skills. We have needs that go beyond the physical and tap into our deepest beliefs about life. How do those beliefs guide you? How will they help you grow whole and live the next part of life with vitality and purpose?

We also need to pay attention to practical issues in the second half of life. As mentioned in Conversation 2 ("Let's Talk about Money," pages 31–58) and discussed more later in this conversation, there are documents that are important to put in place: wills, trusts, power of attorney, healthcare proxy, HIPAA forms, and living wills. Although you may not want to think about these things, it's not a good idea to put it off. The best time to talk about end-of-life issues is when you are healthy and it's not a time of crisis. You don't need to make decisions that are irrevocable, but you do need to start the conversation.

CHOOSING TO AGE WELL

We hear the phrase "health and wellness" all the time. What do they really mean, and how are they connected? Being healthy and physically fit are parts of overall well-being. Are you overweight? Is your blood pressure too high? What about your cholesterol levels? Wellness, on the other hand, is a holistic concept that includes the physical as well as mental, emotional, and spiritual aspects of well-being. How you take care of yourself, how you fuel your body and feed your mind, and how you manage stress are important aspects of wellness. As many couples have found, one partner's health and wellness can have a major impact on the other.

Have You Talked about Taking Care of Yourselves?

In their early sixties, Susan and Ray were enjoying life. Over the years, they had consistently saved a modest amount for their nest egg, made good financial decisions, and were beginning to talk about a time frame for retirement. They felt good about having taken responsibility for their financial future. They were planning to sell their home and buy a small condominium closer to the city, where they would have better access to public transportation, theater, and museums.

Their plans, however, were abruptly interrupted when Susan was diagnosed with colon cancer. She had put off scheduling a routine colonoscopy, even though she knew it was important, particularly with her family history of cancer. The diagnosis was made early enough for Susan to be able to have successful surgery. Had she waited even a few more months, it could have been a very different story. In addition, Ray's mother had died of colon cancer three years earlier. When Susan was diagnosed, Ray went into a major depression and had difficulty being supportive to his wife. It was a rocky time for them both.

All too often, necessary medical treatment is postponed because of fear, procrastination, or financial issues. Although Susan was fortunate to have had adequate healthcare coverage, she still put off scheduling the colonoscopy. No one but you can be responsible for your body, but unfortunately, our own health is often not on the top of our priority list until something wakes us up.

You have the responsibility for being well informed and advocating for what you need. Are you taking responsibility for your health and well-being? Our bodies are the vehicles that carry us through life. Do you take care of your body as well as you take care of your car?

Check Your Attitude about Aging

Harriet is a seventy-one-year-old woman who has bemoaned "getting old" ever since she turned fifty. She rejected well-meaning suggestions from concerned friends and family members who were becoming frustrated with her negativity. Being around someone who is constantly negative can bring everyone down. Harriet refused to accept the reality of aging and became increasingly depressed. Rather than getting help or finding ways to enjoy her life, she was "old" before her time, in a self-fulfilling prophecy.

You don't have a choice about whether you age, but you do have some choice about how you age. Attitude makes a huge difference in your quality of life. As we see above, Harriet's attitude colored how she lived her life. It is impossible to embrace the gifts of aging and continue to grow when we're not able to let go of the past and accept the present. What is your attitude about getting older? Have you noticed that growing older has changed your view of aging? In some societies elders are revered, occupying a special place in the community. In our society, aging has traditionally been viewed negatively, as something to be avoided—as if we have a choice! Words like "declining," "frail," "wrinkled," "decrepit," and "over the hill" are used to describe elders. Anyone over fifty-five who is looking for a job today will probably tell you that ageism in hiring, or discrimination against people because of their age, is alive and well. As millions of baby boomers turn sixty and beyond, hopefully societal perceptions and language will change. If we can't accept growing older ourselves, how can we expect to be respected and taken seriously by others?

🧩 A Note from Dori

Now that I'm in my late sixties, I no longer view seventy and upward as "old." We have so many healthy and vital friends in their seventies and eighties. Many are "young olds," active, energetic, and interested in the world, often in spite of having chronic or terminal illnesses. Others are beset with medical or emotional issues and aren't aging as well. Many of our friends who are healthy and vibrant do admit they struggle with increasing concerns about their mortality and the finite nature of time. They are challenged by how to be realistically optimistic and balance these fears and concerns with living their life as fully as possible.

Messages about looking and feeling younger are unavoidable. Our culture values physical beauty and youth. "You don't look your age" is music to our ears, and why shouldn't it be? It is wonderful to look and feel good. It can be unnerving to look in the mirror and see your mother or father staring back. Many a face-lift has been contemplated or scheduled after having that experience! However, there is a danger when we deny that we are not as young as we used to be and go to extremes to look younger. Some men and women endure costly and sometimes painful cosmetic procedures, yet still do not feel good about their appearance. In some cases, it is an addiction; the more plastic surgery procedures you have, the more you want.

Wanting to enhance your appearance is fine, but not if it's

at the expense of your health or, in some cases, a significant impact on your pocketbook. Getting old isn't "bad"—it's just what happens to the human body. How you choose to age is what can make a difference. (In fact, there is only one sure way to avoid getting older, and that is not a great alternative.)

> At sixty-two, Dave was in a struggle with aging. Once an athlete, he was spending hours at the gym doing strenuous exercise and heavy lifting. One day, exhausted, he collapsed and was taken to the emergency room. Fortunately, it was not a heart attack or stroke, but it was a "wake-up call."

Exercise is important, but not when you are stressing your body beyond its limits, and we do have limits as we age. Dave is learning that he can still be in good shape and look his best, even if he no longer has the body of a young athlete.

A positive attitude involves acceptance of the fact that aging is a natural process. Making good choices for our physical and emotional health is crucial. And the truth is, no matter how often we exercise, how many body parts are repaired or replaced, how much we spend on special vitamins that promise longevity, how well we eat, or how much cosmetic surgery we have, we are still going to get old and eventually die. The hope, however, is that, as we age, we take good care of ourselves and feel vital for as long as possible—hopefully to our last breath.

It is easy to be in denial about aging. On a more superficial level, who wants to see the cellulite or the potbelly that was not there a few years ago? Noticing those telltale signs of aging in your partner before you can see it in yourself is not uncommon. For example:

Joe was upset when his wife gained weight. He somehow overlooked his own potbelly and love handles.

Judy noticed that her husband's scalp was shining through what used to be a thick carpet of hair, while he noticed that her eyelids were looking a little droopy.

We're human, and we react to these signposts. However, if we get stuck on our own or our partner's physical appearance, moving toward a healthier, more accepting place may be difficult, if not impossible.

We all want to be loved for who we are, warts and all. Hopefully, couples who have been together a long time have come to accept what is not going to change. Some couples can look into the eyes of their partner and still see the youthful, beautiful person they fell in love with.

"Denying or trivializing the positive potential of aging prevents people from realizing the full spectrum of their talents, intelligence, and emotions."
—Gene Cohen, MD, PhD, a pioneer in the field
of geriatric psychiatry who studied creativity,
aging, and the potential of the aging brain

REALISTIC OPTIMISM

"Realistic optimism" means accepting positive outcomes while realizing there are limits to what is possible. Life has its twists and turns. We don't always get what we want, but we can make the best of what we have. We have seen that couples who grow together, "in sickness and in health," often develop this sense of realistic optimism and an ability to find humor in the ironies of life. Being able to talk about difficult issues helps us develop ways to respond with resilience to illness, loss, and whatever else life puts in front of us. In the process, we learn to accept what is, make the most of it, and find ways to live each day to the fullest. Remember Dave? His "wake-up call" changed his life. He continues to exercise with a focus on strength training, but now he goes to the gym three times a week and does a moderate—rather than exhaustive—workout. He and his wife are also walking several mornings a week. It gives them time together that they didn't have before.

If physical issues become an obstacle to your dreams, it is time to create new dreams. Hiking in the Rocky Mountains may be at the top of your dream list, but now that you have time, the arthritis in your knees may not be accommodating. Or your knees are fine, but you can no longer tolerate high altitudes. Perhaps you have always wanted to learn to fly an airplane, but you can't pass the vision exam. As we deal with our changing medical and health issues, we are forced to "reality test" what is possible and what is not. The challenge is to realistically live life with possibility while continuing to discover new opportunities for adventure, learning, and fulfillment. We need to set goals and have dreams we can accomplish. Otherwise, we will keep setting ourselves up for disappointment and a sense of always falling short.

Maintaining Realistic Optimism through Serious Illness

Bob, a sixty-two-year-old English professor, planned to retire at age sixty-six on a reasonable pension and Social Security. His wife, Evie, a bank manager, was also thinking about retiring in a few years. But Bob's diagnosis of leukemia four years ago turned their lives and their plans upside down. For a year, all they could focus on was defeating the illness. Evie was able to work part-time so she could take Bob to his appointments and be with him during his chemotherapy treatments.

Although they knew the odds were not good, they maintained a positive attitude and did everything possible to get through this difficult time.

During his year of treatment, Bob did a lot of reflecting and journaling about his accomplishments, which, in one way or another, all came down to helping others. He knew what he wanted to do "when" he recovered. He loved teaching, but after twenty-five years, the passion was gone. Still, all through his illness, he focused on loving life and maintaining a sense of realistic optimism.

After a year of treatment, the leukemia went into remission, and by then Bob was clear about his direction. He and Evie talked, and she agreed she would go back to work full-time until they were both eligible for Medicare and Social Security. Bob loved the outdoors and had always enjoyed backpacking and hiking. Although he needed to regain his strength, he believed that, in time, he would be able to camp and hike again.

Over the years, he and Evie had gone on many backpacking trips, and he had learned a lot about the sport and the equipment. Friends and relatives were always asking for advice about where to go and what equipment they would need. Eventually, Bob applied for a job at a local sporting goods store. Although he had never been in sales, his enthusiasm, knowledge, and love of nature were his strongest attributes. He began working part-time and was probably one of the best salespeople in the company. He enjoyed helping the customers and hearing them talk about their adventures. Being a natural teacher, Bob was able to teach his customers things that most salespeople would never think to talk about. This was Bob's way of giving back through his natural talents and abilities.

Finding the Humor in Life

Humor is an important ingredient in life. Having a partner to share laughter with can be a great tension reliever when things get stressful. Whether it is laughing at yourself, finding the humor in a story, or watching a terrific comedy, laughter is great medicine, physically and emotionally. Laughter releases stress-reducing chemicals in the brain that relax muscles and lower anxiety, stimulate the immune system, decrease blood pressure, enhance mood and creativity, and help us feel more connected to others. All this with your own natural hormones! What could be better?

Likewise, humor and laughter are important ingredients in a marriage. Laughing often helps to create connection even when no one else sees the humor. It can go a long way when there are problems to solve or difficult situations to deal with. Some couples find that laughter, even having a sense of "gallows humor," has helped them to feel more in control at the darkest times, such as when dealing with a life-threatening diagnosis. Laughter is like a vitamin for relationships. It is a universal connector that bonds people together. Humor can relieve stress and tension, soften the rough edges, and clear the way for a renewed perspective. Laughter workshops are becoming popular, and there is now even a new form of yoga called "Laughter Yoga," where laughter is used to bring more oxygen to the body and brain.

Bring Humor and Laughter into Your Relationship

- Find ways to have fun together.
- Share humorous events and stories.
- Find the humor in everyday life.
- Spend time with people who enjoy life and are fun.
- Be able to laugh at yourself.

Having friends to commiserate with is also helpful. Humor can help turn us around when we are feeling "old," and laugh lines are a lot more appealing than a fixed grimace.

🧩 A Note from Roberta

One of the things I love about my husband, Bruce, is his sense of humor. A wonderful storyteller, he makes everyone laugh. He says I have no sense of humor. (He has been known to exaggerate.) I grew up in a family where there was a lot of tension and not a lot of fun. So learning to laugh has been a wonderful gift.

My mother didn't start getting gray until she was in her seventies, so I figure I'm safe for a while. But one day I decided to ask Bruce to do a 'gray hair check' on me. He looked at my brown roots and asked, 'What's wrong with that color?' I told him it was mousy brown, and not very attractive. (My hair is that shade of brown that just begs to be highlighted.) His response was: 'Some people like mice!' It may not seem funny now, but at the time it had me laughing all day. Bruce has taught me about the importance of humor and how to laugh at myself. It helps me lighten up and helps us feel more connected as a couple.

TAKING CARE OF YOURSELF: BODY, MIND, AND SPIRIT

Robert, a ninety-three-year-old retired physician, continues to play tennis twice a week. He has had both knees and one hip replaced and has trouble keeping score, but his backhand can still wipe just about any of his opponents off the court. For over fifty years, tennis has been Robert's primary form of exercise. His strength, determination, and competitive spirit continue to serve him well on the court as well as in life. Robert and his wife also take long walks together almost every day.

Recent research and advances in biotechnology have revolutionized diagnosis and treatment in just about every field of medicine. Knees and hips are being replaced at record rates, allowing people to enjoy physical activities well into their seventies and eighties, and even into their nineties. But as we've seen throughout this book, emotional stressors can wreak havoc on the body too.

What Is Stress?

Stress is often referred to as a "silent killer," because major body systems can be affected well before a diagnosis is made. Stress is a state of tension created in response to both external and internal demands and pressures. Work, family, financial obligations, unrealistic expectations, and negative beliefs, along with a lack of adequate coping mechanisms, can be serious and sometimes fatal. Stress is virtually unavoidable in our society. In fact, studies report that it accounts for a significant proportion of physician visits. Research indicates that stress, particularly long-term stress, is related to high blood pressure and high cholesterol, which themselves are risk factors for heart disease, stroke, digestive and respiratory problems, and cancer. Stress can compromise the immune system, leaving us more vulnerable as we age. Stress may also contribute to the widespread rate of insomnia in our society. Not getting enough sleep can add to stress. Sleep helps to nourish the mind, body, and spirit. More and more physicians are referring their patients to stress-reduction workshops and groups. Learning to relax and lessen stress is an important key to self-care.

It is human nature to want to soothe yourself when you are feeling stressed and anxious. However, resorting to unhealthy coping mechanisms such as drugs or alcohol, overeating or overspending, working too much or driving too fast can put even more stress on your body and on your relationship. We all need strategies to manage stress in order to survive in our modern society. Single men and women may look at their coupled counterparts with envy, thinking, "At least they have someone to share life's burdens." Having a trusted partner and knowing that you can support each other and work together through difficult times can be a great antidote to stress. While this may potentially be true, if couples are not working together and supporting each other in times of uncertainty and change, the results can cause more stress, damaging both the individual and the relationship.

Stress Management Suggestions for Couples

- Laugh together and bring humor into your relationship. Laughter can be a great stress reliever when things are tense.
- Do things that promote health and well-being: exercise, eat well, and get enough sleep. Enjoying a meal you've created together can nourish your relationship as well as your body, mind, and spirit.
- Find activities that you enjoy doing together: see a good movie, go for a bike ride, spend a day in the city, or go to a ball game, concert, or the museum. Just have fun together!
- Get help when you need it. Talk with a therapist or coach, or find a support group. Knowing you're not alone can be extremely helpful when dealing with stress.

Stress and the Mind-Body Connection

For decades, illness and disease were treated with little attention to the effects of thoughts, feelings, and emotions on the physical body. The emerging fields of holistic health and integrative medicine have provided evidence-based data that has had an impact on the diagnosis and treatment of illness. Holistic health is a healing-oriented approach that integrates the whole person—body, mind, and spirit—with environment and lifestyle choices. Meditation, yoga, art, music, dance, and the martial arts all have a place in wellness and mind-body medicine.

Fitness over Fifty

Getting older is a fact of life. No one is exempt. There are many things you can do to take care of your body and, as much as possible, counteract the effects of aging. Along with diet and nutrition, exercise tops the list! Not only does exercise build muscle, but it also improves bone density, joint strength, flexibility, and balance. Exercise releases endorphins in the body, decreasing pain and elevating mood and energy.

However, if you are raring to get started, hold on—don't just hop on the treadmill. If you have been relatively inactive and want to start an exercise program, the first step is to get checked by your physician. You need to know whether there are restrictions or recommendations in order to exercise safely. Just about anybody can start walking, but a more intensive workout can be potentially harmful if you are not prepared. A good program usually includes an aerobic workout, flexibility and balance exercises, as well as strength, endurance, and resistance training. It should also be tailored to you: your body and your needs. Many community adult education and hospital programs offer courses for people at different fitness levels. Check your local YMCA or health clubs. A good physical therapist or personal trainer can be an excellent resource to help you get started or get to the next level. Working with someone who has knowledge of health and exercise physiology can help you benefit from and enjoy your routine and prevent injuries.

Did You Know?

"If exercise could be packaged into a pill, it would be the single most widely prescribed and beneficial medicine in the nation." —Robert N. Butler, MD. Butler coined the term "ageism" and was the author of the Pulitzer Prize-winning book *Why Survive?*

Physical activities that are not as structured as exercise programs can also offer diversity and have additional benefits. Doing things you enjoy can be an important part of your daily or weekly routine, and playing basketball, gardening, walking, taking a dance or spinning class, yoga, tai chi, and many other activities all offer exercise benefits. The operative word is "enjoy." If you do not enjoy what you are doing, chances are the momentum will be short-lived. Discover physical activities that you and your partner like doing together. Both of you will benefit by supporting, encouraging, and coaching each other to stay on track. Committing to and working toward mutual goals is a great way to strengthen your relationship.

Tips for Developing Your Exercise Program

1. Get checked by your doctor before you start an exercise program.
2. Schedule in your exercise time. It's an appointment with yourself.

3. Find activities that you enjoy. If you don't like it, chances are you won't continue.

4. Exercise together. It's great to have a buddy to help keep up the momentum.

5. Set up a buddy system with a friend even if you can't exercise together. Agree, for example, that you'll each exercise thirty minutes at least five times a week, and if you don't, you'll pay $100 to the other person or donate it to a charity. Work on the honor system, and check in at the end of the week. The agreement to pay money if you don't exercise can be a terrific motivator. (Make the amount high enough so it will motivate you to exercise.)

As time passes, the body loses muscle mass and strength. In fact, 30 to 40 percent of lean body mass is lost between ages fifty and eighty. However, according to the National Institute on Aging, when older people lose the ability to do things independently, the cause is not aging alone. More likely, it is inactivity. Studies also indicate that people who are physically active have a lower risk of developing diseases such as Alzheimer's and dementia.

Major Benefits of Staying Active

- Maintaining muscle strength
- Strengthening bones and avoiding or slowing down the process of osteoporosis
- Keeping joints, tendons, and ligaments more flexible
- Strengthening heart and lungs
- Lowering risk of developing Alzheimer's and dementia
- Improving balance and coordination
- Increasing energy
- Promoting a sense of well-being

The Amazing Brain

If you are still not convinced about the positive effects of exercise, read on. Exercise not only helps build physical strength and resilience, but also improves mental function and helps us think and feel better. Research shows that our brain works better when we exercise. When we are younger, we usually have left-hemisphere or right-hemisphere dominance. As we age, brain function is more balanced, with both sides of the brain working together. In other words, the logical mind and the creative mind are working more in concert. In fact, this may be why so many of us search for encore careers or hobbies that are creative and challenge more expressive traits later in life.

Exercising the Brain

Our bodies and our brains thrive on exercise. Physical exercise is important because it influences the rate of creation of new neurons in your brain. Mental exercise is important because it helps determine how those new neurons are used and how long they survive. Current brain research suggests that a simple physical activity, such as walking, can stimulate the brain and improve memory processes. Continuing to learn is one of the best ways to maintain brain fitness. Activities such as learning new skills and abilities, doing a crossword puzzle, playing a musical instrument, reading, playing new games, and anything else that involves having to think and problem solve can promote brain fitness. Remember that learning can be fun. It doesn't have to be a chore.

AGING, LOSS, AND CHANGE

We all grow older, no matter how well we take care of ourselves. Our bodies are not made to last forever, and we become more vulnerable as we age. As much as we like to think we are in control, genetics predisposes us to certain diseases. In addition, life-altering conditions like Alzheimer's, Parkinson's, cancer, and heart disease can happen to anyone. Taking responsibility for your health, staying informed, eating well, and keeping fit all contribute to enhancing your quality of life and help you to be more resilient and able to cope if the unexpected does happen. Life can change on a dime with an accident, an illness, or a dreaded diagnosis. A fifty-nine-year-old colleague was recently diagnosed with early Alzheimer's. Although she is still relatively healthy, the diagnosis means the inevitability of change. Not only will her life change dramatically as time goes by, but her husband will also need to take on more responsibility as her illness progresses.

Did You Know?

According to the Centers for Disease Control, more than 50 percent of our potential for lifelong health is determined by our personal behaviors. And once you reach age sixty-five, your genes play less of a role than your health choices and how you take care of yourself in the future.

Everyone experiences loss at one time or another: loss of health, jobs, loved ones, friends, pets, homes, and other things we count on for security. Change and loss can lead to feelings of sadness, grief, anger, and abandonment. You never know how you will react to loss until you experience it. Being able to acknowledge and accept our feelings is an important part of the process of moving through loss in a healthy way. Profound grief and sadness are normal responses to loss and may take time to work through.

🧩 A Note from Roberta

My husband's Aunt Sophie was a bright, spirited woman who lived into her late eighties. Although less than five feet tall, she was a force to be reckoned with. If she had an opinion about something, there were no holds barred! Although Aunt Sophie never married, she had a partner for many years who was the love of her life. They traveled together, enjoyed doing the same things, and wrote each other love letters when they were apart. When he died, she was devastated. She had lost her best friend.

Aunt Sophie lived with cancer for several years, but it didn't stop her from being actively engaged in life. When we visited she was always dressed to the nines, including high heels and makeup, and usually with a batch of mandel bread—a traditional Jewish almond bread similar to biscotti—fresh out of the oven. She loved her grandnieces and grandnephews and treated them as her own. Emails went back and forth on a regular basis so she could keep up with their lives. Aunt Sophie spent a lot of time with her favorite addictions, reading and computer games, which she played for hours. When her eyesight became so bad that she could no longer read, Bruce started her on a new addiction: books on tape. She loved listening to them and amassed quite a library of volumes, which she traded with friends and neighbors.

As the cancer took hold of her body and she got closer to dying, we brought her to a hospice in Boston where we could be with her every day during the last few weeks of her life. One day we found her sitting up in bed, looking at herself in a mirror. She was upset about how pale she was and asked me to bring her blush to brighten up her face. Image was important to her, and even in the last few days of her life she put on her makeup and earrings. Aunt Sophie died peacefully in her sleep. She was an inspiration and a wonderful role model. The secrets to her

well-lived life were her generosity, love, positive attitude, many
interests, and using her keen and alert mind till the very end.

Bruce and Aunt Sophie had a special relationship. Being
together through her death gave us the opportunity to talk
about our beliefs and wishes for what we would want at the end
of our lives.

Dealing with Depression

When grief is prolonged with increasing depression, isolation, and an inability to engage in life, intervention—such as
talking with a counselor, seeing a doctor, and perhaps getting
medication—may be necessary.

Many of us know people who are dealing with medical and
health issues. You may be in that boat yourself. Serious or life-
threatening illness puts us right up against our own mortality.
We may begin to wonder "What's it all about?" and seek more
of a sense of purpose and meaning in life. People who have had
a history of recurrent depression and difficulty coping with loss
and change may be more prone to serious depression and anxiety in the face of loss. Not having an adequate support system
can also be a major factor in depression. In addition, shame and
guilt are often associated with depression, making it difficult for
people to ask for and accept help. If untreated, depression can
be devastating for everyone.

Living with a partner or family member who is depressed
can be overwhelming. You may blame yourself, try to "fix it,"
or become more distant. Trying to talk with someone who is
depressed can be difficult and frustrating: he or she often cannot
describe what they need, and you may be at a loss about what to
do. The person who is depressed needs help, and you need support. Having a sounding board can take the burden off both of

you. You need to have someone who can listen to you, help you develop coping skills, and support you in taking care of yourself. Depression is an illness that affects the entire family, and everyone needs support through the process.

Recognizing the Signs of Depression

Being alert to the signs and symptoms of depression can be life-saving. If you or someone you care about is experiencing the following symptoms, it may be time to seek professional help:

- Irritability
- Fatigue
- Lack of interest in activities previously enjoyed
- Isolation
- Changes in appetite and sleep patterns
- Self-medicating with alcohol or drugs
- Expressing feelings of hopelessness and not wanting to live
- Preoccupation with death

The "D" Word

Talking openly about death has long been taboo in our society. How often have you heard people say "if he dies" rather than "when he dies"? We shield children from the concept of death, probably because we do not want to deal with it ourselves. The tendency is to avoid the topic but, as we well know, life is finite and death is a reality. Just as you and your partner need to plan for the next part of your lives, it is also important that both of you make provisions for your survivors.

This starts with making sure that all of your legal and other important documents are kept together in a safe place. Your partner and at least one or two other family members or trusted friends should know where this is and how to access it. It is a terrible situation when someone dies and nobody, including the grieving partner, knows where to find the documents. In addition, it is very important for you and your partner to know each other's end-of-life wishes. Being open with your family creates closeness and helps prepare them for when the time comes.

If you or your partner is a caregiver for your parents or anticipate that at some point you will be, it is important to talk with them about all of the above issues while they are still able to talk with you. You need to know where their important documents are kept and be sure that they are in order. Likewise, it is important to talk with them about their end-of-life wishes, finding a way to bring the subject up if they don't. It is unfortunate when we deny the reality of someone who knows they are dying by not being able to acknowledge it ourselves. How sad for that person and for those who are left to grieve, who perhaps never had the opportunity to say what was in their hearts. Don't be afraid to bring up the topic of death and dying. You will know soon enough if someone does not want to talk about it.

People who are chronically ill or near death are often relieved to talk about their feelings with someone who is willing to listen. Being able to say good-bye to a loved one brings closure for both of you. People we love live on in our hearts long after they are gone. All too often, however, these important conversations do not happen because it can be difficult and painful to talk about death and dying.

🧩 A Note from Roberta

My parents had the same group of friends from the time they were fourteen years old. They all grew up in the Bronx and moved to Florida to retire. One by one, they died, and eventually there was only my mother and Uncle Al. Mom and Al lived in the same retirement community and had known each other for seventy-three years, but when she was dying he would not go to see her. He was unable to deal with my mother's death because it reminded him of his own mortality. Uncle Al was the last of a group of friends who had known each other almost all of their lives, but he had never learned how to say good-bye.

A friend tells the story of the celebration of her sister's life in the last few weeks before she died. Family and friends gathered to share stories and honor what she had meant to them, and she was able to do the same. Imagine how the experience of dying could be transformed by creating rituals to honor the life and accept the loss.

Wills, Documents, and Other Important Information

- Wills need to be rewritten upon marriage, divorce, remarriage, birth or adoption of children or grandchildren, or any time you want to change designation of property upon your death.
- Be sure your partner and another trusted person know where your legal documents are located, where there is a list of important accounts and passwords, and the name, address, and phone number of your accountant, lawyer, estate attorney, and any other key people involved in your financial and legal life.
- Make sure you each have a signed copy of your healthcare proxy, living will, and durable power of attorney. Some states require that your signature be notarized. It is important to check the requirements in your state so that your documents are

valid. Reevaluate your documents periodically and update so they reflect your current views. If you are hospitalized, copies of your documents need to be part of your medical record.

- Sign and understand the HIPAA Privacy Act, which gives you rights and protections over your healthcare information.

- Make sure your partner and another trusted person has access to keys for safe deposit boxes, homes, cars, etc.

- Be sure to create a list of your doctors and medications so your healthcare providers can be reached, if needed.

- Talk with your adult children about your financial plans. If there will be an inheritance, however small or large, the receiver benefits from preparation.

- If you have children who are still minors, be sure you have worked out guardianship arrangements if anything happens to both of you.

- Talk with a legal adviser regarding ways to protect any assets for your survivors, such as trusts and beneficiary designation for any pensions and life insurance policies.

It is important for couples to know each other's end-of-life preferences. It may be a difficult subject, one that you would prefer to put off, but if your partner dies unexpectedly, you will be grateful to have had the conversation. Talking together about your end-of-life wishes well before you get there can save a lot of pain and confusion. Putting it off can lead to more stress at a time that is already difficult and stressful, especially for the surviving partner.

The Healthcare Puzzle

Although the healthcare reform bill has passed, there continues to be a great deal of controversy around it. Given the current reality, it's particularly important to stay abreast of changes. Being well-informed and having accurate information is essential in order to understand your options and make healthcare decisions that are best for you.

If either you or your partner is age sixty-five or older, Medicare, a federally funded health insurance program, will be a piece of your puzzle. It doesn't cover everything and there are decisions you will need to make about supplemental health insurance as well as long-term-care expenses. Information about Medicare can be found on the government website. (See "Resources," page 275.) The website is comprehensive but can be confusing, especially if you are just looking for basic information. To get the most accurate and up-to-date information, you can contact the Social Security Administration based in Washington, DC, or an office in your local community. Although Medicare is part of the Social Security Administration, you can apply for Medicare without having to apply for Social Security benefits. You may choose to delay taking your Social Security until you're eligible for full compensation. There is also a "spousal option" if your spouse receives Social Security and you've reached your full retirement age. Depending on your situation there may be a number of options to consider about how and when to begin your Social Security benefits. As we mentioned in Conversation 2 ("Let's Talk about Money," pages 31–58), it's helpful to talk with your financial adviser and/or estate attorney so you can make decisions based on what's in your best interest.

HEALTHCARE PROXY AND LIVING WILLS

A healthcare proxy is a legal document that allows a person to choose someone to make medical decisions on their behalf should they become unable to do so. Knowing that you have designated a trusted person who knows you and will respect your wishes can be very reassuring. A living will is a legal document that states your wishes regarding life-prolonging medical treatments and other end-of-life issues. It is important to have a living will as it informs your healthcare providers and your family about your desires for medical treatment in the event that you are not able to speak for yourself. As with any major decision regarding your will, trusts, and other legal documents, consulting with an elder law or estate attorney is a wise thing to do.

What You Need to Know about Healthcare Proxy, Living Will, and Durable Power of Attorney Documents

- Healthcare proxy, living will, and durable power of attorney documents should be part of your long-term planning.
- You each need to have your own healthcare proxy, living will, and durable power of attorney forms.
- You each need to sign a HIPAA healthcare privacy of information form which stipulates how and to whom your healthcare information can be shared.
- Many legal forms are available online or from an attorney. (See "Resources," page 275.)
- Check the laws in your state governing the requirements necessary for your documents to be binding. Some states require two witnesses, while others may require notarization. Laws vary by state of residence.
- Make sure a copy of your healthcare proxy document is included in your medical records in case you need to be hospitalized.

Estate-Planning Checklist (for each of you)
- Up-to-date will
- Healthcare proxy

- Power of attorney
- Living will
- HIPAA form
- List of what you are bequeathing
- Legacy requests
- Where your important documents are kept
- What assets you have
- Where your accounts are located
- Account numbers, PINs, and passwords
- Names of trusted people who know where your car keys, house keys, and safe deposit box keys are kept
- Important names and contact information:
  - Attorney/financial adviser/CPA
  - Insurance broker
  - Healthcare providers
  - Estate attorney
  - Bank name and branch office location
  - Safe deposit box location and number

Although you may not want to think about end-of-life issues, it is the responsible thing to do. Do you really want your partner or children to have to make difficult decisions when they are caught up in their own confusion and grief? It is important for you and your partner to be aware of each other's preferences so that if and when one of you becomes ill, decisions about medical care and life-prolonging treatment are clear. At some point, usually sooner rather than later, it's also important to talk with adult children, and perhaps other trusted relatives and friends, about your decisions.

🧩 A Note from Dori

As I previously mentioned, my father had a tendency to be controlling, which was difficult much of the time but proved helpful in dealing with end-of-life issues in our family. After he was diagnosed with a debilitating illness in his late sixties, he sat us down to talk not only about financial issues, but also about his wishes and desires in regard to his own death and how he hoped we would care for our mother.

He and my mother discussed and signed their living wills and healthcare proxies. We discussed the various contingencies of what they wanted. This proved invaluable. My mother, as the executor for my father, knew he wanted no heroic efforts and was able to enforce this after he had a major heart attack. In turn, as the executor for my mother's living will and healthcare proxy, I knew that she did not want to be kept alive if there was no quality of life; she did not want to live for the sake of being kept alive in a nursing home if she wasn't able to enjoy being alive. When the time came, with the support of my brother, who also knew her wishes, I was able to make the decision not to extend her life through extraordinary measures.

Given this experience, my husband and I have written our healthcare proxies, living wills, and durable power of attorney, and have long-term care insurance. We are each the executor for the other, with alternative executors if need be. We both know each other's wishes and have promised to carry them out to the best of our abilities. We have also learned that it's important to revisit these wishes as time passes. For example, when my husband recently had surgery, we went over his wishes and some had changed.

Although I don't like to think ahead to our death, I do find it comforting that we have discussed our wishes and desires and have prepared the necessary documents for the end of our lives. In addition we have recently made new decisions about our burial and funeral wishes and have prepaid our funeral expenses. It is our way of controlling the parts of our life that we can control, and it's a loving way of protecting whoever survives and providing for our son.

LONG-TERM-CARE INSURANCE

How much do you know about long-term-care insurance? What are the benefits and costs of having long-term-care insurance and potential consequences if you do not have it? Whether to buy long-term-care insurance can be a confusing piece of your retirement puzzle. Knowing the facts will help you and your partner make decisions that are right for your circumstances.

Long-term-care insurance has become increasingly popular due to the rapidly growing elderly population and the advanced medical technology that enables people to live healthier for more years. Many people think about buying long-term-care insurance to protect their assets. But more accurately, long-term-care insurance is a plan for providing an income stream that allows you to remain in your home or community and receive care for an extended period of time. It can protect your loved ones from the emotional, physical, and financial burden a chronic illness places on a family. Rather than being the actual caregiver, your partner or family can manage care provided by paid caregivers.

Having long-term-care insurance can be a great reassurance and protect your partner and family financially and emotionally. But it is important to know if it is the best choice for you. As with other major decisions, get the facts and be a well-informed consumer. Take the time to get accurate information and do comparative research so that you understand what you are buying. Read between the lines and know the details of the plan you are considering. Meet with a reliable agent who can answer your questions, provide information, and help you look at your unique situation. You may not agree on whether to buy long-term-care insurance, or you may find out that one or both of you is ineligible, but in any case, talking together and planning ahead can save a lot of pain and hardship in the future.

Long-Term-Care Insurance: Things to Consider

- Do you have assets that should be protected?
- How important is it to you to stay in your home and maintain your independence?
- Do you and your partner have money for care in your home or in a facility if one or both of you needs it?
- Would your children have the finances or ability to care for you? How would they feel about it?
- What kind of coverage does the plan provide?
- What is the cost of premiums over the years?
- Is there a cost-of-living increase for coverage benefits?

Negative Inheritance

As mentioned, the cost of long-term care can be a major burden for families. In some situations parents who don't plan ahead for long-term-care costs may leave their children with what is called a "negative inheritance," a term credited to Boston University economics professor Laurence Kotlikoff. Basically, the term describes a situation where the costs to children who care for their aging relatives may exceed any inheritances they might have received. This can be especially difficult for families who also have expenses for their children and/or were planning on saving funds for their own retirement.

While advisers say planning ahead can preempt much of the emotional and financial duress that caring for a sick and aging parent entails, the most crucial, and often most elusive, ingredient is proactive family discussion.

🧩 A Note from Dori

When David, my husband, was in his late sixties and I was in my midfifties, we decided to apply for long-term-care insurance. We weren't sure if we would qualify because of some prior health issues but were pleased to discover we would be eligible for coverage. We needed to prepare for the application by getting our medical records together for review. We had two pressing reasons:

1. We wanted to be sure we had coverage if either one of us needed care.
2. We didn't want our health care needs and costs to become a burden on our son.

For us it felt like an "act of love" as an insurance and assurance for the future. We explored a few options, talked with some experts in the field, and found a plan that provides what we felt we would need. Despite the cost of the yearly premiums, we're glad we made the decision. We take out car insurance and have insurance on our house and property, so for us long-term-care insurance helps us feel we also have some protection for our future medical needs.

SUMMARY

Most of us want to age well, but we don't always have the resources or know how to do that. The intent of this chapter is to offer practical information and suggestions as well as encourage both of you to think about what aging well means to you. There are many ways to get information today. Hopefully, the resources in this book will help you get started. How you take care of yourself and each other throughout your lives and the lifestyle choices you make will have an enormous impact on your health and wellness now, as well as in the years to come. There are many important decisions that will need to be made along the way, and the ones you make today will have a ripple effect into tomorrow. Ultimately, aging well is about growing whole rather than growing old.

Talking It Through: Creating Your Shared Vision

Spend some time thinking about the following issues. Use your journal to write down your thoughts and feelings, as well as anything you want to talk about with your partner. If you need a refresher on how to communicate effectively, go back to "Getting to Yes Together: The Importance of Communication," pages xxxiii–xlv.

As you get started, remember the five tips and "Have a BLAST!"

- **B**laming gets in the way
- **L**isten without interrupting
- **A**gree to disagree and don't make assumptions
- **S**et a safe space for discussion
- **T**ake time to talk without distractions

Exercise 1

Go it solo: Things to think about on your own

1. Are there medical or health issues that need to be addressed?
2. Am I conscientious about self-care (for example, exercise, nutrition, and regular visits to my doctor)?
3. How do I handle stress?
4. Have we talked together about our current and future healthcare needs?
5. Have we discussed healthcare proxies, living wills, and long-term-care insurance?
6. Do we have the information we need to plan for our future?

Exercise 2
Couple time: Things to talk about together

1. Take turns sharing your responses to each question in Exercise 1, one at a time.
2. Share something positive that you learned about each other.
3. Take time to question anything that was not clear.
4. Make a list of the things that you agree on.
5. Set a time for your next conversation.

It is important to remember that these are big questions that take time to resolve. You are probably not going to agree on everything; most couples don't. Being able to communicate effectively can help you come to solutions, one conversation at a time.

Puzzle Piece: Health and Wellness
What one or two things could you do to improve your health and wellness? How can you support your partner to reach

his or her wellness goals? Write your discoveries in the
Puzzle Piece section at the end of the "Creating Your Shared
Vision" chapter, page 263.

Funwork
Do individually

Make a list of activities that you would enjoy doing with
your partner that would support you both in aging well. For
example:

- Take a walk in nature.
- Learn to tango.
- Do a crossword puzzle together.
- Learn something new together.
- Join a health club.
- Allow your imagination to guide you and have fun.

Now share your list with your partner and create your
shared list. Pick one of the activities from your shared list.
Then, get out your calendar and pick a date and time. Make
a commitment to each other to follow through. By scheduling it, there is a greater chance that you will keep the commitment and make it happen.

Continue with other activities; keep doing the one you
chose, or both, on a regular basis.

By the way, many spas do offer reasonable off-season rates
or days when two people can go for the price of one. But don't
expect Medicare or other insurance to pay. We checked, and it's
not covered.

Choosing Where and How to Live: Staying Put or Exploring New Frontiers?

Prior to retiring in their midsixties, Bonnie and Bill had talked about the possibility of moving from the Northeast to a warmer climate. But they loved their home, which was near an urban center and in close proximity to shops, restaurants, and entertainment. They had a wonderful network of friends, an active social life, and excellent medical facilities nearby. Most importantly, Bonnie and Bill realized they would miss their children and grandchildren. They decided that staying put was the best choice for them. They could always rent a place in Florida if they wanted to get away for a month or two during the winter.

As time went by, Bonnie and Bill were glad they had made the decision to stay in their home. Bonnie worked three days a week in the local library, while Bill taught ESL (English as a second language) at the high school. They got involved in church activities, where they reconnected with old friends and made new ones. Although they dealt with some medical issues, such as arthritis, high cholesterol, and diabetes, they were conscientious about their health and took good care of themselves.

By her early seventies, the arthritis was interfering more with Bonnie's life. She had a great deal of pain and stiffness, which made walking up and down stairs several times a day difficult. Bonnie and Bill decided to renovate their home, making accommodations for their physical needs. They converted the first floor to a primary living space, with a master bedroom and full bath equipped with hand rails and supports, a guest bathroom, TV room and office, and a separate laundry room. Living safely and comfortably in their home for as long as possible was their goal.

Bonnie and Bill decided early on to stay in their home for as long as possible. They planned for the future and had many conversations about what kind of care they wanted if one or both became ill and unable to care for themselves or each other. They talked with their children about their choices and decisions for the future. Their children were relieved to hear about their parents' wishes and plans and wanted to support and honor their decision to stay in their own home. Although the conversation was initially uncomfortable, they found it helped to have the issues on the table, so everyone could be part of the discussion.

Talking with your children about what you want as you get older is important for everyone. It can be comforting for you and your partner to know that your wishes will be honored, and a relief to your children to know that, when the time comes, they can make decisions according to your wishes.

HAVE YOU TALKED ABOUT YOUR LIFESTYLE AND WHERE YOU WANT TO LIVE?

Ted and Kate had worked hard for many years in stressful corporate careers. They raised three children, who were all doing well. They had planned carefully and would be able to retire at age sixty-six, which was a few years away. Then it would be "their time" to do something totally different. They both wanted a simple life that would allow them to be in nature, ride horses, and have time for their hobbies. Until they started talking seriously about where they wanted to live, the topic of relocation had never come up. But having the lifestyle they wanted would probably mean relocating, possibly out of state. As the conversation progressed over time, they thought about where they had traveled and the places they most enjoyed staying.

For both Ted and Kate, it was the wonderful bed-and-breakfasts they'd stayed in while traveling where they had always felt most at home. A light went on for them. They knew that running a B&B was a lot of work, but with retirement savings and the sale of their home, they would be able to hire enough staff to help out. Kate loved cooking but rarely had time for it, and Bill enjoyed fixing things and working in the garden. Together, they had a lot of skills to get started. The first step was doing research into the economic realities of running a B&B, where the best locations might be, and visiting areas where they might want to live.

It was a big risk, but one that Ted and Kate wanted to take. They had always been a good team and worked well together raising the kids and running a busy household, even while both had high-pressure jobs. They knew this new venture wouldn't be easy. Many B&Bs never make it, especially in a down economy, but the adventure seemed worth the risk, and they were excited about doing it together.

Did You Know?

"Creating a vocation vacation—spending a few vacation days actually working in the profession you've always wanted—can be the first step toward making that dream come true." —Brian Kurth, author of *Test-Drive Your Dream Job: A Step-by-Step Guide to Finding and Creating the Work You Love*

We go through many changes in life, and often what we wanted in our thirties or forties no longer fits our vision for the life we want to live now. When couples talk together, they may discover things they never knew before. What if your partner's dream is to work on a dude ranch in Montana? Or maybe the dream is to sell most of your belongings and build a log cabin in Vermont, or join the Peace Corps. Will you be on board, or do you have dreams of your own? If you are lucky, you may get to share a dream like Ted and Kate, but it might not happen that way. It is important to talk about the kind of life you want to retire to. There are many options today that are worth exploring. Deciding what's right for you will probably take some research and many conversations.

Did You Know?

According to an AARP survey, 80 percent of seniors in America want to remain in their own homes as they grow older. In order to do that, in addition to possibly renovating their home to accommodate changing physical needs, they need community support, accessible medical care, and adequate transportation.

For several years, Gary and Lyn literally and figuratively went back and forth; Gary's heart was in their Vermont home, which Lyn also loved, but Lyn's friends and social and professional lives were in Boston. With Lyn approaching sixty and Gary turning sixty-five, the tipping point had been reached. They needed to make a plan they could both agree to.

After many discussions, Gary and Lyn finally decided to work three days a week in the city, where they would be able to see family and friends, and spend long weekends in Vermont. They wanted to live more simply and have the freedom to more deeply explore the creative aspects of their character. Doing so required many concessions but gave them the time to continue to work on finding balance in their lives.

Many couples face the dilemma of where to live and what kind of lifestyle they want. It is not a decision made overnight, but one that results from having many conversations, sometimes over the course of several years. Beginning the conversation before you get to a decision-making place can help pave the way for an easier transition.

🧩 A Note from Roberta

Bruce moved to Boston from Atlanta in January 1999. Imagine moving to New England in the dead of winter from the more temperate South. He has never really acclimated, and every year, as the first snowflakes fall, he starts talking about how much he hates the cold. His dream is to move to California, but I can't imagine leaving my children, grandchildren, and friends. I love the change of seasons, including winter (though I wish it was shorter), but recently have begun to understand why people move to warmer climates as they get older. As we begin to talk about the dilemma, we will need to think more creatively. Maybe it doesn't have to be one or the other. Although we are not yet ready to explore options, I can see that over the next few years, we may be asking ourselves, "Do we want to stay put or explore new frontiers?"

Do You Need to Be Thinking about All This Now?

You may be wondering why it is important to think about all of this, especially if you're not yet ready to retire. It's true that what you want or need at your current age may change as the years pass, but it is better to explore options ahead of time rather than waiting until you are feeling pressured to make a decision. What you need when you are active and independent may be different from the assistance you require later on, when you may be less self-reliant.

Do We Stay or Do We Go?

Talking together about where to live is an important part of retirement transition. The decision is usually based on lifestyle choices, geographical preferences, proximity to family and friends, health issues and needs, and, of course, financial considerations. Many couples, like Bonnie and Bill, choose to stay in their home and make accommodations over time. Others decide to downsize and either buy or rent a smaller home or condominium, or consider other alternative living options. Recreational vehicles are becoming more popular for full- or part-time living and travel. And some more adventurous couples take off for parts unknown, in the United States or abroad. If you and your partner are thinking about relocating to another state or country, do yourself a favor and invest the time and money to see what it would really be like to live there.

Reasons to Think Ahead about Lifestyle and Housing Decisions

- You have the opportunity to think individually and talk together about what you both want.
- Knowing the lifestyle you want can help you make better financial decisions.

- It takes time to work out a plan, especially if you and your partner have different visions.
- You have time to explore possibilities you may want to consider by talking with others, getting accurate information, and using the Internet to research ideas.
- You can travel to get a sense of an area you're considering, but avoid making decisions prematurely.
- You also have the opportunity to rent in the area for a few months, if possible, to see what it is like on a day-to-day basis.

You would be surprised at the number of people who move to a place they have "fallen in love with" only to realize, after the glow wears off, they made a very costly mistake.

Dan and Carolyn spent a few weeks in Costa Rica every year. They loved the lifestyle, the diverse wildlife, the culture, and the warmth and friendliness of the people. They thought it would be a wonderful place to live when they retired. When Carolyn left nursing and Dan sold his small auto parts business, they sold their modest home and took money from retirement funds to buy a beautiful two-bedroom condominium on the beach. They looked forward to visits from family and friends.

Within a few months after moving, Carolyn was miserable. She missed her friends and family, her hair dresser, and the conveniences of home that she had taken for granted. For several months, Dan enjoyed being on a permanent vacation. He loved fishing and scuba diving and taking day trips around the area. But eventually, Dan admitted that he, too, missed their old life. Dan and Carolyn had to face the fact that they had made a costly mistake. Costa Rica was a wonderful place to visit, but they hadn't anticipated what it would be like after the novelty wore off. Six months later, they sold the condo for less than they had paid, but were relieved to be moving back home.

Carolyn and Dan made the decision to move to Costa Rica without checking the reality of living there for more than a few weeks at a time. It might have been wiser to spend the money and rent a place for several months before making a major decision that would impact their life.

Judy and Greg approached their move in a very different way. For years, they had talked about retiring to North Carolina. They loved being there for a month each year, but actually moving and leaving family and friends was a difficult decision that they hadn't been ready to make.

Over the years, while they vacationed in North Carolina, they developed friendships with people who lived in the area as well as other vacationers like themselves. As each northern winter seemed harsher than the one before, Judy and Greg looked forward to going south, where the climate was more moderate. They loved playing golf, enjoyed the arts and crafts festivals, and appreciated the slower pace of living.

They finally both agreed that North Carolina was their "retirement destination." Before buying a home, they decided to rent for a year and give themselves a chance to adjust to the change. Judy moved to their rented condo to start fixing it up, while Greg was in the process of selling the house they had lived in for many years. They had made the decision to sell their home whether or not the move was permanent. Both of them felt the house was bigger than they needed, and they were more than ready to give up shoveling snow.

Things to Consider:
Do We Stay or Do We Go?

Relocating is a major life transition, especially if you are leaving family, friends, and your social network. It is easy to focus on one aspect of the new environment, such as climate, culture, or aesthetics. But there are many questions to ask and factors to consider before the final decision is made.

If you are staying in your home, consider:

- renovating to accommodate to your changing needs
- renting out a room
- trading a room for household or caregiving help

Consider downsizing or relocating when:

- your children move out
- you retire
- the house seems too big and the upkeep is too much to handle
- it is a good time to sell and you would get a good price
- you or your partner's medical needs change

To help you make informed decisions about where to live, consider:

- affordability
- climate
- diversity in age in the community
- taxes
- medical and healthcare resources
- cost of living

- crime rate
- cultural, educational, and recreational opportunities
- geographical closeness to family
- proximity to a religious community
- proximity to public transportation, airport, and trains
- availability of shopping
- amenities such as marina, golf course, tennis, swimming pool, fitness center, or hiking, walking, and bicycle trails
- proximity to the ocean, lakes, or mountains

🧩 A Note from Dori

David, Louie, and I live in a town house in Boston with many stairs just to get inside, and more stairs within to get to the bedrooms. We bought this unit when David was fifty and I was in my late thirties. We did some initial renovations and put in an extra bathroom with a seat in the shower, anticipating it might be good to have as we got older. We love the location, which is within walking distance to stores, restaurants, the library, town hall, and public transportation, and close to our work and medical care. Our intention is to stay there as long as we can. There is a space downstairs with a ground-floor entry that could house a caregiver, if the need arises, or be modified so we could, depending on the cost, install an elevator or lift to get upstairs. At present, we feel the living space and stairs help keep us in shape. I do, however, get people to help carry heavy grocery items up the stairs. Although we love Boston, we have discovered it helps to break up the winter with a vacation to a warm spot. Prior to Louie's birth, we went away for long weekends every four to six weeks. Now we work around school vacations. Although we like sun and warmth in winter, we also have used some winter vacations for family skiing and some for "staycations" since we all also love being at home.

IS A RETIREMENT COMMUNITY RIGHT FOR YOU?

Retirement communities catering to people fifty and older have become very popular. Some are designed as residential communities, offering facilities for people who want to stay physically active and socially involved. Others focus on sports such as golf, tennis, or sailing. Not all retirement communities have costly amenities; some provide an affordable lifestyle for individuals and couples who want to live in a community environment with people their age. There are communities with a specific religious orientation, but most are nondenominational and diverse. In addition, continuing care retirement communities (CCRCs) are springing up all around the country. They offer graduated levels of care, ranging from residential to assisted living and nursing care facilities. Most require initial health, independence, and financial criteria for inclusion. Some are set up so you purchase your unit, while others provide rental units. A reason given by many who are considering a CCRC is that they don't want to worry about being a burden to their children or finding appropriate facilities when they are older. Many residents of retirement communities say it is like being in a "camp for adults," with stimulating activities, new friends, and opportunities to feel needed and helpful.

Craig and Marion decided in their late sixties to move into a retirement community. Marion had been responsible for her mother's care during the last few years of her life and couldn't believe how difficult it had been to find appropriate resources. Craig and Marion agreed that they didn't want their children to have to go through the same pain and frustration. Their friends thought they were crazy to make this decision at such a young age, but Craig and Marion felt it was right for them. They had visited many retirement communities and found one they both liked not far from their children, grandchildren, and friends.

Now, they love their new lifestyle. They either have meals with other residents, cook at home, or go out with friends. The community offers a wide range of classes and activities to choose from. Craig is studying French, and Marion has begun exploring her artistic side in painting classes. They've become friends with older adults in the community and admire how many of them are still active and aging well. Craig and Marion are healthy and active, and they feel reassured that as their health needs change, they'll receive appropriate care without having to be a burden to their children.

Finding a retirement community that will suit your needs takes time and research. Talking about your requirements and criteria and knowing the specifics about what is and isn't included at the place you're considering is important. Communities usually have rules and regulations that you are expected to follow. Make sure that you understand the rules before signing up so that you don't end up surprised and disappointed.

Some Questions to Consider When Choosing a Retirement Community

- What are the up-front costs, what are the monthly costs, and what services are included?
- What amenities do you want the residence to have, such as a gym, tennis courts, golf course, or a pool?

- What are the additional fees for these services?
- If you have a pet, what are the rules and regulations for pets?
- Do you want your children or grandchildren to visit for more than a week or two? If so, is this allowed?
- Are grandchildren allowed to use the pool, and, if so, starting at what age?
- What happens to your unit if you need to relocate to another phase of assistance? What happens if you need the additional assistance and your partner doesn't?

Sometimes, retirement communities are affiliated with universities and require that residents take classes. This may appeal to older adults who thrive on lifelong learning. You may like the accommodations, but if you're not interested in taking classes, then this probably isn't the right choice for you.

Whatever you are considering, make the time to visit, ask questions, talk with residents, eat a few meals in the dining room, and walk around the premises. Where to live is a decision that you need to make together. Whatever you decide, remember it is the place you may be calling home for many years. Be sure that what you're signing up for is something that you both like and will feel comfortable living in. It is true that you can rethink your decision if you're not happy, but finding another place and moving again is not only stressful, but also costly. Don't feel rushed to make a decision. Take your time and think it through.

🧩 A Note from Dori

When my parents were in their late sixties, they considered the possibility of a retirement community and put a down payment on a unit. A few of their friends lived in the community. At the last minute, however, they changed their minds and decided they didn't want to live in a community with everyone the same age. Instead, they wanted to buy a single-family house in a residential area with young families. The house they found was in an isolated neighborhood with no public transportation to supermarkets, shops, or medical facilities. Wherever they wanted to go, they had to drive. Although I understood their wishes to be in a multigenerational community, I brought up my concerns about the location and lack of public transportation nearby prior to the purchase. They thought I was being overcautious and decided to buy the house anyway.

Shortly after moving into their new home, my father's health took a turn for the worse, and he died the following year. My mother thought she would be able to maintain the new house with the help of neighbors, but she began to feel isolated from her friends. Visiting was difficult, because she was no longer able to drive in the dark, and neither were her friends. We explored a variety of possibilities, such as having a college student move in who could offer some help and companionship in exchange for rent, but this did not work out since the students were already set in their living situations. Six months later, on a visit to the East Coast, my mother had a stroke. My brother and I sold their house to pay for her care and expenses.

In hindsight, had my parents followed their initial plan and bought the unit in the retirement community, my mother would have been able to move to the community's assisted-living facility, where she would have received care and had friends nearby.

Alternative Communities

Hundreds of different kinds of alternative communities for individuals and couples are springing up across the country.

Nationwide, there is a pioneering movement toward developing more intergenerational living and working communities and some communities affiliated with colleges and universities. Such programs appeal to boomers and others who are interested in intergenerational living, lifelong learning, cooperative living, cohousing, or intentional communities. There are also models developing around the country allowing seniors to "age in place." Here are a few examples of the options:

- Beacon Hill Village in Boston, Massachusetts, is a self-developed community group. Members live in separate residences but share services and activities. The village model is being replicated in other communities throughout the country.
- Lasell Village, on the Lasell College Campus in Newton, Massachusetts, is an award-winning senior housing community that emphasizes active, intellectually enriched living for seniors. Residents are required to take courses at Lasell College.
- An intergenerational cooperative community in Berkeley, California, has young families and older adults living together and providing services to each other. Elders, as "grandparenting" figures, help out with babysitting and child care.
- Intergenerational Living and Health Care, based in Minneapolis, Minnesota, is a nonprofit program. Part of its mission is "to strengthen connections between generations through intergenerational programs that link children and older adults." It provides health care, assisted living, and residential settings for elders, combined with early childhood education centers where children and elders are able to interconnect.

- Project Independence in North Hempstead, New York, is a "daily life assistance" program for senior citizens who wish to remain in their own homes instead of moving to assisted-living communities. Community resources are utilized to enable seniors to remain independent for as long as possible.

Cohousing, another option to consider, is a collaborative model that brings together living in a private home with the benefit of sharing mutual aid and social support. Communities are usually small-scale neighborhoods that provide a balance between personal privacy and living among people who know and care about each other. Some cohousing communities, such as Elder Spirit in Abingdon, Virginia, and Silver Sage in Boulder, Colorado, advertise as environmentally safe and ecologically friendly. Some cohousing communities are for seniors and others are multigenerational.

Intentional Communities

An intentional community is planned and created by a group of people who share similar social, political, religious, or spiritual values. Often, the aim of the community is living together cooperatively in order to foster a lifestyle that reflects shared values. You may also want to explore the possibility of starting your own intentional community with "kindred spirits."

Jane and Jim have been talking with a group of other couples about forming an intentional community together. They are all in their sixties and seventies, and at least one, if not both, members of the couples still work either full- or part-time. They all have active lifestyles and similar interests. They enjoy culture and learning and physical activities like golf, hiking, and bicycling and love being near the ocean. Being close to medical facilities and a fitness center are also important considerations. Although they don't necessarily need to live near their children, they do want to have easy access to a local airport so they can visit with children and grandchildren and have family visit them. Jane, Jim, and their friends have been planning for their retirement transition for years and are in the process of discussing possible locations. They're hoping to have the health and resources to develop their community and also be able to maintain close contact with their families.

There are other kinds of communities that draw people with special interests or needs, such as a residential land trust or a housing cooperative. Some are in residential communities and others are housed in the broader community. The least clearly planned form of an intentional community is a city, some known to be more progressive and others more conservative. In the United States, for example, certain cities attract like-minded residents simply by virtue of their reputation for shared values or fostering an attractive lifestyle. There are also similar communities developing in other countries. An industrious second-half-of-life project might be identifying your needs as well as your values and interests and creating a community where one has not previously existed.

Other kinds of alternative communities that you might want to explore are eco-villages (where the emphasis is on a "green environment"), communes, and urban housing cooperatives. One of the major advantages to any of these living environments is being part of a community where you can have connection with like-minded people. There are many intentional and alternative communities such as these around the country. (For additional information, see "Resources," page 275.)

RV Communities

Retirement transition can be a time to fulfill your wanderlust. For many couples, the RV (recreational vehicle) community is a great way to explore the country and become identified with a traveling group. For people who don't want the hassle of airline or train travel, prefer taking pets along with them, or like having their own kitchen and bathroom, an RV can be an effective and efficient way to travel. Although RVs are not inexpensive, you may be able to buy a used RV or an older model without all the amenities at a reasonable price. RV aficionados like to have control of their itineraries, where they go, how long they stay, and where they're going next. There is a whole culture attached to the RV community, which you learn when you're part of it. Traveling in an RV gives you the opportunity to meet a lot of people from this country and from around the world. In addition, you get to have all kinds of adventures along the way.

Louise and Fred had decided that after they retired, they wanted to travel around the country and visit places they had never seen before. But Roscoe, a loyal family member who happened to be a dog, was part of the family. Since most hotels and motels don't allow pets, Louise and Fred decided that a traveling home would be perfect for the three of them.

They bought a used RV and took off—with Roscoe's ears flapping in the breeze and his tail happily wagging. They loved their RV experience. They enjoyed meeting interesting people from all over the country and the world and being part of a new community with its own values, rules, and ethics. There were times they changed their itinerary to spend more time with people who had become friends. They shared a "pioneering" spirit with other RV owners, in a community where people valued freedom, mobility, and adventure.

There are many RV communities around the country where you can live full-time or stay for short periods during your travels. Some communities are well-established and have town meetings and a sense of neighborhood. They may provide separate areas for "transients" who are just passing through. Many RV communities welcome families with children, while others are established retirement communities. As with other housing options, talking together, learning from others, and visiting different communities enables you to find a community that meets the needs of you and your partner.

When you rent or buy an RV, you are making a choice about "where you want to live," whether it is temporary or permanent. There are many factors that need to be considered, just as if you were renting or buying a house or condo. It is important to consider costs, whether to buy new or used, how comfortable it is, whether it has the amenities you need for the kind of lifestyle you want, and where you will park it when you are not on the road. Although living in a recreational vehicle for any amount of time may seem like "roughing it," many RVs are quite luxurious, often including the latest in technology and cooking facilities and up-to-date bathrooms. (See "Resources," page 275.)

READJUSTING TO CHANGING CIRCUMSTANCES

In their midforties, Suzanne and Tom bought land in an isolated but beautiful area in the Midwest. It was their dream location, with nature, mountains, and a lake nearby. They envisioned hiking and horseback riding during the day and sharing dinner around a glowing fire in the evening when it got cold. But when they reached their late fifties, they could not afford to retire, and their dream location no longer seemed as ideal. Although they had visited many times and still loved the area, they began to realize how difficult it might be to actually live there. Tom had a mild heart attack when he was fifty-three, and he and Suzanne both had arthritis, which flared up in the cold. Suzanne and Tom had also not considered their aging parents, who would need their help at some point. They realized they needed to be near a good medical facility and have access to a swimming pool and yoga studio.

Suzanne and Tom talked about their options and acknowledged a sense of disappointment about having to let go of their dream. They also realized that they couldn't afford to take early retirement as they had planned and would both need to work for at least another five years. Selling the property in a few years would give them enough money to buy a lakefront cottage in a less isolated but beautiful area closer to a community with medical and other facilities and closer to an airport when they needed to visit their parents. They could also consider staying in their home and living in a warmer climate during the winter months, where they could enjoy the outdoors and have the best of both worlds. Given that their time frame for retirement had changed and there were other factors to consider, they had the opportunity to talk about the pros and cons and begin to explore their options. Their love for the outdoors and living a healthy lifestyle will surely influence their decisions.

Did You Know?

In *The Paradox of Choice: Why More Is Less*, Barry Schwartz cautions against the conventional wisdom that more choice brings greater contentment. His studies show that we may not choose well when offered too many options, and thus, we enjoy the fruits of our decisions less.

In general, we have more options today than our parents ever had. Sometimes the choices are overwhelming. In addition, what you needed five, ten, or fifteen years ago may be very different from what you need now and what will be important in the future. The key is being able to think far enough ahead to make informed decisions and talking together about your needs, values, and goals. You may not always agree, but at least you have a starting point.

Staying or Going: Transition, Change, and Emotions

Even when you have made a difficult but well-thought-out decision to downsize or relocate, the actual process of going through the move can bring up feelings of ambivalence, sadness, loss, and sometimes conflict. There may be emotional decisions about what to keep, what to sell, and what to give away. If you are moving out of a home that holds a lifetime of memories, there are myriad feelings about how to part with possessions that you value but no longer need. And your move may affect the lives of family members who have relied on you and are used to having you close by. It can be an overwhelming time when you need each other's support. Any kind of move is stressful, but the added pressure at this point in your life can exacerbate issues and feelings, even if you have made a decision that feels right for both of you.

Sometimes people benefit from the help of an "organizer" or coach who can help you to de-clutter and go through the process of deciding what to keep and what to let go of. You may also want to have some items appraised for their monetary value. (For more information, see "Resources," page 275.)

SUMMARY

Retirement transition can be a time of living out dreams, starting your dream "to-do" list, developing a new vision together, or just staying put. There are many things that need to be taken into consideration before decisions are made. Choosing where and how to live is not a one-time conversation.

Whatever you decide together, though not irrevocable, puts a process in motion that has many ramifications. The more thorough and well-informed you are, the more you'll be able to talk together about the pros and cons of your options. It is an ongoing process that requires flexibility and being able to adapt to change. Many couples discover that there is nothing stopping them from living their dream. Others may find finances and health present obstacles. Although the dream may have to be altered, there are usually ways to have some of what you really want in your life.

Talking It Through: Creating Your Shared Vision

Spend some time thinking about the following issues. Write down things that you want to talk about with your partner. If you need a refresher on how to communicate effectively, go back to "Getting to Yes Together: The Importance of Communication," pages xxxiii–xlv.

As you get started, remember the five tips and "Have a BLAST!"

- **B**laming gets in the way
- **L**isten without interrupting
- **A**gree to disagree and don't make assumptions
- **S**et a safe space for discussion
- **T**ake time to talk without distractions

Exercise 1
Go it solo: Things to think about on your own

1. Do I want to explore a different lifestyle?
2. What options do I want to consider?
3. What kind of community would I want to be part of?
4. Would I be willing to relocate?
5. What criteria are important to me regarding where and how to live?

Exercise 2
Couple time: Things to talk about together

1. Take turns sharing your responses to each question in Exercise 1, one at a time.
2. Share something positive that you learned about each other.
3. Take time to question anything that was not clear.
4. Make a list of the things that you agree on.
5. Set a time for your next conversation.

Remember, these are big questions that take time to resolve. You are probably not going to agree on everything; most couples don't. But being able to communicate effectively can help you come to solutions, one conversation at a time.

Puzzle Piece: Choosing Where and How to Live
Based on what is important to both of you, what are the criteria you want to consider for your future lifestyle options? Write your discoveries in the Puzzle Piece section at the end of the "Creating Your Shared Vision" chapter, page 263.

Funwork
Do individually

- If you did not have to worry about finances, what would your ideal lifestyle and location look like?
- Write a brief description about what you most like about this lifestyle, including how it satisfies your needs.
- Share with your partner.

Social Life, Friends, and Community: I Signed Us Up for Hip-Hop

Ruth and Norm were part of a group of couples who had been friends for over forty years. Together they raised their children and vacationed as families, and when their kids grew up, they were there for each other through many of the ups and downs of life. Together, they celebrated holidays and significant life events and consoled each other during times of loss and grief. The illness or death of one spouse impacted them all. Over the years, many of the friends took classes and workshops together, helped each other with career endeavors, and supported cultural, spiritual, and creative pursuits. In many cases, the relationships were closer than those with their siblings.

HAVE WE TALKED ABOUT OUR SOCIAL LIFE, FRIENDS, AND COMMUNITY?

"As couples rediscover one another post-career, their relationships to each other, friends, and community become increasingly important."
—Helen Dennis, coauthor, *Project Renewment: The First Retirement Model for Career Women*

We all need a "village" for support and a sense of belonging. Who are the friends you have known the longest? The ones who knew you "when," the ones who hold your secrets? Old friends have a different perspective than those you meet in later years, who may know your history but didn't live through it with you. Old friends, new friends and acquaintances, and community are all part of your village and bring a sense of belonging to your life. There is almost nothing better than having a sense of belonging and connection with like-minded people who know and care about you. It is one of the reasons that people bond around common beliefs or a mission and join community groups, religious and spiritual organizations, and special interest groups. As individuals and as a couple, investing in activities that you enjoy with each other or with friends can enrich and bring meaning to your life. This is especially true in the second half of life, when your children may be off living on their own.

Having your "place" with friends and community and experiencing the satisfaction of connection and engagement fosters a sense of well-being and satisfaction. The older you get, the more important it is to create community, especially if work no longer serves that purpose. Isolation can be dangerous to your health, but may be easy to fall into when the familiar structure of day-to-day life is gone and there is nothing to replace it. Although it may be harder to make friends as you get older, when you do things that you enjoy, you're more likely to meet people with similar interests.

Social Life

Gene and Joan loved to dance but felt they didn't have time to take classes or go dancing together. When they went to parties, weddings, or other events and watched couples having fun on the dance floor, they always said, "We should learn how to do that." Gene finally decided to take the step and enrolled them in swing dancing and hip-hop. They're now also learning the tango. They made time for this shared interest. Not only is it great exercise, but they also have fun and meet other couples who also love to dance.

Sarah and Simon had talked for years about wanting to explore spirituality through meditation. They signed up for a meditation class at a local center, where they found camaraderie with others. The center was a welcoming community that offered what they were looking for: social, intellectual, and spiritual connection.

Helena and Skip bought a small condominium in a large development. Leaving their old friends and neighbors had been difficult, but they needed to sell their home for financial reasons. They had chosen this particular development because it had a pool, clubhouse, and community center where they could meet other couples. Although it took awhile, they eventually signed up for bridge lessons, where they got to know people who also wanted to have fun and develop new relationships.

There is a growing trend toward lifelong learning and adult education. Many community adult education programs offer courses on business and career development, finance, health and well-being, dance, exercise, computers, and just about anything else you want to learn. Over five hundred universities and community colleges across the country have lifelong learning institutes (LLIs) with courses that are intellectually stimulating and offer opportunities to connect with like-minded people. You might even want to consider teaching a course. Adult education and LLI programs are always looking for experienced people to teach courses that educate and fill a need in the community. (See "Resources," page 275, for more information.) The opportunities for continued learning and growth, meeting people and having fun, are available—you just need to find them. That might mean taking a risk or stepping out of your comfort zone by doing something you never thought you could do. It is well worth it to feel that you are engaged in life and part of a community where you are giving as well as receiving.

Fun Is Good for Your Brain

For many years, Marty and Beth had talked about living in France for a year. When Marty finally sold his business and retired, they began thinking more seriously about the idea. They talked with their sixteen-year-old son, who thought it would it be "cool" to finish high school in another country. Their two older children, who were attending college, made plans to visit.

Through the Internet, Marty and Beth found a French family interested in a house swap for the year. Beth was hoping to volunteer in a bilingual program and enrolled in a French immersion course to prepare, while Marty began to think about writing a book on food and wine. He intended to use the year to do research and write. Six months later, they began their adventure, looking forward to an exciting and stimulating year ahead.

Activities that involve having to think and problem solve can be fun as well as good for your brain. For instance, you might try doing crossword puzzles with your partner, learning to play a musical instrument, or learning a foreign language. Choosing one or two things that you enjoy separately or together can be a great start. The point is to learn something new, do something differently, and have fun.

Some of these activities may also be a way for the two of you to develop new friendships based on shared interests. Having fun together can help your heart as well as your brain. When you share interests and activities, not only are you spending time together and expanding your social network, but you are also making an investment in your relationship, which fosters a sense of togetherness.

Activities to Stimulate Your Brain and Connect with Others

- Take a course.
- Learn how to play bridge.
- Invite friends over for an evening of fun and games such as Scrabble, cards, Trivial Pursuit, Bunco, or watching a movie or sports game together.
- Go to a museum exhibit and learn about the artist.
- Take an art class.
- Take a computer class.
- Learn to play a musical instrument.
- Go on a trip where learning and travel are combined.

Old and New Friendships

Women often say, "I don't know what I would do without my friends." Women form bonds that last over time. On the other hand, men often, though not always, develop relationships around a common interest, such as work, sports, or involvement with a community or civic group. When the common interest ends, the relationships often end as well. It is less likely for a man to call a friend and say, "Let's have lunch."

Katy and Nelson both had a close network of friends through work. When Katy retired, she kept in touch with the women she felt close to. They got together for dinner once a month, sometimes met for lunch when Katy was in the area, and occasionally went to the theater together. But Katy also met new friends when she started doing things she didn't have time for while she was working: practicing yoga, taking a dance class, and doing volunteer work.

Having had very little free time all his life, Nelson was not sure what to do with his time when he retired. It did not occur to him to reach out to his former work friends, and he had a difficult time making new connections. Nelson said, "It's not easy for a seventy-year-old man to develop new friendships."

Even if you are in a relationship, one person cannot meet all of your needs. It is important to have other people in your life, whether they are family members or friends. Lack of friendships and support can actually lead to stress in your marriage. For example, when Nelson no longer had his work group buddies, he felt dependent on Katy to spend more time with him, make social connections, and plan activities. Katy, who loved spending time with friends, felt burdened by Nelson's dependence on her. The equilibrium in their relationship was thrown off. Katy and Nelson needed to find more balance in their relationship. Unlike Nelson, many men do bond with friends and maintain relationships over time.

Josh had a group of six friends from college who had stayed in contact for many years after graduation. They gradually lost touch as marriages ended, jobs changed, moves happened, and one of the men passed away. When he was in his late sixties and reminiscing about the past, Josh decided it would be fun to get the group together again. He emailed the group to get input and see if they were interested in a reunion. Everyone got back to him, and they set a date for a weekend of golfing and fun.

Josh found that it was extremely rewarding to connect with old friends who knew him in his "wild and crazy days." The men had all changed, and yet the bond of friendship was still there. Given their shared past, they were able to talk about their lives and what it was like to grow older. It was validating for Josh and the others to talk about things that were on all of their minds: relationships, health issues, retirement, and what was next for all of them. At the end of the weekend, they agreed to stay in touch and plan for another reunion the following year.

🧩 A Note from Dori

My husband, David, has maintained strong friendships with his college roommates, whom he has known for more than fifty years. The men meet periodically and play golf. On occasion, the wives, and sometimes children, are also part of the gatherings. One of the couples lives an hour away and we often see them for dinner and the theater. The other couples live in North Carolina, and we try to get together for occasional special gatherings. They all joined us to celebrate our son's bar mitzvah and recently, during one of Louie's vacations, we visited with them in North Carolina.

When I think about friendships, I often hear the words in my head of a song I learned years ago as a Girl Scout. We sang it as a round: "Make new friends but keep the old; one is silver and the other gold." I particularly liked the song since we moved around a lot as I grew up, and I was often leaving old friends and having to make new ones. As an adult, I reconnected with a family who were special to me when I was in elementary school. I have also maintained two friendships with women I met as a teenager; one became my college roommate. Although we don't see each other often, each time we meet, we pick up as though we had just talked yesterday.

My husband and I also have developed some good friends individually and as a couple: some through our travels and work, others through our son's school and activities and other shared interests. We have also made friends in our religious community and our neighborhood. We use email and phone calls to stay connected, and at times travel with some of our friends or travel to visit with them. As often as our schedules permit, we try to get together with friends individually, as a couple, or as a family. We realize it "takes a village" for all of us, and being part of a community and connected with others is important to both of us.

Couple Friendships

Deep bonds can develop between couples when they get to know each other over time. In fact, sometimes friends may become closer than biological siblings. Close friends are there for each other in good times and bad. Whether they travel together, go out to dinner, or just stay home playing cards, couples often develop a sense of closeness and trust that goes beyond many friendships. Sometimes groups form around specific interests or topics: gourmet groups, book and game clubs, or pizza and bowling on Friday night. The ritual of getting together and having fun with others gives people a sense of belonging and connection.

🧩 A Note from Roberta

Several years ago, a few friends decided to start a couples' "salon group." Six couples met to get to know each other, share ideas and suggestions, and talk about what we wanted to get out of the group. Some couples said they just wanted to have fun and connect with friends, others were interested in discussing books they wouldn't ordinarily read, and still others were open to whatever the experience might bring. We all agreed that food was an important ingredient. Over the course of six years, we read many books, some more interesting and absorbing than others. We had some wonderful and elucidating conversations and some that didn't go so well. Although we tried to avoid talking about politics, there were a number of impassioned conversations that went beyond where most of us wanted to go.

Eventually, one couple decided to leave the group and a few more followed. We had invited a new couple in just before things began to fall apart, but we assured them that they had nothing to do with the group dissolving. It was just the natural attrition that happens in groups. Several couples have developed close relationships and see each other frequently. A few couples travel to second homes on weekends and rarely have the time to get together. But several times a year, one couple will initiate a get-together and whoever is around shows up. Although the group did not continue, the relationships have enriched our lives with caring friendships and an ongoing sense of connection.

Be a "Trendsetter"

Start a book club or discussion group for couples who want to talk about second-half-of-life issues. Suggest reading a book that would stimulate conversation. The group may want to consider discussing

The Couple's Retirement Puzzle and talking about the "10 Must-Have Conversations." Invite some friends over for food and drink and get the conversation rolling. It is validating to know that others are traveling a similar path and that you are not in this alone.

There is no "right way" to develop friendships and support systems. As we age, there are a variety of ways to expand our social network—through hobbies, religious affiliations, courses, volunteer work, encore careers, or through the Internet and social networks. Some couples enjoy venturing out and learning new things, and others stick with old standbys. Either way, you have to be out there to develop new relationships; they will not come knocking at your door.

LIVING IN COMMUNITY

How do you know what the opportunities are for involvement and activities in your community? Most local newspapers have a community activities section or online blog that lists information about upcoming programs, talks, and events. Radio or the local cable TV networks often provide good information about community politics and events. The town library will have postings for book clubs, workshops, and talks that are coming up, and you may also discover that your town has its own Facebook page for up-to-the-minute information. You may have lived in a community for years but have no idea about what really goes on. Being in retirement transition is a good time to explore and find out what's available.

Where you live can be an important part of your sense of belonging and feeling connected to people. You may want to refer to Conversation 8, "Choosing Where and How to Live: Staying Put or Exploring New Frontiers?" on pages 193–216 to learn about different types of living situations that can provide activities as well as a sense of community and connection for you. Knowing your neighbors or connecting around common interests and values helps create a sense of community.

Virtual Communities

Communities are no longer just face-to-face. The world of the Internet has provided us with virtual communities that expand the parameters of what we thought was possible. In addition to social media websites such as Facebook and Twitter, there are chat groups as well as message boards and online forums that cover every topic imaginable, and some you would not want to imagine. You can get support, opinions, and ideas with just a password and the click of a button. You can create a network of your own in a few minutes and be connected to it in about a nanosecond. If you love chess, Scrabble, or just about any other game, you can find a virtual opponent any time of the day or night. Is this a good thing or bad? It does not matter—it just is!

Some older boomers who did not grow up with computers feel overwhelmed by the thought of turning one on. Others spend half their life in front of the screen, to the chagrin of their partners. Whatever your thoughts about the Internet, the fact is that it offers possibilities for information, connection, support, and sharing that have never existed before. You can put a word out into cyberspace and suddenly find a network of people who want to connect around issues, books, politics, aging, health issues, or any number of topics. Whatever it is, you can be sure that someone out there wants to chat about it.

A word of warning: If a virtual community becomes more important than your "real" relationships, it is time to step back, reflect, and possibly get some help. The Internet world can be addictive, especially if you have a lot of time on your hands. There are limits to living in a virtual world, and crossing the line can be risky. The other caution is that we need to know how to protect ourselves; it is not hard to be a target for scammers.

Conference calls—local, statewide, and global—are another popular way for people to form discussion or special interest groups and participate in teleconferences about a variety of different topics. Anyone can access a free conference line and invite others to call in or join a call organized by others. Once you get your call-in number and a PIN number, you can invite other participants to join your call. Teleconference calls are usually set up online and participants receive a specific time to call, a number, and a PIN number. There are also free videoconferencing and teleconferencing services available. (See "Resources," page 275.)

It may push you out of your comfort zone to reach out to others to form a group in person, online, or via the telephone, but you will probably discover that other people also want to connect and will welcome possibilities.

🧩 A Note from Dori

I created two virtual communities. One is the Boomers and Beyond Special Interest Group I started in 2007 as a way to bring together "kindred spirits" from around the world who wanted to explore positive, creative, and successful aging. These interdisciplinary professionals are themselves boomers or beyond or are working with people in that age group. We meet twice a month on the telephone and discuss issues, often with speakers as a springboard for our discussions. As an offshoot of this group, some of the members formed a book group that also meets monthly by phone. Beginning in 2012, I also began to offer a monthly "Revolutionize Your Retirement Interview with Experts Series to Help You Create a Fulfilling Second Half of Life" for professionals and the public. This series is available via phone or the Internet. We make a point of meeting each other in person whenever the opportunity arises.

🧩 A Note from Roberta

Historically, women have bonded together in groups to support and learn from each other. If the need and momentum is there, some grassroots groups, such as The Transition Network, grow into organizations. The Transition Network (TTN) is a national nonprofit organization for women fifty and forward who are going through transition and exploring what's next in their personal and professional lives. Women join TTN to meet other interesting women, get a fresh perspective on their own opportunities, learn about resources and supports, and explore new possibilities. They usually discover that they are energized by the opportunity to define this new period of healthy older adulthood.

In 2012, recognizing the value of TTN, I took the lead in getting the Boston chapter off the ground. With the help of the national organization and a small but dedicated group of women, Boston officially became a chapter in October 2013. To find out if there is a TTN chapter near you, go to www.thetransitionnetwork.org. If you don't have a chapter in your area, consider starting one. You can also join the national chapter and become part of a phone or online peer support group. TTN is a warm, welcoming nationwide community of women who have open arms and are eager to support you.

VOLUNTEERING

Volunteering has become very popular at a time when jobs are hard to come by, particularly for older workers. It's an opportunity to stay engaged, use your skills and talents, expand your network, and give back. Although volunteering sometimes results in a paid job, don't count on that outcome.

There are numerous opportunities to volunteer depending on your interests and skills. You can use the Internet to find volunteer opportunities in and around your community or around the world. It can be an exciting opportunity for couples to travel and share in giving back locally and globally. Organizations such as the Peace Corps have certain health requirements and time commitments. Other organizations, such as AmeriCorps and Experience Corps, have less stringent health and time requirements. (See "Resources," page 275, for more information.)

With the occurrence of a natural disaster, such as Hurricane Katrina, the earthquake in Haiti, the typhoon in the Philippines, or other serious threats such as the devastation of the attacks of 9/11 and the 2013 Boston Marathon bombing, people are often inspired to volunteer time, energy, skills, and resources to help in any way possible. There are times when one partner may feel compelled to help because of medical or other needed skills, but the other does not. The challenge for couples is staying connected and supportive even when they are not physically or emotionally interested in doing the same thing.

Another organization, the Service Corps of Retired Executives (SCORE) is a national nonprofit formed to educate entrepreneurs and help small businesses grow. You might become involved with SCORE as a volunteer mentoring others, or as a client looking for help in developing your encore business. ReServe, another nonprofit organization, was founded in New York and has begun to expand to other states. ReServe matches workers with nonprofit organizations and offers a small stipend for a short-term project.

If volunteering is new to you, start small and see how it feels. For example, you could volunteer a few hours to help paint a community building or plant flowers at city hall. It is a good way to meet interesting people and become more involved in your community.

Many corporations have organizations to foster their employees' and retirees' involvement in community affairs with the resources of the company behind them. For some businesses, this has become the community component of their corporate strategy, contributing services and expertise to build and sustain strong communities. Check with your employer to see if they offer this capability and how you can participate.

Did You Know?

National and local networks of volunteer agencies are available to help you match your skills to the need for volunteers. An example of a unique opportunity in one community in Massachusetts is Service Opportunities after Reaching 55 (SOAR 55). SOAR 55 is an organization that helps meet local community needs through the volunteer service of adults fifty-five and older. SOAR 55 serves as a volunteer connector between individuals and a variety of nonprofit and public organizations. For example, a former CEO with expertise in organizational development might be matched with a developing nonprofit organization. There are also faith-based programs that match skilled people with volunteer opportunities.

You can also create your own opportunities by approaching organizations that could benefit from your experience and interests. It might be helpful to brainstorm ideas with your partner or with friends and colleagues. It is always great to have a sounding board and a "community voice" to help you to think bigger. You might decide you would like to do volunteer work in a totally different arena and learn while you are contributing.

SUMMARY

We all need a village to sustain involvement and vitality. Even if you have a wonderful partner, no one can or should be expected to meet all of your needs and desires. Finding your "place" and developing friendships, relationships, and community are critically important for continued growth and connection. There are many ways that lifelong learning and contributing your skills for the benefit of others can help you stay vital and connected. As we age, there is often the desire to reach out and give back, to find the balance to both savor and save the world. Family is one way we seek connection and meaning in life. Having friendships and being involved with community are other ways. We can be intentional in our choices and use our energy productively for the betterment of family, community, and the planet.

Talking It Through: Creating Your Shared Vision

Spend some time thinking about the following issues. Use your journal to write down your thoughts and feelings, as well as anything you want to talk about with your partner. If you need a refresher on how to communicate effectively, go back to "Getting to Yes Together: The Importance of Communication," pages xxxiii–xlv.

As you get started, remember the five tips and "Have a BLAST!"

- Blaming gets in the way
- Listen without interrupting
- Agree to disagree and don't make assumptions
- Set a safe space for discussion
- Take time to talk without distractions

SOCIAL LIFE, FRIENDS, AND COMMUNITY 233

Exercise 1

Go it solo: Things to think about on your own

1. What do I most enjoy doing with friends?
2. What activities connect me with others?
3. How can we create community around us?
4. Is my social life satisfying? If not, what would make it better?
5. What is important for us to do as a couple?

Exercise 2

Couple time: Things to talk about together

1. Take turns sharing your responses to Exercise 1, one at a time.
2. Share something positive that you learned about each other.
3. Take time to question anything that was not clear.
4. Make a list of the things you agree on.
5. Set a time for your next conversation.

It is important to remember that these are big questions that take time to resolve. You are probably not going to agree on everything; most couples don't. But being able to communicate effectively can help you come to solutions, one conversation at a time.

Puzzle Piece: Social Life, Friends, and Community

What are two or three things that would enhance your social life, relationships with friends, and connection to your community? Write your discoveries in the Puzzle Piece section at the end of the "Creating Your Shared Vision" chapter, page 263.

Funwork
Do individually or together

- Get together with friends for any of the suggested activities. This may be an opportunity to get to know new people and broaden your social network. The goal is to connect with your partner, to connect with others, and to have fun.
- Have a potluck or progressive dinner.
- Go dancing alone or with friends.
- Start a book group with friends or for couples.
- Have a karaoke evening.
- Go to a movie with friends and have dessert afterward.
- Go bowling.
- Plan or host a game night.
- Organize a community fund-raiser.
- Join a community volunteer project.
- Check the activities section in your local paper, find something that interests you as a couple, and meet others in the process.
- Sign up for an adult education class with the intention of meeting new people.
- Have a totally outrageous experience of your own devising or one that is totally low key.
- If you did some of these activities individually, share your experiences with your partner.

Purpose, Meaning, and Giving Back: What's It All About?

For many years Sam, an energetic, inquisitive seventy-two-year-old, has been searching for answers. He wants to understand the meaning of life. "Why are we here?" he asks. Sam believes there has to be something more, a greater purpose for our existence. He does not want to leave this world without understanding the master plan.

His search has led him to many conversations about the meaning of life, books related to past lives, questions about the existence of God, and, finally, back to religion. Although he still questions, Sam is now more connected to community and to a deeper part of himself. What he is just beginning to see is that the answers he seeks are in his daily life—his relationships with his children, and the support, connection, and humor he shares with family and friends, community, and colleagues. Sam once asked his "higher power" to reveal itself. It responded, "I am you."

HAVE YOU TALKED ABOUT PURPOSE AND GIVING BACK?

It is not uncommon to reach midlife and wonder, "What's it all about?" After so many years of "doing" and working hard to achieve, midlife can feel like an ending, with all of the important parts in the past and nothing to look forward to. Like Sam, we may begin to search for something deeper, something to live for to help us find meaning in life. Although most people look outside themselves, one of the best ways to find meaning is to look inward. All too often, we spend our lives searching for answers we already have.

An Opportunity for Couples

"There's more to retirement than money and medicine— much more...Finding individual and collective meaning is essential for couples of any age who hope to grow old together in a vital relationship."

—Richard Leider, author of *The Power of Purpose* and *Repacking Your Bags*

Talking with your partner about what is really important in life and how you want to be remembered can deepen and enrich your relationship. You may be able to help each other see how you make a difference in the world. Couples sometimes begin to consider ways they can make a difference together, such as volunteering, civic engagement, entrepreneurial projects, or involvement with a greater cause. Sharing what is most important and how you want to live the next part of life is an opportunity to begin talking about your legacy.

Phil and Sherry are both attorneys who specialize in family law, divorce, and mediation. Their greatest concern is always what is best for the child. Over the years, they have seen many situations where children were treated as property and used as pawns in divorce. Several years ago, they made the decision to only work with couples who were committed to

what was best for their children and who were open to thera-
peutic intervention, if necessary. They are now training other
attorneys who have a similar philosophy. In addition, Phil
and Sherry hold free monthly seminars in the community for
divorcing parents.

Through their belief, commitment, knowledge, and generosity,
Phil and Sherry are living their legacy and saving many children
from the potential trauma of a litigious and acrimonious divorce.

RELIGION AND SPIRITUALITY

What role do religion and spirituality play in the search for meaning, and how do couples deal with differences in their beliefs?
Even couples who grew up in the same faith may not agree on
how traditional and religious rituals should be practiced. We
generally understand religion through the paradigm in which
we were raised. You may have continued to practice the religion
you were raised in, converted to the other's religion, or abandoned institutional religion altogether. But as you grow older
and face the inevitability of mortality, you may feel the desire to
connect with something greater than yourself. You might return
to your religious roots, deepen the connection with a religious
community, or search for something else that you can believe
in. For many, religion is a great source of comfort and support,
especially in times of crisis.

Gladys, a seventy-one-year-old mother of four and grandmother
of eight, has been battling cancer for the past nine years. Gladys
has found that her faith in God is what helps her through the
pain and suffering she has endured. Her husband, Paul, lost
his faith in God and religion many years ago when their youngest daughter was killed by a drunk driver. Since then, Gladys

and Paul have had many conversations about their beliefs. They do not try to change each other's minds, but they want to understand and respect each other's feelings.

Steve has struggled with his relationship to religion and questions his belief in God. He thinks that having a strong belief would help him to be less afraid of death, but he has not yet found something he can believe in. Steve's wife, Janet, also struggles with her feelings about religion, but she believes in a higher power, which she finds comforting as she ages.

Feelings and beliefs about religion and spirituality are very personal. Understanding what your partner believes and how he or she feels can foster mutual respect and acceptance of your differences.

A Note from Dori

When I was thirteen years old, I began to question organized religion. I did, however, love the traditions and family gatherings, and to this day embrace those aspects and share them with family and friends. When our son was born, we wanted him to learn about his heritage, and we joined a temple that was welcoming and accepting. We also wanted him to have the traditional bar mitzvah when he turned thirteen. When I was growing up, girls were just beginning to be allowed to have the ritual of a bat mitzvah, and I did not have one. In the back of my mind, I held the thought that maybe one day I would study for this ceremony.

As I got older, and especially since our son was born, I found myself thinking more about my beliefs. A number of years ago an adult study class was being offered at our temple. I decided to join it, learn Hebrew, and study for a bat mitzvah. At age sixty-three, I joined with seven other adults, men and women ranging in age from thirty to their early eighties, and we shared what is called a b'nai mitzvah, literally defined as the son or daughter of the commandments. It was very meaningful for me to make this decision, and it reaffirmed that it is never too late to learn; education continues throughout our lives if we are open to it. My husband, son, and friends were supportive and proud of me for this undertaking. I am still somewhat unsure about the role of institutional religion in my life. In my own way, I am exploring my beliefs and spirituality, both within and outside of my religion.

Spirituality implies something greater than oneself, but is less well defined and generally less prescriptive than religion. It is a more abstract concept that encompasses existence as well as relationship with self, others, and the universe. Many boomers, who came of age in the 1960s, have embraced mindfulness and spirituality as important factors in their lives.

Both religion and spirituality may play an important role in the second half of life as we are faced with questions of meaning and mortality. Having a belief in something greater than oneself is comforting and can provide a sense of belonging to a larger group or community. Research tells us that people who are grounded in a belief are happier, healthier, and often better able to cope with loss and other difficult life circumstances. It is not uncommon for older adults to return to religion or begin to explore spirituality as a way of understanding and bringing meaning to their lives. It may be going to a place of worship, singing in the choir, beginning a meditation or yoga practice, or spending more time in nature. Whatever you choose, it is probably something that brings you back to yourself and helps you connect with something greater.

🧩 A Note from Roberta

I started to become disillusioned with religion in early adulthood when my father died. It was reinforced by other life events that left me wondering: Where is the compassion in religion? Where are the religious "leaders" who are supposed to know how to comfort you in your grief? How does religion manifest itself in day-to-day life, or is it just for special days when prayers are recited? Prayers are just words if we don't understand their meaning. Although I've maintained a cultural and more humanistic connection to my religious background, it is not the same as practicing or believing. For many years something was missing in my life, something that connected me to a greater sense of "being."

In my early fifties, I was invited to join a group that was being formed to explore spirituality. Six women came together from varied backgrounds and religious orientations. Together, we created a safe place to share our perspectives and experiences, define what "spirituality" means in our lives, and attempt to understand the breadth and depth of spirituality in the everyday. Almost twenty years later, we continue to meet monthly at one another's homes, sharing our life paths (as well as amazing food) through the prism of a spiritual lens. The group has become a touchstone in my life, a place to be that brings me back to myself.

MAKING A DIFFERENCE

"Bequeathing our internal wealth is, in my view, our most precious gift to those who follow us."

—Meg Newhouse, founder of the
Life Planning Network

The terms "purpose," "meaning," and "giving back" ultimately relate to how we make a difference in the lives of others. Sometimes known as "life purpose," it is really just about being who you are and sharing your unique talents and gifts. You may question if and how you have made a difference, or think that making a difference means giving something tangible. But making a difference is in the everyday "gifts," shared in small ways that can be seen in the patterns of your life: the choices you have made, how you've coped with life's challenges, the many ways you have helped and supported others. For one person, it might be working in a community organization or volunteering at the senior center a day or two a week. For another, it's in the stories remembered by grandchildren, or how you taught them to fly a kite or bake brownies. Whether your contribution is large or small, whenever you make a difference in the lives of others, you are living your purpose.

Charlotte is a seventy-year-old former realtor, community activist, and talented writer who unexpectedly learned how she had created a rich and enduring legacy by making a difference in the lives of many children merely by living her values and being who she was. Charlotte was attending a workshop on legacy sponsored by her town library. Participants were guided through a brief meditation exercise and asked to imagine that they were at a gathering where they were being acknowledged for a real or imagined accomplishment. The following story is about an actual event in Charlotte's life, told in her own words.

"It was 1975, and I was in the dining room of a lovely hotel near my home. It was a luncheon for the naming of the 'Realtor of the Year.' This award was given to a person who had achieved recognition for service to their community, participation in the Board of Realtors, and ethics. The name of the honoree was announced right after lunch. I had not planned on attending this luncheon, but my husband had insisted. Distracted by thoughts of promising to help my parents wallpaper their kitchen, I never heard the introduction for the honoree. When my name was called, I was stunned. What had I done to deserve this distinguished award? I was always volunteering for programs to help out where needed, but that was in conjunction with other people. Then it hit me! For several years, I had been on a committee called 'Make America Better.' We planted flowers and shrubs in ten communities, but they died over the winter. I didn't think we were putting the Realtors' money to a good enough cause. I told the board president that I thought there were other ways we could help our community and at the same time bring recognition to the Board of Realtors. I shared my idea about a program for helping to identify dyslexic and learning disabled preschool children. She asked me to write up a proposal to present to the Board of Realtors and appointed me chairwoman of the 'Make America Better' committee. Several weeks later, I presented a proposal to the board of directors and got full support."

Charlotte's work over the next several years involved community education, public involvement, and working closely with the director of a local nonprofit school for children with learning disabilities. She was instrumental in bringing attention to the importance of mainstreaming more children with learning disabilities back into the public school system so they could receive the kind of education that would support their growth and development.

At the end of the workshop, Charlotte said:

"I learned something new about myself today. I was not just a housewife stepping in to assist her husband in his real estate business. I was a professional in my own right, recognized by my peers. I have my own legacy to hand down to my grandchildren and great-grandchildren. I learned that I made a difference!"

It took thirty-four years and a few minutes of inner reflection and writing for Charlotte to recognize and appreciate her legacy, the difference she had made in the lives of so many children and families. This awareness helped Charlotte see her life through a different lens, giving her a new sense of meaning and purpose. She was confident she had been a good mother to her children and a loving wife who had supported her husband's career. But until that moment, she had not appreciated the difference she had made in the world. Like Charlotte, you may be unaware of how you make a difference until you honor what you bring to others through your work, volunteering, community involvement, or merely being who you are and doing what you love.

THE MANY MEANINGS OF LEGACY

The word "legacy" usually brings to mind inheritance of money, property, or family heirlooms that are designated in a will. But a legacy is not always tangible, and it is not necessarily about the future. Leaving a legacy can be about living your life so that each day is an opportunity to make a lasting difference. Charlotte lives her legacy every day, and it is one that will be remembered long after she is gone. A legacy can also relate to a deed or a call to action that inspires change. Some legacies are left as a whisper, others with a cry for change in a memorable speech, such as Martin Luther King's "I Have a Dream" speech. Who have you been inspired by and who have you inspired? Whether or not a legacy is intentional, it reflects your values, what is most important, and how that manifests in your life.

We also need to consider a different but equally important form of legacy. Living in a time of global societal change, we are increasingly concerned about the environment, social issues, and what kind of world we will be leaving to our children and grandchildren. We have a responsibility to do as much as we can to ensure a sustainable planet and a safe and secure future for those who come after us.

🧩 A Note from Dori

One of my favorite memories of my mother, and part of her legacy, was a wonderful story she told to me, my brother, and my cousins. We have all told the story to our children and hope they will pass it on to their children. It was a simple folktale called "Tikki Tikki Tembo." This is an ancient Chinese folktale about a boy with a very long name who falls into a well. His brother runs to get help, but people have trouble understanding what he is saying because Tikki Tikki Tembo's name is so long. The moral of the story is, if you love your children, give them short names. (See "Resources," page 275.)

My mother used dramatic hand motions and feeling as she told the story, and she used our names to make it come alive. I would listen, spellbound, and would practice telling the story to her, being sure that I was telling it right. Although my mother died before my son was born, he knows of her through "Tikki Tikki Tembo." The telling and retelling of this story is one way that her spirit lives on for us.

My father's legacy was very different. I was born at the end of the war when he was in Germany working with displaced persons who had been freed from concentration camps. He wrote many letters to my mother during those months, describing his experiences in Germany and separation from his family during my birth and my brother's early years. He eventually began to put the letters together into a book.

When he died, my mother continued this project, and the letters were eventually published by a Jewish Museum in California, where my parents had lived. It took me a number of years to read his letters. When I finally did, I realized what a wonderful legacy he had left, not only to my brother and me, but also for many others who wanted to understand the heartbreak of those years through the eyes of a young man and father.

Both my mother's and father's legacies have helped me think about the importance of legacy in my own life. I write letters to my son, being conscious of wanting him to know the values that are important to me and conveying my hope he will incorporate them into his life.

There are many ways that couples can give their children, grandchildren, and others the gift of legacy. Legacy can be a conversation, honest words shared from the heart, or something you "give" that makes a difference to others. You can enliven your life by creating today what you want to be remembered for tomorrow.

🧩 A Note from Roberta

My four grandchildren are very dear to me and I love spending time with them, but my younger years were often about competing priorities. When my daughter's children, Caitlyn, Jake, and

Lauren, were young, I didn't have the kind of time I would have liked to spend with them. I was a single mother, managing a full-time job and a private practice. Life was hectic. As they got older, I was able to plan more individual time with each of them. Those are wonderful, treasured memories.

Kids can be very different when sibling dynamics are not in play. One of our rituals has been to have a special day for birthdays when the "birthday grandchild" and I do something they want to do. I've spent hours at malls helping one or the other pick out an outfit for a special stuffed bear, played video games in a club where earplugs would have helped, or watched the youngest being made up into a miniature princess with sparkles all over her beautiful little face. But for me, one of the most wonderful parts of being a grandparent is witnessing the emergence of their unique personalities. I see curiosity, talents, interests, compassion, and many other qualities developing in each of them.

When Caitlyn, my oldest granddaughter, turned twelve, we went on an intergenerational trip to the Grand Canyon. Having this extraordinary adventure together was one of the highlights of my life. It wasn't just sharing the beauty and majesty of the canyon or the thrill of white-water rafting, it was also watching a movie together in our hotel room, talking over dinner, and the pride in seeing her step forward to help some of the other grandparents make it up a particularly steep incline. My hope is that part of the legacy I leave will be held in Caitlyn's memory as a special time together. I'm planning to have similar experiences with Jake and Lauren, although in a few years the destination may be one that doesn't involve hiking. We now have Genevieve, my son's daughter, who is just a year and a half. She brings us joy, laughter, and a sense that we can enrich her life and make a difference as we live our legacy every day.

> I want to be remembered as a loving, generous grandmother who lived with vitality, believed in taking risks for the sake of learning and relationships, and who aged well by growing whole.

Treasured stories and memories get lost if they're not told, and storytelling is one of the best ways to pass down family history. Almost everyone enjoys a good story, even if they may have heard it several times before. If you enjoy writing, keeping a journal or creating a narrative can be a wonderful gift to yourself and others. Writing lends itself to reflection: it is a way to review your life and pass on what you feel is important. Another powerful way to share your legacy is through a "life story interview," which can be recorded or videotaped. You may think that younger generations are not interested in the past, but that isn't necessarily true. It may come with maturity and perspective but, at some point, most of us want to know where we came from, and we want to "meet" the characters in our family dramas. It may be time for you to carry the torch of family history forward.

Sentimentality and Legacy

Most families have photo albums, scrapbooks, or other memorabilia that hold memories and meaning from the past. Although filled with sentiment, they are often stashed away in the basement or the attic, in boxes that have not been opened for years. They may have been put away for "safekeeping" and forgotten over time.

🧩 A Note from Dori

When my parents moved from one home to another, my brother and I visited and helped them go through their belongings to decide which things to keep and which to give away. Many items from our childhood were there; some we threw away and others were moved to our respective homes.

Sometime later, after my father died and my mother could no longer live in their home, and then again after my mother died, we had to go through the remaining items in her home. Many of the photos, albums, letters, and other heirlooms that we saved are now in my basement. I vowed that I would not leave so much for my son to have to go through when I die. Now I am faced with the challenge of what to do with the family memories. Who will want them? Should they be saved? How should they be chronicled, and for whom?

Some cousins and I have talked about pulling the material together as our shared family history. Part of the challenge is that we do not live near each other, and it is a huge undertaking to go through everything. I view it as a project I would like to eventually tackle, but finding the time is a challenge. I have talked with a number of friends who share similar stories. It is often hard to let go of family memorabilia.

Many of the sentimental possessions that were important to our parents may have little or no meaning for us. Yet we are often the ones left to figure out what to do with them when our parents become debilitated or die. Although it can be time-consuming, it could also be a very rewarding project to make a "family history scrapbook" for future generations.

🧩 A Note from Roberta

When my oldest niece, Debbie, celebrated her fiftieth birthday, I wanted to give her something special that had belonged to my mother. I thought about the gold watch my mother had given me before she died. My mother had tiny wrists and the watch-band was too small for me to wear. But it was perfect for Debbie. I found it in the back of my closet tucked away in a beautiful velvet bag. When I gave it to Debbie, we cried together. She had been close to Mom and remembered her well. Although the gift itself was beautiful, the deeper meaning that it had for both of us was more precious than a gold watch could ever be.

Just about every form of legacy can be shared with loved ones and others while you are alive. You may have heard the term "ethical will" in relation to legacy. An ethical will is a personal letter to your loved ones in which you share your values, your story and life lessons, your hopes and dreams for the future, as well as any other information that you think is important to pass on. It is also an opportunity to express love, regrets, and forgiveness. In addition to being a gift to your loved ones, writing an ethical will can bring you peace of mind. Many people leave a legacy through service or philanthropic donations to a cause, an organization, or a community. Some are never formally acknowledged for what they have contributed, and others receive plaques or have buildings in their name.

What matters most is that "gifts" of legacy come from the heart and serve others in a way that makes a difference.

CREATING A JOINT LEGACY

Peter and Hinda have celebrated fifty-plus anniversaries. They have both had long careers in the nonprofit world and also enjoyed doing volunteer work in their home state of Washington. Several years ago, they decided to explore international volunteer opportunities. They had three goals in mind: to travel, to give something back, and to continue to learn. Before committing to an assignment, they wanted to test out the waters to see if they would really enjoy international volunteer work. They were both able to take a leave of absence from work for a trial run.

Peter and Hinda did some research and discovered that the American Jewish World Service had a volunteer program that matched people and their skills to the needs of organizations in developing countries. Over the course of the next several years, they volunteered in many programs, traveling to different countries and returning home between trips for a break and their work. Their first three-month assignment took them to northern Thailand, where they taught Burmese refugees about democracy and leadership skills. On subsequent volunteer trips, they traveled to India, Namibia, Uganda, Ghana, and Kenya. They also spent time in Mexico where they helped to build an eco-village. Peter retired first and helped immigrants prepare for citizenship. He feels that because the United States is a country of immigrants, it is an honor to work with people who want to become American citizens. Hinda continued to work a little longer but then semiretired, and they continued their travels and work together. They celebrated their fiftieth anniversary visiting friends they made over the years.

Peter and Hinda are an exceptional couple who have made courageous choices that have enriched their lives and the lives of people in remote parts of the world. They have traveled a path very different from the majority of their peers. They share a similar desire to empower people and teach them skills to help them succeed. During the many years they have spent together, Peter and Hinda have learned a great deal about their similarities and differences. Peter gets very attached to people and places, and although Hinda loves the many places they have been, she has less difficulty saying good-bye.

At one point, Peter went back to a village in Africa to complete a project he had worked on for a charitable organization. Hinda was not keen on going back, nor was she able to take time off from work. Peter went alone and enjoyed the opportunity to live with a family in the village. Although Hinda was lonesome and did not like being alone, she understood Peter's passion to return and finish the project.

Peter and Hinda acknowledge that their choices would not be for everyone. Even when couples are adventurous, there is a lot of communication that has to happen before deciding to embark on a lifestyle that challenges you in body, mind, and spirit. Hinda adds, "You really need to be sure that you're making the decision for yourself and not because it's what your spouse wants. Communication, compromise, and negotiation are important to make this work." From the start, Hinda made it clear that she wouldn't live without plumbing and running water, although this was not as important to Peter. They knew that being in a developing country would mean being isolated and having to depend on each other 24/7. For some couples, this is a deal breaker, but for Peter and Hinda, being married for all those years had taught them resilience and how to negotiate so that both of their needs could be met. They have been an inspiration to family and friends, especially their children and grandchildren, who have raised and donated money for important causes. Their lives have been anything but ordinary, and through example they have modeled giving back. People all over the world read their blogs and see that it is possible to live life with passion and purpose.

Peter and Hinda have been dedicated to their path and worked hard to make it happen together. Their life has been a continuing adventure. They would love to introduce others to international volunteer work and have considered bringing together a professionally diverse group of friends to work on a service project in a developing country. Peter says that some people retire and play golf and some retire and want to do nothing. That would not work for them. They want to continue to do things that are socially useful to make the world a better place. It has been a consistent philosophy of their life: to keep doing for others is part of their Jewish and cultural tradition of *tikkun olam*, or "repairing the world."

What If You're on Different Pages?

Peter and Hinda are a wonderful example of a couple who share similar values and views on legacy and giving back. But beliefs about legacy are very personal, and couples may be at different points on the spectrum. One partner may want to donate a valuable book collection to a library, while the other thinks they should sell the books and put the money in a trust fund for their grandchildren.

There may be disagreement regarding who should inherit a family heirloom or piece of property. If one partner clearly has ownership, it is less complicated than if things are held jointly, which is often the case. And it can get even more complicated if there are children and grandchildren from previous relationships. Resolving such issues goes back to communication, being able to talk about differences and negotiate an equitable solution, or having an objective third party or trusted adviser to facilitate the conversation.

SUMMARY

Our footprints are left in the sands of time through work, relationships, contribution, and service; in ways big and small, we have an impact. The question "What's it all about?" can be a wonderful opening for understanding how we have made a difference and how to make more intentional choices in life. It is never too late to leave a lasting legacy. Through "purpose," we have the opportunity to live in ways that make a difference to others and bring meaning to life. As individuals and as couples, we can choose to share the gifts of our life with those we love. The process of living and leaving a legacy can teach us what it is that makes life worth living. Whether it is leaving a big endowment, being a meaningful presence in the lives of grandchildren, or volunteering in a hospice program, we can each make a difference in someone's life. Giving to one means giving to many.

> *Lives of great men all remind us*
> *We can make our lives sublime,*
> *And, departing, leave behind us,*
> *Footprints on the sands of time.*
>
> —Excerpt from "A Psalm of Life,"
> Henry Wadsworth Longfellow

Talking It Through: Creating Your Shared Vision

Spend some time thinking about the following issues. Use your journal to write down your thoughts and feelings, as well as anything you want to talk about with your partner. If you need a refresher on communicating effectively, go back to "Getting to Yes Together: The Importance of Communication," pages xxxiii–xlv.

As you get started, remember the five tips and "Have a BLAST!"

- **B**laming gets in the way
- **L**isten without interrupting
- **A**gree to disagree and don't make assumptions

- Set a safe space for discussion
- Take time to talk without distractions

Exercise 1

Go it solo: Things to think about on your own

1. What values or principles have been most important in my life?
2. What are my guiding beliefs about life?
3. What lessons have had the greatest impact on
   my life?
4. How have I made a difference in the lives of others?
5. What is important for my children, grandchildren,
   and others to know about my life?
6. How do I want to be remembered?

Exercise 2

Couple time: Things to talk about together

1. Take turns sharing your responses to Exercise 1,
   one at a time.
2. Share something positive that you learned about
   each other.
3. Take time to question anything that was not clear.
4. Make a list of the things that you agree on.
5. Set a time for your next conversation.

These are important life questions. Give yourself time to
think about them and share your responses with each other.
Being able to communicate on a deeper level can enhance
your connection and intimacy.

Even though you are coming to the end of the book,

your conversations should still continue. Life goes on and circumstances change. Be sure to schedule a regular time without interruption when you can spend time together to talk.

Puzzle Piece: Purpose, Meaning, and Giving Back

Discuss together how you can live a purposeful life that is aligned with your values and reflects how you want to make a difference. Choose two or three ideas that capture the essence of your discussion, and write them in the Puzzle Piece section at the end of the "Creating Your Shared Vision" chapter, page 263.

Funwork
Do individually

- Write a letter to someone you love, such as your children, grandchildren, partner, or someone else who is special to you. Share what you want them to know about you and how they have made a difference in your life.
- Share your letter or your experience of writing the letter with your partner.

Creating Your Shared Vision

"The best way to predict your future is to create it."
—Abraham Lincoln

We hope that the information, tools, and exercises in *The Couple's Retirement Puzzle* have helped you and your partner have some of the important conversations central to creating your Shared Vision for retirement transition. By now, you probably have a good sense of where things flow smoothly in your relationship, what keeps you stuck, which conversations have been most important, and what you need to continue to work on. Having these conversations is a continuing process of adjusting to changing life circumstances.

Each of the ten conversations in this book represents a piece of your retirement puzzle and has its own shape and size depending on your priorities. Through the choices and decisions you make, your puzzle will begin to take shape. As your vision emerges, you may begin to see patterns and possible solutions you had not noticed before. Communication continues to be the fuel for moving forward. If you are not in agreement about something and the conversation begins to escalate into an argument, you always have the option of calling for a time out. It works for kids, and it can work for you. A cooling-down period gives you time to think differently about the situation, and you may even come up with creative ideas and solutions for solving the dilemma. But if you find yourselves immovably stuck on opposite sides of an issue, it may be helpful to work with a third party, such as a coach or therapist.

CREATING YOUR SHARED VISION

A Shared Vision is a plan that you create together describing how you want to live the next part of your lives. The best Shared Vision reflects each partner's values, goals, desires, and individual vision. But your visions for the future may not be exactly the same, which is where negotiation and compromise come in. There may be times when you will decide to let go of something for the sake of the relationship, and other times when you stand firm because of your own values or needs. Trying to balance your own needs with the needs of the relationship can be a challenge. We don't always get what we want, but what we end up with may be more valuable. Remember, this is not a rigid, right-or-wrong process. The process of creating your Shared Vision is meant to be a dynamic and fluid guide that can help you move forward and enjoy what could be the best time of your life. As circumstances change, you may need to go back to the drawing board. Having the skills to communicate more effectively can help you make decisions together throughout life.

Step One: Create Your Individual Vision List

How many times have you said something like, "I have always wanted to learn Italian and spend a month traveling in Italy," or "I hope that someday we will have enough money to buy a vacation home on a lake in Maine"? Maybe you want to learn how to create a stained-glass window, take your grandchildren on an adventure trip, or reconnect with a friend or relative whom you haven't seen in years. Most of us live our lives as if there are endless tomorrows, putting things off that we would really love to do or want to accomplish. A Vision List is a list of the goals you want to achieve, dreams you want to fulfill, and experiences you want to have in your lifetime. Creating a Vision List can remind you of what is most important in your relationship and in your life.

The first step is for both of you to create an individual list that includes your vision for yourself as well as your vision for the relationship. Include as many ideas as possible, even if you think they are unrealistic. Then prioritize the ten most important ideas on your list. Before filling out the individual Vision Lists on page 266 at the end of the chapter, make several copies so that you can return to the exercise and revise your visions over time. Take as much time as you need, giving yourselves some time to work on your individual lists before talking together.

The following questions are a guide to thinking about what is most important to you in your life:

- What have you always wanted to do, but have not yet done?
- What would you do if you had unlimited time, money, and resources?
- What are your biggest goals and dreams?
- What more do you want to accomplish in your life?
- What skills or activities do you want to learn?
- Where have you always wanted to go, but have never been?
- What do you most want to see or experience?
- What relationships, if any, do you want to resolve?
- What dreams do you have for you and your partner?
- What do you most want to achieve in different areas of your life?
- How can you live your life with a greater sense of meaning and purpose?

Step Two: Share Your Prioritized Vision Lists

The objective of this step is to hear what is important to your partner and share what's important to you. Listening is a tool for learning, and being a good listener involves staying present and keeping focused on what your partner is saying without interrupting. (You may want to return to "Getting to Yes Together: The Importance of Communication," pages xxxiii–xlv for a communications refresher.) What dreams and goals do you share? What do you both want for the future and how can this fit into your plan? Make sure you have enough time to talk and ask questions. This is an opportunity to see where your visions are similar and where they may differ. If you find that there are differences, don't worry. It's possible to make space for both your individual and joint visions.

Step Three: Putting the Puzzle Together to Create Your Shared Vision

It's time to put the pieces of your puzzle together and create your Shared Vision, which includes both short- and long-term goals. The process of creating a Shared Vision involves integrating what's important to each of you individually with what you both want for your relationship and how you want to live the next part of life together. Focusing on the next one to five years may be more realistic than thinking about the rest of your life. Over time, your vision will change depending on what's happening in your lives and what your priorities are for the coming years.

Remember, this is a first draft, and it can be revised at any time. In fact, it's a good idea to revisit your vision at least once a year as things change. Before filling out your Shared Vision at the end of the chapter (see page 266), make several copies of the page so you can return to the exercise and revise your vision over time.

- Review what you've written in the Puzzle Piece section on pages 263–265 while reading the book. Does this still reflect what you want to include in your Shared Vision? Is there anything that should be taken out?
- What else have you discovered from your individual Vision Lists and conversations that you want to include in your Shared Vision?
- Decide together what this version of your Shared Vision will include. Write your Shared Vision on page 266.
- Create a time frame and action steps that will help you reach each of your goals.

The following example illustrates how Jeremy and Kim, both sixty-three and married thirty-seven years, put their retirement puzzle together. This was their first attempt at writing a Shared Vision.

- *If, When, and How to Retire*: We will both continue to work until age sixty-six, when we can collect our full Social Security. Before that time we'll consult with a Social Security adviser and decide whether to use the spousal benefit option until Kim reaches age seventy or both collect individual benefits at age sixty-six.
- *Let's Talk about Money*: Save enough money to supplement a trip to Italy for our fortieth anniversary by eating out no more than twice a week and putting the money we would have spent into a "vacation" savings account.
- *Changing Roles and Identities*: In the next year, start to explore what we might want to retire to. Jeremy: begin to take courses in restoring antique furniture. Kim: explore options for working with victims of domestic violence. Together: reassess household chores and find ways to share responsibilities.

- *Time Together, Time Apart*: Spend one weekend day together doing something we both enjoy.
- *Intimacy and Romance*: Take turns planning a romantic date night twice a month.
- *Relationships with Family*: Set a time in the next six months to talk with our children about our wills and tell them where other legal documents are kept.
- *Health and Wellness*: Schedule physical exams and develop our fitness routines. Start walking together three mornings a week for at least thirty minutes.
- *Choosing Where and How to Live*: Make a decision within the next three years about whether we want to move to a retirement community or renovate our home so that we will be able to age in place.
- *Social Life, Friends, and Community*: Start a couples' book group to combine socializing, good food, and intellectual stimulation.
- *Purpose, Meaning, and Giving Back:* Put together a family album for our children and grandchildren. Plan a family reunion to celebrate our retirement in three years.

Seeing all of your puzzle pieces together will provide an overview of possibilities and help you clarify your priorities and set goals based on what is realistic. Don't be surprised if one or more of your puzzle pieces conflict. For example, if you are committed to taking that "trip of a lifetime" next summer but your house needs a new roof, you may need to find ways to save money, explore creative financing, or put one or the other on hold. Accomplishing your goals involves gathering information and setting realistic timelines based on finances and other important factors. Creating a Shared Vision is one part of the equation, but making it happen is something you will need to work on together.

SUMMARY

We hope that this book has helped you, as individuals and as a couple, to "puzzle out" the most important pieces of your unique plan for retirement transition. Because life is unpredictable, the best plan is a balance of optimism and realism. It takes courage and commitment to take risks, step out of your comfort zone, and create a life that reflects what you really want. The process of reassessing outdated roles and letting go of what is no longer relevant can give you the freedom to open up to new possibilities, both individually and together. You may discover that your "bonus years" offer the opportunity to accomplish many of your individual and shared dreams. *Remember, retirement isn't a destination—it's a journey. Enjoy the places you visit along the way.*

PUZZLE PIECE: CREATING OUR SHARED VISION

Write out your responses to the Puzzle Piece sections at the end of each chapter to the corresponding conversations here. Then compile your individual and shared visions.

If, When, and How to Retire

_____

_____

_____

_____

Let's Talk about Money

_____

_____

_____

_____

Changing Roles and Identities

_____

_____

_____

_____

Time Together, Time Apart

_____

_____

_____

_____

Intimacy and Romance

_____

_____

_____

_____

Relationships with Family

_____

_____

_____

_____

Health and Wellness

_____

_____

_____

_____

Choosing Where and How to Live

_____

_____

_____

_____

Social Life, Friends, and Community

_____

_____

_____

_____

Purpose, Meaning, and Giving Back

_____

_____

_____

_____

Your Individual Vision (Partner One)

_____

_____

_____

_____

Your Individual Vision (Partner Two)

_____

_____

_____

_____

Your Shared Vision

_____

_____

_____

_____

_____

_____

_____

Afterword

Detours: When Life Doesn't Work Out the Way You Want

As we know from the ebb and flow of life and relationships, things do not always work out as we hope they will. Jobs are lost, friends come and go, children choose lifestyles we do not approve of, marriages end, and loved ones die. Life is full of unexpected events we have no control over. You and your partner may have planned for your ideal retirement, only to find that one of you has a serious illness or that you don't have enough money to retire. Maybe you believe marriage is forever but, all of a sudden, you are alone, whether by choice or circumstance. Life has its moods: it can be generous, forgiving, and joyful, as well as harsh and bewildering. But as we grow through the process of surviving, we learn to be more resilient and to deal with life on life's terms.

WHAT IF YOUR PARTNER DOESN'T WANT TO TALK?

You may have picked up this book with the hope that you could finally get your partner to talk about planning for retirement. After all, time is passing, and you may not even know whether you can afford to retire. It would be great to bring the book home, read it together, create your vision, and go merrily on your way to the next chapter of your lives.

But what if that doesn't happen? Your partner may not have any interest in reading a self-help book, or may think you don't need a book to figure out your life. Maybe you're ready to plan for retirement but your partner isn't. Feeling disappointed or angry is understandable, but becoming reactive won't help. It can be frustrating when you come across something that could be helpful and your partner rejects it. That doesn't mean you have to throw the book out the window. The best thing to do is accept that you are not on the same page, hope that will change, and continue to explore and even share your own vision for retirement with your partner. It may spark an interest that opens the conversation.

If you are reading the book on your own, you can still benefit from the information, suggestions, and exercises. For instance, consider practicing some of the suggestions in "Getting to Yes Together: The Importance of Communication," pages xxxiii–xlv, such as listening more attentively when your partner is talking, using "I" statements to express how you feel, and avoiding interrupting or making assumptions. Your partner may feel like he or she is being heard and react in a more positive way. A lot can happen when old patterns of communication begin to change.

We know from our experience working with couples that one partner can be a "change agent" in a relationship, even if the other is unwilling to participate. Imagine a pebble being dropped into the water—when it hits the water, there is a ripple effect all around it. In a similar way, you can be the change agent, creating a ripple effect in your relationship.

Change is inevitable. We either choose to make changes or we get pushed along, and over time, things inevitably change, whether we like it or not. Many people prefer to initiate change and have choice about their lives rather than just leaving things up to chance. But others may resist because they fear loss, thinking, "If our relationship changes, I could lose my partner." Change means letting go of something that may no longer be working to allow the space for something different. If your partner is resistant, don't be surprised if he or she gets angry or tries to make you feel guilty for doing something new. Your wish to have a more positive relationship may be threatening to a partner who is more comfortable with the status quo.

You can suggest getting help from a therapist or coach, but if your partner refuses, take care of yourself. There are two people in a relationship, and nobody is always right or always wrong. We all need to take responsibility for our behavior. Once you begin to gain a clearer understanding of your role in the relationship, you may find new, nonthreatening ways to engage your partner.

WHAT IF YOU GET DIVORCED?

Older boomers born in the late 1940s and '50s grew up on TV shows and movies where everyone lived happily ever after. But life does not always parallel art, and not every story has a happy ending. Midlife and beyond can be a time of questioning and searching for a new identity. Men and women may find themselves attracted to someone who will listen and be empathic, or who will bring out a long-lost, youthful, and more exciting part of themselves. However, affairs undermine trust and can wreak havoc on families and relationships. They can even, though not always, lead to divorce.

Another fairly common reason for divorce in midlife is when couples find that, without the kids and the old familiar roles, they have nothing in common. People grow in different ways, and it can be difficult to bridge the gap, especially if they have dissimilar visions for the future. This can happen even if you still love and care about each other. You may decide that you are better off going your separate ways and remaining friends, or you might choose to separate for a period of time and come back together after you have both had a chance to pursue a dream or passion. Both of these options take a great deal of mutual understanding, trust, and maturity.

For couples who have a history of marital conflict and poor communication, retirement decisions can cause more stress and may even bring the marriage to a crossroads. This may be a time of opportunity in crisis, which can force some couples to address and resolve long-standing issues. Other couples may find themselves questioning whether to stay together if their needs and goals are different and their issues appear irreconcilable. There has been an increase in divorces for people over fifty. If problems cannot be resolved, some people are deciding they don't want to spend another twenty-plus years in an unhappy marriage. Divorce can feel very much like a death—it is certainly a loss, even if it was your choice to end the marriage. Both divorce and loss of a partner are very high on the stress scale. In either case, having a support network is extremely important. Couples who get divorced face many of the same challenges as widows or widowers, though they rarely get the same compassion or support. Their status and identity change as they go from being married to being single. Going from two to one is a huge adjustment, whether through getting divorced or through the death of a partner. It is not uncommon to hear single people say that it is a couple's world, and they don't feel like they "fit in."

WHAT IF YOUR PARTNER DIES?

We tend to live our lives thinking that we will "grow old together." In reality, we know that is not necessarily true. By the time you reach your fifties, sixties, and seventies, you have probably experienced the loss of one or more of your parents, siblings, friends, colleagues, or possibly your partner. Death adds a component of shock and trauma—whether suddenly from a heart attack, stroke, or accident that takes a life in a flash, or as a result of a terminal illness that has gone on for a long time before the person succumbs. Even when a death is expected, you may feel unprepared when it actually happens.

When a partner dies suddenly, it is not uncommon to go into shock, at first disbelieving that it happened, or to feel totally numb. An enormous sense of loss usually follows, along with feelings of grief and sadness. It is also not uncommon for the surviving partner to have a variety of other feelings including anger and guilt, which can sometimes be compounded by a sense of "unfinished business." When a loved one dies, the surviving partner, family, or friends may feel ashamed to admit feeling guilt, as if it was their fault, or anger about being left. Some survivors may recall memories of the last interaction, perhaps wishing to say what had not been spoken or take back the words that were said.

There is usually a massive rallying around the surviving partner and family when a partner dies. Friends bring food, send flowers, and write heartfelt notes of condolence. It is helpful to have loving people around when your life has just turned upside down. The real shock and loneliness often come when friends and family have gone and you are left alone in a home you have shared with your partner through all your ups and downs, good times and bad. It takes time to grieve and mourn the loss of a loved one, as well as all of the wishes, dreams, and hopes that were involved. You will need time to readjust and find your way on your own. It is important to be patient with yourself and accept support and help from others. Some people find it helpful to see a grief counselor or join a support group. Being isolated can lead to lack of self-care, disconnection, depression,

272 The Couple's Retirement Puzzle

or ignoring important legal and financial issues, all of which, if not dealt with, can have devastating effects.

You and your partner may have planned for your retirement transition and growing old together. Now you may be going it alone, trying to adjust to a changing identity and marital status. There you are, having no choice but to reinvent yourself.

There is no question how difficult it can be when life throws you a curve ball, and what you thought would be a shared retirement transition is not going to happen. Death has a way of helping us realize that life is very special and precious—and that it is important to do the best you can to figure out a way to move on, creating the best possible life for yourself in spite of the challenges ahead.

SUMMARY

Life is an unpredictable journey, with ecstatic moments of joy, devastating losses, and everything in between. The more resilient and resourceful we can be, the easier it is to get through the tough times. We need friends and family for support and much-needed hugs, and we also need a belief that things do change and time can indeed heal. Sometimes it is a stretch to think we can learn from loss and pain, but in retrospect, there is usually something in the experience that has made us wiser and helped us to move on in our lives.

Reading Group Guide for Individuals and Couples

The following questions are meant to encourage group discussion about various aspects of retirement transition and issues related to the second half of life. In this book, the term "retirement transition" has been used to reflect a process of letting go of what is no longer necessary and opening the space for creating what will come next in life.

1. What does the word "retirement" mean to you?

2. What are your fears about retirement?

3. In retrospect, what do you wish you and your partner had discussed earlier in your relationship?

4. What have you and your partner done to prepare for retirement transition? Where are you in the process?

5. If you have already retired, what do you wish you had known prior to retiring?

6. What are your hopes and dreams for the future? How similar or different are they from your partner's hopes and dreams?

7. What have you always wanted to do but never had time for?

8. How do you envision what's next? Do you plan to travel, explore hobbies, work, volunteer, or develop an encore career?

9. What skills do you have that you would like to be able to use more often?

10. What, if anything, would you like to learn about or study?

11. What are your priorities at this point in your life?

12. What brings you happiness?

13. How would you define "aging well"? What role models do you have for aging well?

14. What, if anything, gets in the way of having the life you want to be living? (For example: finances, family obligations and responsibilities, caring for aging parents, or health issues.)

15. What do you need to let go of to have more of what you want in your life?

16. What would enhance your relationship with your partner?

17. What resources and supports do you need to successfully navigate retirement transition?

18. What do you most want to accomplish in your life?

Resources

ON THE ROAD TO TRANSITION

Astor, Bart. *AARP Road Map for the Rest of Your Life: Smart Choices About Money, Health, Work, Lifestyle...and Pursuing Your Dreams.* Hoboken, NJ: John Wiley & Sons, 2013.

Ballard, Phoebe, and Jack Ballard. *Turning Points: Create Your Path through Uncertainty and Change.* Bloomington, IN: AuthorHouse, 2002.

Bateson, Mary Catherine. *Composing a Further Life: The Age of Active Wisdom.* New York: Vintage Books, 2011.

Borchard, David C., and Patricia A. Donohoe. *The Joy of Retirement: Finding Happiness, Freedom, and the Life You've Always Wanted.* New York: AMACOM, 2008.

Bridges, William. *Managing Transitions: Making the Most of Change,* 2nd ed. Boston: Da Capo Press, 2003.

Butler, Robert N. *The Longevity Revolution: The Benefits and Challenges of Living a Long Life.* New York: PublicAffairs, 2008.

Chimsky, Mark Evan, ed. *65 Things to Do When You Retire: More than 65 Notable Achievers on How To Make the Most of the Rest of Your Life.* South Portland, ME: Sellers Publishing, 2012.

Corbett, David D., and Richard Higgins. *Portfolio Life: The New Path to Work, Purpose, and Passion After 50.* San Francisco: Jossey-Bass, 2006.

Cullinane, Jan. *The Single Woman's Guide to Retirement*. Hoboken, NJ: John Wiley & Sons, 2012.

Davidson, Sara. *Leap! What Will We Do with the Rest of Our Lives?: Reflections from the Boomer Generation*. New York: Random House, 2007.

Dychtwald, Ken. *Age Power: How the 21st Century will be Ruled by the New Old*. New York: Tarcher, 2000.

Dychtwald, Ken, and Daniel Kadlec. *The Power Years: A User's Guide to the Rest of Your Life: Pursue Your Dreams, Deepen your Relationships, Achieve Financial Freedom*. Hoboken, NJ: John Wiley & Sons, 2005.

Ferrin, Kelly. *What's Age Got to Do With It? Volume II: Secrets to Aging in Extraordinary Ways*. Libertyville, IL: Red Zone Publishing, 2007.

Fonda, Jane. *Prime Time: Love, Health, Sex, Fitness, Friendship, Spirit: Making the Most of All of Your Life*. New York: Random House, 2011.

Freedman, Mark. *The Big Shift: Navigating the New Stage Beyond Midlife*. New York: PublicAffairs, 2011.

Freudenheim, Ellen. *Looking Forward: An Optimist's Guide to Retirement*. Stewart, Tabori & Chang, 2004.

Goodman, Miriam. *Reinventing Retirement: 389 Ideas about Family, Friends, Health, What to Do and Where to Live*. San Francisco: Chronicle Books, 2008.

Greenbaum, Stuart, ed. *Longevity Rules: How to Age Well into the Future*. Carmichael, CA: Eskaton, 2010.

Gullette, Margaret Morganroth. *Agewise: Fighting the New Ageism in America*. Chicago: University of Chicago Press, 2011.

Jay, Gary R., ed. *Remarkable and Real: Remarkable Questions, Real Possibilities in the Second Half of Life*. Thomson, GA: Business Expert Publishing, 2012.

Jeffers, Susan J. *Feel the Fear...And Do it Anyway*. New York: Ballantine Books, 2006.

Lawrence-Lightfoot, Sara. *The Third Chapter: Passion, Risk and Adventure in the 25 Years after 50.* New York: Sarah Crichton Books, 2009.

Leider, Richard J., and David A. Shapiro. *Repacking Your Bags: Lighten Your Load for the Good Life.* San Francisco: Berrett-Koehler Publishers, 2012.

Life Planning Network. *Live Smart After 50! The Experts' Guide to Life Planning for Uncertain Times.* Boston: Life Planning Network, 2013.

Lynch, Frederick R. *One Nation Under AARP: The Fight Over Medicare, Social Security, and America's Future.* Berkeley, CA: University of California Press, 2011.

Mandell, Fred, and Kathleen Jordan. *Becoming a Life Change Artist: 7 Creative Skills to Reinvent Yourself at Any Stage of Life.* New York: Avery, 2010.

Marohn, Stephanie, ed. *Audacious Aging.* Santa Rosa, CA: Elite Books, 2009.

McGraw, Robin. *What's Age Got to Do With It? Living Your Healthiest and Happiest Life.* Nashville: Thomas Nelson, 2008.

Moody, Harry R., and Jennifer R. Sasser. *Aging: Concepts and Controversies,* 7th ed. Los Angeles: Sage Publications, 2011.

Morris, Barbara. *Put Old on Hold.* Escondido, CA: Image F/X Publications, 2004.

Pauley, Jane. *Your Life Calling: Reimagining the Rest of Your Life.* New York: Simon & Schuster, 2014.

Prochaska, James O., John C. Norcross, and Carlo C. Diclemente. *Changing for Good: A Revolutionary Six Stage Program for Overcoming Bad Habits and Move Your Life Positively Forward.* New York: Avon Books, 1994.

Radu, Mary, and Cheryl Mann. *The Road Map to Meaningful Mid-life: Create Your Vision and Your Action Plan, Audio and PDF Workbook.* Saint Helena, CA: Pathmaker Coaching and Goals InSight, 2007.

Rimm, Allison. *The Joy of Strategy: A Business Plan for Life*. Brookline, MA: Bibliomotion, 2013.

Rosenblatt, Roger. *Rules for Aging: Resist Normal Impulses, Live Longer, Attain Perfection*. San Diego, CA: Harcourt, 2000.

Schlossberg, Nancy K. *Revitalizing Retirement: Reshaping Your Identity, Relationships, and Purpose*. Washington, DC: American Psychological Association, 2009.

Schulz, James H., and Robert H. Binstock. *Aging Nation: The Economics and Politics of Growing Older in America*. Baltimore: John Hopkins University Press, 2008.

Spector, Alan, and Keith Lawrence. *Your Retirement Quest: 10 Secrets for Creating and Living a Fulfilling Retirement*. Cincinnati: Cincinnati Book Publishers, 2010.

Trafford, Abigail. *My Time: Making the Most of the Rest of Your Life*. New York: Basic Books, 2004.

GETTING TO YES TOGETHER

Bernstein, Jeffrey, and Susan Magee. *Why Can't You Read My Mind? Overcoming the 9 Toxic Thought Patterns that Get in the Way of a Loving Relationship*. Boston: Da Capo Press, 2003.

Cohen, Herb. *You Can Negotiate Anything: How to Get What You Want*. Sydney: Angus & Robertson, 1994.

Colvalt, Patricia. *What Smart Couples Know: The Secret to a Happy Relationship*. New York: AMACOM, 2007.

Fisher, Roger, William L. Ury, and Bruce Patton. *Getting to Yes: Negotiating Agreement Without Giving In*. New York: Penguin, 1991.

Gottman, John, and Nan Silver. *The Seven Principles of Making Marriage Work*. London: Orion Publishing Group, 2004.

Hendrix, Harville. *Getting the Love You Want: A Guide for Couples, 20th Anniversary Edition*. New York: Henry Holt, 2008.

Kardasis, Arline, Rikk Larsen, Crystal Thorpe, and Blair Trippe. *Mom Always Liked You Best: A Guide for Resolving Family*

Feuds, Inheritance Battles & Eldercare Crises. Norwood, MA: Elder Decisions, 2011.

Lerner, Harriet. *The Dance of Connection: How to Talk to Someone When You're Mad, Hurt, Scared, Frustrated, Insulted, Betrayed, or Desperate.* New York: Quill, 2002.

———. *Marriage Rules: A Manual for the Married and the Coupled Up.* New York: Gotham Books, 2012.

McKay, Matthew, Patrick Fanning, and Kim Paleg. *Couple Skills: Making Your Relationship Work.* Oakland, CA: New Harbinger Publications, 2006.

Nichols, Michael P. *The Lost Art of Listening: How Learning to Listen Can Improve Relationships.* New York: Guilford Press, 2009.

Notarius, Clifford, and Howard Markman. *We Can Work It Out: How to Solve Conflicts, Save Your Marriage, and Strengthen Your Love for Each Other.* New York: Berkley Publishing Group, 1994.

Parker-Pope, Tara. *For Better: The Science of a Good Marriage.* New York: Dutton Adult, 2010.

Robinson, Jonathan. *Communication Miracles for Couples: Easy and Effective Tools to Create More Love and Less Conflict.* San Francisco: Conari Press, 2009.

Scott, Susan. *Fierce Conversations: Achieving Success at Work & in Life, One Conversation at a Time.* New York: Berkley Publishing Group, 2004.

Shem, Samuel, and Janet Surrey. *We Have to Talk: Healing Dialogues Between Women and Men.* New York: Basic Books, 1998.

Ury, William. *Getting Past No: Negotiating Your Way from Confrontation to Cooperation.* New York: Bantam Books, 1993.

CONVERSATION 1: IF, WHEN, AND HOW TO RETIRE

Alboher, Marci. *The Encore Career Handbook: How to Make a Living and a Difference in the Second Half of Life.* New York: Workman Publishing, 2013.

Allen, Catherine, Nancy Bearg, Rita Foley, and Jaye Smith. *Reboot Your Life: Energize Your Career and Life By Taking a Break*. New York: Beaufort Books, 2011.

Anderson, Nancy. *Work with Passion in Midlife and Beyond: Reach Your Full Potential & Make the Money You Need*. Novato, CA: New World Library, 2010.

Beauregard, Jack. *Finding Your New Owner: For Your Business, For Your Life: A Guide to a New Paradigm for Baby Boomer Business Owners*. Cambridge, MA: STPI Press, 2011.

Bernstein, Alan, and John Trauth. *Your Retirement, Your Way: Why It Takes More Money to Live Your Dream*. New York: McGraw Hill, 2007.

Bolles, Richard. *What Color Is Your Parachute? 2014: A Practical Manual for Job-Hunters and Career-Changers*. New York: Ten Speed Press, 2013.

Byron, William J. *Finding Work Without Losing Heart: Bouncing Back from Mid-Career Job Loss*. Fort Collins, CO: Adams Media, 1995.

Erickson, Tamara. *Retire Retirement: Career Strategies for the Baby Boomer Generation*. Boston: Harvard Business School Publishing, 2008.

Fideler, Elizabeth F. *Men Still At Work: Professionals Over Sixty and On the Job*. Lanham, MD: Rowman & Littlefield, 2014.

———. *Women Still At Work: Professionals Over Sixty and On the Job*. Lanham, MD: Rowman & Littlefield, 2012.

Freedman, Marc. *Encore: Finding Work That Matters in the Second Half of Life*. New York: PublicAffairs, 2007.

———. *Prime Time: How Baby Boomers Will Revolutionize Retirement and Transform America*. New York: PublicAffairs, 1999.

Hannon, Kerry. *Great Jobs for Everyone 50+: Finding Work that Keeps You Happy and Healthy...and Pays the Bills*. Hoboken, NJ: John Wiley & Sons, 2012.

———. *What's Next? Finding Your Passion and Your Dream Job in Your Forties, Fifties and Beyond*, rev. ed. New York: Berkeley Trade, 2014.

Hively, Jan, Carleen MacKay, and Dorian Mintzer. *The Career Playbook: Second Half Plays For Boomers & Beyond*. Boston: Boomers and Beyond Special Interest Group, 2014.

Ibarra, Herminia. *Working Identity: Unconventional Strategies for Reinventing Your Career*. Boston: Harvard Business School Press, 2004.

Kurth, Brian, and Robin Simons. *Test-Drive Your Dream Job: A Step-By-Step Guide to Finding and Creating the Work You Love*. New York: Business Plus, 2008.

Levoy, Gregg. *Callings: Finding and Following an Authentic Life*. New York: Three Rivers Press, 1997.

MacKay, Carleen. *Plan B for Boomers*. San Diego, CA: San Diego Workforce Partnership, 2009.

———, Phil Newbold, and Brad Taft. *The Return of the Boomers—A Leaders Guide: Crossing the Bridge to the Future with the Help of the Mature Workforce*. Scottsdale, AZ: Cambridge Media, 2008.

———, and San Diego Workforce Partnership. *Playbook 1 of the Career Playbook Series*. San Diego, CA: San Diego Workforce Partnership, 2014.

Newman, Betsy Kyte. *Retiring As a Career: Making the Most of Your Retirement*. Westport, CT: Praeger, 2008.

Orszag, Peter R. "Retirement Will Kill You," *Bloomberg View*, June 11, 2013. www.bloombergview.com/articles/2013-06-11/retirement-will-kill-you.

Portzline, Larry. *Follow Your Enthusiasm: How 12 Ordinary Men Discovered Extraordinary Encore Careers*. Williamsport, PA: Larry Portzline, Publisher, 2013.

Rich-New, Kathleen. *Plan B: The Real Deal Guide to Creating your Business*. New York: Morgan James Publishing, 2013.

Rogoff, Edward G., and David L. Carroll. *The Second Chance Revolution: Becoming Your Own Boss after 50.* New York: Rowhouse Publishing, 2009.

Roiter, Bill. *Beyond Work: How Accomplished People Retire Successfully.* Mississauga, Ontario: John Wiley & Sons Canada, 2008.

Rosenberg, Renée Lee. *Achieving the Good Life After 50: Tools and Resources for Making It Happen.* New York: Five O'Clock Books, 2007.

Schofield, George H. *After 50 It's Up to Us: Developing the Skills and Agility We'll Need.* Lakewood Ranch, FL: The Clarity Group, 2007.

Sedlar, Jeri, and Rick Miners. *Don't Retire, Rewire!: 5 Steps to Fulfilling Work That Fuels Your Passion, Suits Your Personality, and Fills Your Pocket,* 2nd ed. New York: Alpha Books, 2007.

Shifman, Julie. *Act Three: Create the Life You Want After Your First Career and Fulltime Motherhood.* Austin, TX: Greenleaf Book Group Press, 2012.

Stone, Marika, and Howard Stone. *Too Young to Retire: 101 Ways to Start the Rest of Your Life.* New York: Plume, 2004.

Strewler-Carter, Joan, and Stephen T. Carter. *What's Next in Your Life? How to Find Meaning Behind the Money: A Boomer's Guide to a New Retirement.* Kansas City, MO: Rockhill Books, 2008.

Transition Network, Gail Rentsch, and Lynn Sherr. *Smart Women Don't Retire—They Break Free: From Working Full-Time to Living Full-Time.* New York: Springboard Press, 2008.

Trausch, Susan. *Groping Toward Whatever: Or How I Learned to Retire (Sort Of).* Hingham, MA: Free Street Press, 2010.

Weinstein, Bob. *So What If I'm 65: Get a Job, Get the Most Out of Your Best Years.* Ghent, NY: Bob Weinstein Media, 2012.

Zelinski, Emie. *How to Retire Happy, Wild and Free: Retirement Wisdom That You Won't Get from Your Financial Advisor.* Edmonton, Alberta: Visions International Publishing, 2009.

Web Resources (If the website is no longer available, search the title to find the updated website listing)

AARP: www.aarp.org

Ageless in America: www.agelessinamerica.com

Audacious Aging: www.audaciousaging.com

Encore Careers: www.encore.org

Life Planning Network: www.lifeplanningnetwork.org

National Council on Aging (NCOA): www.ncoa.org

Pivot Planet (previously Vocation Vacations): www.pivotplanet.com

Revolutionize Retirement: www.revolutionizeretirement.com

San Diego Mature Workforce Coalition: www.sdmatureworkers.org

Senior Job Bank: www.seniorjobbank.org

Workforce 50: www.Workforce50.com

2Young2Retire: www.2young2retire.com

CONVERSATION 2: LET'S TALK ABOUT MONEY

Annino, Particia M. *Women & Money: A Practical Guide to Estate Planning.* CreateSpace, 2011.

Anspach, Dana. *Control Your Retirement Destiny: Achieving Financial Security Before the Big Transition.* New York: Apress, 2013.

Bachrach, Bill. *Values-Based Financial Planning: The Art of Creating an Inspiring Financial Strategy.* Valley Village, CA: Aim High Publishing, 2003.

Benson, April Lane. *To Buy or Not to Buy: Why We Over Shop and How to Stop.* Boston: Trumpeter, 2008.

Blayney, Eleanor. *Women's Worth: Finding Your Financial Confidence.* McLean, VA: Direction$, 2010.

Bradley, Susan with Mary Martin. *Sudden Money: Managing a Financial Windfall.* Hoboken, NJ: John Wiley & Sons, 2000.

Carlson, Robert C. *The New Rules of Retirement: Strategies for a Secure Future.* Hoboken, NJ: John Wiley & Sons, 2005.

Clifford, Denis, Frederick Hertz, and Emily Doskow. A *Legal*

Guide for Lesbian & Gay Couples, 16th ed. Berkeley, CA: Nolo Publishing, 2012.

Ealy, C. Diane, and Kay Lesh. *Our Money Our Selves for Couples: A New Way of Relating to Money and Each Other.* Herndon, VA: Capital Books, 2003.

Glover, Ryan. *Preparing for Retirement: A Comprehensive Guide to Financial Planning.* Greensboro, NC: Tarheel Advisors, 2013.

Hegland, Kenney F., and Robert B. Fleming. *Alive and Kicking: Legal Advice for Boomers!* Durham, NC: Carolina Academic Press, 2007.

Holland, David D. *Confessions of a Financial Planner: Secrets to a Secure Retirement.* Holland Productions, 2011.

Kahler, Rick, and Kathleen Fox. *Conscious Finance. Uncover Your Hidden Money Beliefs and Transform the Role of Money in Your Life.* Rapid City, SD: Fox Craft, 2005.

Kinder, George. *The Seven Stages of Money Maturity: Understanding the Spirit and Value of Money in Your Life.* New York: Dell Publishing, 1999.

Kingsbury, Kathleen Burns. *Wealth from the Inside Out Workbook.* Easton, MA: KBK Wealth Connection, 2010.

Klontz, Brad, Rick Kahler, and Ted Klontz. *Facilitating Financial Health: Tools for Financial Planners, Coaches, and Therapists.* Cincinnati: National Underwriter Company, 2008.

Knuckey, Deborah. *Conscious Spending for Couples: Seven Skills for Financial Harmony.* Hoboken, NJ: John Wiley & Sons, 2003.

Mauterstock, Robert. *Can We Talk? A Financial Guide for Baby Boomers Assisting their Elderly Parents.* Rogers, AR: Soar with Eagles Press, 2008.

Mellan, Olivia, and Sherry Christie. *Money Harmony: A Road Map for Individuals and Couples.* Washington, DC: Money Harmony Books, 2014.

————. *Overcoming Overspending: A Winning Plan for Spenders and Their Partners*, 2nd ed. New York: Walker Books, 2009.

Miller, Mark. *The Hard Times Guide to Retirement Security: Practical Strategies for Money, Work, and Living*. Hoboken, NJ: John Wiley & Sons, 2010.

Mor, Eva. *Making the Golden Years Golden: Sources of Information to Guide You in Making the Right Decisions for Living Better, Healthier, Independently and Stress Free*. Bloomington, IN: AuthorHouse, 2009.

Onerheim, Mayuri. *Money. Spirituality. Consciousness: A Guided Inquiry into our Personal Relationship to Money*. Sydney: ReadHowYouWant, 2012.

Orman, Suze. *Suze Orman's Action Plan: New Rules for New Times*. New York: Spiegel & Grau, 2010.

Piper, Mike. *Social Security Made Simple: Social Security Retirement Benefits and Related Planning Topics Explained in 100 Pages or Less*. St. Louis: Simple Subjects, 2012.

Ricco, Cia, and Belinda Rosenblum. *Self-Worth to Net Worth: 12 Key Ways to Creating Wealth Inside and Out*. Littleton, MA: Rich Life Publishing, 2012.

Rich, Jonathan. *The Couples Guide to Love and Money*. Oakland, CA: New Harbinger Publications, 2003.

Ruffenach, Glenn, and Kelly Greene. *The Wall Street Journal Complete Retirement Guidebook: How to Plan It, Live It and Enjoy It*. New York: Random House, 2007.

Singer, Mark, ed. *The Six Secrets to a Happy Retirement: How to Master the Transition of a Lifetime*. Medford, MA: ATA Press, 2012.

Singer, Mark. *The Changing Landscape of Retirement—What You Don't Know Could Hurt You*. Medford, MA: ATA Press, 2011.

Solin, Daniel R. *The Smartest Retirement Book You'll Ever Read*. New York: Perigee Books, 2009.

Thomas, Holly P. *The Mindful Money Mentality: How to Find Balance in Your Financial Future*. Tampa: Porchview Publishing, 2013.

Twist, Lynne, and Teresa Barker. *The Soul of Money: Reclaiming the Wealth of our Inner Resources*. New York: W. W. Norton, 2006.

Vernon, Steve. *Live Long and Prosper: Invest in Your Happiness, Health and Wealth for Retirement and Beyond*. Hoboken, NJ: John Wiley & Sons, 2004.

———. *Turn Your IRA and 401(k) into a Lifetime Retirement Paycheck*. Oxnard, CA: Rest-of-Life Communications, 2012.

Yochim, Dayana. *The Motley Fool's Guide to Couples & Cash: How to Handle Money with Your Honey*. Alexandria, VA: Motley Fool, 2003.

Zimmerman, Susan. *Mindful Money for Wealth and Well-Being*. CreateSpace, 2013.

Web Resources (If the website is no longer available, search the title to find the updated website listing)

Association for Integrative Financial and Life Planning (AIFLP): www.aiflp.org

Certified Financial Planning Board of Standard's site for consumers: www.cfp.net

Debtors Anonymous: www.debtorsanonymous.org

Financial Industry Regulatory Authority (FINRA): www.finra.org

Financial Planning Association's site for consumers: www.fpanet.org

Free Legal Documents: www.findforms.com

Gamblers Anonymous: www.gamblersanonymous.org

Kinder Institute: www.kinderinstitute.com/dir/

National Association of Personal Financial Advisors: www.napfa.org

Paladin Registry: www.paladinregistry.com

Shopaholics Anonymous: www.shopaholicsanonymous.org

Social Security: www.ssa.gov

Stopping Overshopping: www.shopaholicnomore.com

CONVERSATION 3: CHANGING ROLES AND IDENTITIES

Arp, David H., Claudia S. Arp, Scott M. Stanley, Howard J. Markman, and Susan L. Blumberg. *Fighting for Your Empty Nest Marriage.* San Francisco: Jossey-Bass, 2000.

Battaglia, Beverly. *Changing Lanes: Couples Redefining Retirement.* Charleston, SC: BookSurge Publishing, 2008.

Brown, Brené. *Daring Greatly: How the Courage to Be Vulnerable Transforms the Way We Live, Love, Parent, and Lead.* New York: Gotham Books, 2012.

————. *I Thought It Was Just Me (But It Isn't): Making the Journey from "What Will People Think?" to "I Am Enough."* New York: Gotham Books, 2007.

Buckingham, Marcus, and Donald O. Clifton. *Now, Discover Your Strengths.* New York: Free Press, 2001.

Emmons, Roberts A. *Thanks! How Practicing Gratitude Can Make You Happier.* New York: Mariner Books, 2007.

Floyd, Mary Louise. *Retired with Husband: Superwoman's New Challenge.* Acton, MA: VanderWyk and Burnham, 2006.

Goldman, Connie. *Who Am I...Now That I'm Not Who I Was?* Minneapolis: Nodin Press, 2009.

Jacobs, Ruth Harriet. *Be an Outrageous Older Woman.* New York: Harper Perennial, 1997.

Lerner, Harriet. *The Dance of Anger: A Woman's Guide to Changing the Patterns of Intimate Relationships.* New York: William Morrow, 2005.

Linley, Alex. *Average to A+: Realising Strengths in Yourself and Others.* Coventry, England: CAPP Press, 2008.

Miller, Nancy Bost. *Creative Aging: Discovering the Unexpected Joys of Later Life Through Personality Type.* Davies Publishing, 1998.

Polston, Betty L., and Susan K. Golant. *Loving Mid-Life Marriage: A Guide to Keeping Romance Alive from the Empty Nest Through Retirement*. Hoboken, NJ: John Wiley & Sons, 1999.

Richo, David. *How to be an Adult in Relationships: The Five Keys to Mindful Loving*. Boston: Shambhala, 2002.

Sadler, William A. *The Third Age: 6 Principles of Growth and Renewal After 40*. Boston: Da Capo Press, 2000.

———, and James H. Krefft. *Changing Course, Navigating Change After 50*. The Center for Third Age Leadership Press, 2008.

Sharf, Maggie. *September Songs: The Good News about Marriage in the Later Years*. New York: Riverhead Books, 2009.

Wood, Amy. *Life Your Way: Refresh Your Approach to Success and Breathe Easier in a Fast Paced World*. Portland, ME: Modern Sage Press, 2010.

Zander, Rosamund Stone, and Benjamin Zander. *The Art of Possibility: Transforming Professional and Personal Life*. New York: Penguin Group, 2000.

Web Resources (If the website is no longer available, search the title to find the updated website listing)

Authentic Happiness: www.authentichappiness.sas.upenn.edu

Discovering What's Next, a program of ESC of New England: www.escne.org

Discover Your Strengths: www.gallupstrengthscenter.com

VIA Signature Strengths—a free strength assessment: www.authentichappiness.sas.upenn.edu/questionnaires.aspx

What's Next in Life Values Assessment: www.whatsnext.com/content/life-values-self-assessment-test

CONVERSATION 4: TIME TOGETHER, TIME APART

Battaglia, Beverly. *Changing Lanes: Couples Redefining Retirement*. Charleston, SC: BookSurge Publishing, 2008.

Fredrickson, Barbara. *Positivity: Top-Notch Research Reveals the 3 to 1 Ratio that will Change Your Life*. New York: Three Rivers Press, 2009.

Goodman, Miriam. *Too Much Togetherness: Surviving Retirement as a Couple*. Springville, UT: Bonneville Books, 2011.

Reivich, Karen, and Andrew Shatte. *The Resilience Factor: 7 Keys to Finding Your Inner Strength and Overcoming Life's Hurdles*. New York: Broadway Books, 2002.

Vandervelde, Maryanne. *Retirement for Two: Everything You Need to Know to Thrive Together as Long as You Both Shall Live*. New York: Bantam Dell, 2007. Kindle edition.

Yogev, Sara. *For Better or For Worse...But Not for Lunch: Making Marriage Work in Retirement*. New York: Contemporary Books, 2001.

CONVERSATION 5: INTIMACY AND ROMANCE

Butler, Robert N., and Myrna I. Lewis. *The New Love and Sex After 60*. New York: Ballantine Books, 2002.

Goldman, Connie. *Late-Life Love: Romance & New Relationships in Later Years*. Minneapolis: Fairview Press, 2006.

Hall, Kathryn. *Reclaiming Your Sexual Self: How You Can Bring Desire Back Into Your Life*. Hoboken, NJ: John Wiley & Sons, 2004.

Klinger, Leah, and Deborah Nedelman. *Still Sexy after All These Years: The 9 Unspoken Truths about Women's Desires Beyond 50*. New York: Berkley Publishing Group, 2006.

Nelson, Tammy. *Getting the Sex You Want: Shed Your Inhibitions and Reach New Heights of Passion*. Beverly, MA: Quiver Books, 2012.

Ogden, Gina. *The Heart & Soul of Sex*. Boston: Trumpeter Books, 2006.

———. *The Return of Desire: A Guide to Rediscovering Your Sexual Passion*. Boston: Trumpeter Books, 2008.

Price, Joan. *Better Than I Ever Expected: Straight Talk about Sex after Sixty.* Emeryville, CA: Seal Press, 2006.

Sheehy, Gail. *Sex and the Seasoned Woman: Pursuing the Passionate Life.* New York: Ballantine Books, 2007.

Westheimer, Ruth K. *Dr. Ruth's Sex After 50: Revving Up the Romance, Passion & Excitement!* Fresno, CA: Quill Driver Books, 2005.

Web Resources (If the website is no longer available, search the title to find the updated website listing)

American Association of Sexuality Educators, Counselors, and Therapists (AASECT): www.aasect.org

CONVERSATION 6: RELATIONSHIPS WITH FAMILY

Abramson, Alexis. *The Caregiver's Survival Handbook: How to Care for your Aging Parents Without Losing Yourself.* New York: Perigee Books, 2004.

Adams, Jane. *I'm Still Your Mother: How to Get Along with Your Grown-Up Children for the Rest of Your Life.* Lincoln, NE: iUniverse.com, 2001.

Atkins, Dale. *I'm Ok, You're My Parents: How to Overcome Guilt, Let Go of Anger, and Create a Relationship that Works.* New York: Henry Holt, 2004.

Berman, Claire. *Caring for Yourself While Caring for Your Aging Parents: How to Help, How to Survive,* 3rd ed. New York: Henry Holt, 2006.

Bottke, Allison. *Setting Boundaries with Your Adult Children: Six Steps to Hope and Healing for Struggling Parents.* Eugene, OR: Harvest House Publishers, 2008.

Cain, Madelyn. *The Childless Revolution: What It Means to be Childless Today.* New York: Perseus Publishing, 2001.

Capossela, Cappy, Sheila Warnock, and Sukie Miller. *Share the*

Care: How to Organize a Group to Care for Someone who is Seriously Ill. New York: Fireside Press, 2004.

Carson, Lillian. *The Essential Grandparent's Guide to Divorce: Making a Difference in the Family.* Deerfield Beach, FL: Health Communications, 1999.

Delehanty, Hugh, and Elinor Ginzler. *Caring for Your Parents: The Complete AARP Guide.* New York: Sterling Publishing, 2006.

Gambone, James V., and Rhonda Travland. *Who Says Men Don't Care? A Man's Guide to Balanced and Guilt-Free Caregiving.* Charleston, NC: CreateSpace, 2011.

Goldman, Connie. *The Gifts of Caregiving: Stories of Hardship, Hope, and Healing.* Minneapolis: Fairview Press, 2002.

Gore, William Willis. *Long-Distance Grandparenting: Connecting with Your Grandchildren from Afar.* Sanger, CA: Quill Driver Books/Word Dancer Press, 2008.

Hegland, Kenny F., and Robert B. Fleming. *Alive and Kicking: Legal Advice...for Boomers.* Durham, NC: Carolina Academic Press, 2007.

Isay, Jane. *Walking on Eggshells: Navigating the Delicate Relationship Between Adult Children and Parents.* New York: Flying Dolphin Press, 2007.

Kornhaber, Arthur. *The Grandparent Guide: The Definitive Guide to Coping with the Challenges of Modern Grandparenting.* New York: Contemporary Books, 2002.

———. *The Grandparent Solution: How Parents Can Build a Family Team for Practical, Emotional and Financial Success.* San Francisco: Jossey-Bass, 2004.

Nemzoff, Ruth. *Don't Bite Your Tongue, How to Foster Rewarding Relationships with Your Adult Children.* New York: Palgrave Macmillan, 2008.

———. *Don't Roll your Eyes: Making In-Laws into Family.* Palgrave MacMillan, 2012.

Perman, Barbara, and James Ballard. *No Ordinary Move: Relocating Your Aging Parents.* Bloomington, IN: AuthorHouse, 2008.

Scott, Laura S. *Two is Enough: A Couple's Guide to Living Childless by Choice.* Berkeley, CA: Seal Press, 2009.

Sheehy, Gail. *Passages in Caregiving: Turning Chaos into Confidence.* New York: William Morrow, 2010.

Simon, Sidney, and Suzanne Simon. *Forgiveness: How to Make Peace with Your Past and Get on With Your Life.* Princeton, NJ: Philip Lief Group, 1998.

Web Resources: (If the website is no longer available, search the title to find the updated website listing)

Adult Family Conflict Resolution: www.elderdecisions.com

Alzheimer's Association: www.alzfdn.org

CaringBridge (connecting family and friends when a loved one is ill): www.caringbridge.org

Eldercare Locator: www.eldercare.gov

Elder Law Answers: www.elderlawanswers.com

Empowering Caregivers: www.care-givers.com

Grandparents.com: www.grandparents.com

Grand Times: www.grandtimes.com

Grandparents Today: www.tcpnow.com/guides/gptoday.html

Health Care Elder Law Programs, Inc.: www.help4srs.org

Long Distance Grandparenting: www.longdistancegrandparenting .com

Lotsa Helping Hands: www.lotsahelpinghands.com

National Academy of Certified Care Managers: www.naccm.net

National Academy of Elder Law Attorneys: www.naela.org

National Association of Professional Geriatric Care Managers: www.caremanager.org

National Association of Professional Organizers: www.napo.net

National Eldercare Mediator Network: www.eldercaremediators .com

CONVERSATION 7: HEALTH AND WELLNESS

Aging With Dignity. *Five Wishes Document: Helps You Control How You are Treated if You Get Seriously Ill.* Aging with Dignity.com, 2009.

Amen, Daniel G. *Making a Good Brain Great.* New York: Harmony Books, 2005.

Benson, Herbert, and William Proctor. *Relaxation Revolution: Enhancing your Personal Health Through Science and Genetics of Mind Body Healing.* New York: Scribner, 2010.

Boston Women's Health Book Collective. *Our Bodies, Ourselves: Menopause.* New York: Touchstone Books, 2006.

Bourne, Edmunds J. *The Anxiety and Phobia Workbook.* Oakland, CA: New Harbinger Publications, 2011.

Buettner, Dan. *The Blue Zone: Lessons for Living Longer from the People Who've Lived the Longest.* Washington, DC: National Geographic, 2008.

Butler, Robert N. *The Longevity Prescription: The 8 Proven Keys to a Long, Healthy Life.* New York: Penguin Group, 2010.

————. *Why Survive? Being Old in America.* Baltimore: John Hopkins University Press, 2002.

Callanan, Maggie, and Patricia Kelley. *Final Gifts: Understanding the Special Awareness, Needs and Communication of the Dying.* New York: Simon & Schuster, 2012.

Charlesworth, Edward A., and Ronald G. Nathan. *Stress Management: A Comprehensive Guide to Wellness.* New York: Ballantine Books, 2004.

Cohen, Gene D. *The Creative Age: Awakening Human Potential in the Second Half of Life.* New York: Quill, 2001.

————. *The Mature Mind: The Positive Power of the Aging Brain.* New York: Basic Books, 2005.

Collins, Joseph. *Discover Your Menopause Type: The Exciting New Program That Identifies the 12 Unique Menopause Types & the Best Choices for You.* New York: Three Rivers Press, 2000.

Crowley, Chris, and Henry S. Lodge. *Younger Next Year: A Guide to Living Like 50 Until Your 80's and Beyond*. New York: Workman Press, 2005.

Csikszentmihalyi, Mihaly. *Flow: The Psychology of Optimal Experience*. New York: Harper and Row, 1990.

Diller, Vivian, and Jill Muir-Sukenick. *Face It: What Women Really Feel as Their Looks Change and What to Do About it*. Carlsbad, CA: Hay House, 2011.

Gardner, Howard. *Five Minds for the Future*. Boston: Harvard Business School Publishing, 2006.

Gilbert, Daniel T. *Stumbling on Happiness*. New York: Vintage Books, 2007.

Goldman, Connie, and Richard Mahler. *Secrets of a Late Bloomer: Staying Creative, Aware, and Involved in Mid-Life and Beyond*. Minneapolis: Fairview Press, 1995.

Kessler, Lauren. *Counterclockwise: My Year of Hypnosis, Hormones, Dark Chocolate and Other Adventures in the World of Anti-Aging*. New York: Rodale Books, 2013.

Kiernan, Stephen P. *Last Rights: Rescuing the End of Life from the Medical System*. New York: St. Martin's Griffin, 2006.

Kind, Viki. *The Caregiver's Path to Compassionate Decision Making: Making Choices for Those Who Can't*. Austin, TX: Greenleaf Book Group, 2010.

Kübler-Ross, Elisabeth. *On Death and Dying*. New York: Scribner, 1997.

Lachs, Mark. *Treat Me, Not My Age: A Doctor's Guide to Getting the Best Care as You or Your Loved One Gets Older*. New York: Viking, 2010.

Langer, Ellen J. *Counterclockwise: Mindful Health and the Power of Possibility*. New York: Ballantine Books, 2009.

Lear, Martha Weinman. *Where Did I Leave My Glasses?: The What, When, and Why of Normal Memory Loss*. New York: Hachette Book Group, 2008.

Lustbader, Wendy. *Counting on Kindness: The Dilemmas of Dependency.* New York: Free Press, 1991.

Mezirow, Jack. *Learning as Transformation: Critical Perspectives on a Theory in Progress.* San Francisco: Jossey-Bass, 2000.

McCullough, Dennis. *My Mother, Your Mother: Embracing "Slow Medicine": The Compassionate Approach to Caring for Your Aging Loved Ones.* New York: Harper Perennial, 2009.

Murray, Bob, and Alicia Fortinberry. *Creating Optimism: A Proven, Seven-Step Program for Overcoming Depression.* New York: McGraw Hill, 2004.

Nuland, Sherwin B. *The Art of Aging: A Doctor's Prescription for Well-Being.* New York: Random House, 2008.

———. *How We Die: Reflections on Life's Final Chapter.* New York: Alfred A. Knopf, 1994.

Okun, Barbara, and Joseph Nowinski. *Saying Goodbye: A Guide to Coping with a Loved One's Terminal Illness.* New York: Berkley Publishing Group, 2012.

Rock, David. *Your Brain at Work: Strategies for Overcoming Distraction, Regaining Focus, and Working Smarter All Day Long.* New York: HarperCollins, 2009.

Seligman, Martin E. P. *Authentic Happiness: Using the New Positive Psychology to Realize Your Potential for Lasting Fulfillment.* New York: Free Press, 2002.

———. *Flourish: A Visionary New Understanding of Happiness and Well-Being.* New York: Free Press, 2012.

———. *Learned Optimism: How to Change Your Mind and Your Life.* New York: Pocket Books, 1998.

Sheehy, Gail. *Menopause: The Silent Passage: Revised and Updated.* New York: Pocket Books, 1998.

———. *Predictable Crises of Adult Life.* New York: Ballantine Books, 2006.

———. *Understanding Men's Passages: Discovering the New Map of Men's Lives.* New York: Ballantine Books, 1999.

Strauch, Barbara. *The Secret Life of the Grown-Up Brain: The Surprising Talents of the Middle Aged Mind.* New York: Viking, 2010.

Thompson, Edward H. Jr., and Lenard Kaye. *A Man's Guide to Healthy Aging: Stay Smart, Strong and Active.* Baltimore: John Hopkins Press, 2013.

Tindle, Hilary. *Up: How Positive Outlook Can Transform Our Health and Aging.* New York: Hudson Street Press, 2013.

Vaillant, George E. *Aging Well: Surprising Guideposts to a Happier Life from the Landmark Harvard Study of Adult Development.* New York: Little, Brown, 2002.

———. *Triumphs of Experience: The Men of the Harvard Grant Study.* Cambridge, MA: Belknap Press, 2012.

Viorst, Judith. *Necessary Losses: The Loves, Illusions, Dependencies, and Impossible Expectations That All of Us Have to Give Up in Order to Grow.* New York: Fireside, 1998.

Warner, Jan, and Jan Collins. *Next Steps: A Practical Guide to Planning for the Best Half of Your Life.* Fresno, CA: Quill Driver Books, 2009.

Weil, Andrew. *Healthy Aging: A Lifelong Guide to Your Physical and Spiritual Well-Being.* New York: Alfred A. Knopf, 2005.

Willcox, Bradley J., D. Craig Willcox, and Makoto Suzuki. *The Okinawa Program: How the World's Longest-Lived People Achieve Everlasting Health—And How You Can Too.* New York: Three Rivers Press, 2001.

Web Resources: (If the website is no longer available, search the title to find the updated website listing)

Aging With Dignity: www.agingwithdignity.org

The Cards I've Been Dealt: www.thecardsivebeendealt.com

Consider the Conversation: www.considertheconversation.org

The Conversation Project: www.theconversationproject.org

Five Wishes: fivewishesonline.agingwithdignity.org

Free Legal Documents online: www.findforms.com
Go Wish Card Game: www.gowish.org
Infinite Wellness Solutions: www.infinitewellnesssolutions.com
Medicare: www.medicare.gov
Music and Happiness: www.musicandhappiness.com
Prepare: www.prepareforyourcare.org
Sharp Brains: www.sharpbrains.com
Social Security: www.aarp.org/work/social-security
Social Security: www.ssa.gov

CONVERSATION 8: CHOOSING WHERE AND HOW TO LIVE

Corcoran, Barbara, and Warren Berger. *Nextville: Amazing Places to Live the Rest of Your Life.* New York: Springboard Press, 2008.

Cullinane, Jan, and Cathy Fitzgerald. *The New Retirement: The Ultimate Guide to The Rest of Your Life.* New York: Rodale Books, 2004.

Durett, Charles. *The Senior Cohousing Handbook, 2nd Edition: A Community Approach to Independent Living.* Gabriola Island, BC: New Society Publishers, 2009.

Felton, Sallie. *If I'm so Smart, Why Can't I Get Rid of This Clutter? Tools to Get It Done!* Washington, DC: Journey Grrrl Publishing, 2011.

Golson, Barry. *Gringos in Paradise: An American Couple Builds Their Retirement Dream House in a Seaside Village in Mexico.* New York: Scribner, 2006.

———. *Retirement Without Borders: How to Retire Abroad—in Mexico, France, Spain, Costa Rica, Panama, and Other Sunny, Foreign Places (And the Secret to Making It Happen Without Stress).* New York: Scribner, 2008.

Kompes, Gregory A. *50 Fabulous Gay-Friendly Places to Live.* Franklin Lakes, NJ: Career Press, 2005.

Marcus, Clare Cooper. *Home as Mirror of Self: Exploring the Deeper Meaning of Home*. Newburyport, MA: Conari Press, 1995.

Peddicord, Kathleen. *How to Retire Overseas: Everything You Need to Know to Live Well (for Less) Abroad*. New York: Hudson Street Press, 2010.

Schwartz, Barry. *The Paradox of Choice: Why More is Less*. Harper Collins Publishers, 2005.

Van Booven-Whitsell, Valerie. *The Senior Solution: A Family Guide to Keeping Seniors Home for Life!* St. Louis: LTC Expert Publications, 2007.

Ware, Ciji. *Right Sizing Your Life: Simplify Your Surroundings While Keeping What Matters Most*. New York: Springboard Press, 2007.

Web Resources: (If the website is no longer available, search the title to find the updated website listing)

AARP: www.aarp.org

Cohousing: www.cohousing.org

Guide for Retirement Communities and "Best Places to Live": www.cnnmoney.com/retirement

Home Exchange: www.homeexchange.com

Home Link International: www.homelink.org

National Association of Senior Move Managers: www.nasmm.org

National Resource Center on Supportive Housing and Home Modifications: www.homemods.org

Met Life Report on Aging in Place 2.0: www.metlife.org/mmi/research/aging-in-place

Retirement RVs: www.retirementrvs.com

RV Forum: www.rv.net

Senior Resource: www.seniorresource.com/house.htm

Society of Certified Senior Advisors: www.csa.us (search housing and other topics)

Village Concept: www.vtvnetwork.org

Where to Retire magazine: www.wheretoretire.com

CONVERSATION 9: SOCIAL LIFE, FRIENDS, AND COMMUNITY

Bourke, Penelope Stuart, ed. *Journeys Outward, Journeys Inward: Travel and Transformation*. Chapel Hill, NC: Second Journey Publications, 2013.

Bratter, Bernice, and Helen Dennis. *Project Renewment: The First Retirement Model for Career Women*. New York: Scribner Press, 2008.

Chimsky, Mark. *65 Things to Do When You Retire: Travel*. South Portland, ME: Sellers Publishing, 2013.

Kelm, Jacqueline Bascobert. *Appreciate Living: The Principles of Appreciate Inquiry in Personal Life*. Wake Forest, NC: Venet Publishers, 2005.

Sellers, Ronnie. *70 Things to Do When You Turn 70: More than 70 Experts on the Subject of Turning 70*. South Portland, ME: Sellers Publishing, 2013.

Sheehy, Sandy. *Connecting: The Enduring Power of Female Friendship*. New York: William Morrow, 2000.

Web Resources: (If the website is no longer available, search the title to find the updated website listing)

The Aging Adventurer: www.TheAgingAdventurer.com

Bernard Osher Foundation: www.osherfoundation.org

Boomer Living Plus: www.boomer-livingplus.com

Eldertreks: www.eldertreks.com

National Center for Creative Aging: www.creativeaging.org

Osher Lifelong Learning Institute (formerly North Carolina Center for Creative Retirement): olliasheville.com

Road Scholar (formerly Elderhostel): www.roadscholar.org

www.freeconferencecall.com
www.freeconferenceservice.com
www.instantconference.com
www.skype.com

CONVERSATION 10: PURPOSE, MEANING, AND GIVING BACK

Arrien, Angeles. *The Second Half of Life: Opening the Eight Gates of Wisdom.* Boulder, CO: Sounds True, 2005.

Baines, Barry. *Ethical Wills: Putting your Values on Paper.* Boston: Da Capo Press, 2006.

Baldwin, Christina. *The Seven Whispers: A Spiritual Practice for Times Like These.* Novato, CA: New World Library, 2002.

————. *Storycatcher: Making Sense of Our Lives through the Power and Practice of Story.* Novato, CA: New World Library, 2005.

Bronson, Po. *What Should I Do with My Life? The True Story of People Who Answered the Ultimate Question.* New York: Ballantine Books, 2005.

Burgess, Gloria. *Dare to Wear Your Soul on the Outside: Live Your Legacy Now.* San Francisco: Jossey-Bass, 2008.

Byock, Ira. *The Four Things That Matter Most: A Book About Living.* New York: Atria Books, 2004.

Chopra, Deepak. *The Seven Spiritual Laws of Success: A Practical Guide to the Fulfillment of Your Dreams.* San Rafael and Navato, CA: Amber-Allen Publishing/New World Library, 1994.

Chopra, Deepak, and Rudolph E. Tanzi. *Super Brain: Unleashing the Explosive Power of Your Mind to Maximize Health, Happiness, and Spiritual Well-Being.* New York: Harmony Books, 2012.

Daniel, Lois. *How to Write Your Own Life Story: The Classic Guide for the Nonprofessional Writer,* 4th ed. Chicago: Chicago Review Press, 1997.

Dass, Ram. *Still Here: Embracing Aging, Cha.*
New York: Riverhead Books, 2000.

Davidson, Sara. *The December Project: An Extrao.
and a Skeptical Seeker Confront Life's Greatest N.*
York: HarperOne, 2014.

Dychtwald, Ken, and Daniel J. Kadlec. *With Purpose: Gc
Success to Significance in Work and Life.* New York: \
Morrow, 2009.

Frankel, Bruce. *What Should I Do With the Rest of My Life? 1
Stories of Finding Success, Passion, and New Meaning in t*
Second Half of Life. New York: Avery, 2010.

Freed, Rachel. *Women's Lives, Women's Legacies: Passing Your
Beliefs and Blessings to Future Generations.* Minneapolis:
Fairview Press, 2003.

Grout, Pam. *The 100 Best Volunteer Vacations to Enrich Your Life.*
Washington, DC: National Geographic, 2009.

Hachmyer, Caitlin, ed. *Alternatives to the Peace Corps: A Guide
to Global Volunteer Opportunities,* 12th ed. Oakland, CA: Food
First Books, 2008.

Hollis, James. *Finding Meaning in the 2nd Half of Life: How to
Finally, Really Grow Up.* New York: Gotham Books, 2005.

Johnson, Robert A., and Jerry M. Ruhl. *Living Your Unlived Life:
Coping with Unrealized Dreams and Fulfilling Your Purpose in
the Second Half of Life.* New York: Jeremy P. Tarcher, 2009.

Kayne, Sheryl. *Volunteer Vacations Across America: Immersion
Travel USA.* Woodstock, VT: Countryman Press, 2009.

Kelley, Tim. *True Purpose: 12 Strategies for Discovering the
Difference You Are Meant to Make.* Berkeley, CA: Transcendent
Solutions Press, 2009.

Kelm, Jacqueline. *The Joy of Appreciative Living: Your 28-day Plan
to Greater Happiness in 3 Incredibly Easy Steps.* New York:
Jeremy P. Tarcher, 2008.

ner, Jerome. *Be It Ever So Humble: A Dialogue at the Threshold of Family, Ancestors, Culture and Home.* Charleston, SC: BookSurge Publishing, 2009.

itaj, Karma. *Women Who Could...And Did: Stories of 26 Exemplary Artists & Scientists.* Chestnut Hill, MA: Huckle Hill Press, 2002.

Kushner, Harold S. *Living a Life That Matters.* New York: Alfred A. Knopf, 2001.

Lama, Dalai, and Howard C. Cutler. *The Art of Happiness: A Handbook for Living.* London: Hodder & Stoughton, 1998.

Lieder, Richard J. *The Power of Purpose: Find Meaning, Live Longer, Better,* 2nd ed. San Francisco: Berrett-Koehler Publishers, 2010.

Lieder, Richard J., and David A. Shaprio. *Something to Live For: Finding Your Way in the Second Half of Life.* San Francisco: Berrett-Koehler Publishers, 2008.

Leider, Richard J., Alan M. Webber, and Emilio Pardo. *Life Re-Imagined: Discovering Your New Life Possibilities.* San Francisco: Berrett-Koehler Publishers, 2013.

Lesser, Elizabeth. *The Seeker's Guide: Making Your Life a Spiritual Adventure.* New York: Villard, 2000.

Longfellow, Henry Wadsworth. *The Complete Poetical Works of Longfellow.* Cambridge, MA: Houghton, Mifflin, 1893.

McMillon, Bill, Doug Cutchins, and Ann Geissinger. *Volunteer Vacations: Short-Term Adventures That will Benefit You and Others,* 10th ed. Chicago: Chicago Review Press, 2009.

Merck, Ed. *Sailing the Mystery: My Journey into Life's Remaining Chapters.* Victoria, BC: FriesenPress, 2013.

Moberg, David O., ed. *Aging and Spirituality: Spiritual Dimensions of Aging Theory, Research, Practice, and Policy.* New York: Routledge, 2001.

Moody, Harry R., and David Carroll. *The Five Stages of the Soul: Charting the Spiritual Passages that Shape our Lives.* New York: Anchor Books, 1998.

Mosel, Arlene, and Blair Lent. *Tikki Tikki Tembo*. New York: Square Fish, 2007. First published 1968 by Holt, Rinehart, and Winston.

Oliver, Mary. *New and Selected Poems, Vol. 1*. Boston: Beacon Press, 2004.

———. *New and Selected Poems, Vol. 2*. Boston: Beacon Press, 2007.

Papineau, Andre. *Breaking Up, Down and Through: Discovering Spiritual and Psychological Opportunities in Your Transitions*. Mahwah, NJ: Paulist Press, 1997.

Richo, David. *The Five Things We Cannot Change...and the Happiness We Find by Embracing Them*. Boston: Shambhala, 2006.

Schachter-Shalomi, Zalman. *From Age-ing to Sage-ing: A Profound New Vision of Growing Older*. New York: Warner Books, 1995.

Shula, Jean Deitch. *The Coming of Aging: Learning to Live from the Inside Out*. Baltimore: Publish America, 2006.

Spence, Linda. *Legacy: A Step-By-Step Guide to Writing Personal History*. Athens, OH: Swallow Press, 1997.

Stretcher, Victor J. *On Purpose: Lessons in Life and Health from the Frog, the Dung Beetle, and Julia*. Ann Arbor, MI: Dung Beetle Press, 2013.

Tolle, Eckhart. *A New Earth: Awakening to Your Life's Purpose*. New York: Penguin, 2008.

———. *The Power of Now: A Guide to Spiritual Enlightenment*. Novato, CA: New World Library, 1998.

Vaillant, George E. *Spiritual Evolution: How We Are Wired for Faith, Hope, and Love*. New York: Harmony Books, 2009.

Williams, Terry Tempest. *When Women Were Birds: Fifty-Four Variations on Voice*. New York: Sarah Crichton Books, 2012.

Web Resources: (If the website is no longer available, search the title to find the updated website listing)

Action Without Borders: www.idealist.org

AmeriCorps: www.nationalservice.gov/programs.americorps

Coming of Age: www.comingofage.com
Create the Good: www.createthegood.org
Cross Cultural Solutions: www.crossculturalsolutions.org
Earthwatch Institute: www.earthwatch.org
Experience Corps: www.experiencecorps.org
Global Exchange: www.globalexchange.org
Global Vision International: Volunteer abroad and travel around
the world: www.gviusa.com
Global Volunteer Network: www.globalvolunteernetwork.org
GoEco: Volunteer Abroad for Ecological & Humanitarian Projects:
www.GoEco.org
Habitat for Humanity International: www.habitat.org
The Legacy Center: www.thelegacycenter.net
National Park Service: www.nps.gov/gettinginvolved/volunteer
Peace Corps: www.peacecorps.gov
Peter and Hinda Schnurman's blog: www.peterandhindas
.blogspot.com
Peter and Hinda Schnurman's videos: www.youtube.com
/hindapeter
ReServe: Innovation Staffing for Nonprofits: www.reserveinc.org
Sage-ing International: www.sage-ing.org
SCORE: Volunteering and Mentoring: www.SCORE.org
Spiritual Eldering Institute: www.spiritualelderinginstitute.org
Storycorps: www.storycorps.org
Teach for America: www.teacherforamerica.org
Volunteer Match: www.volunteermatch.org
Who Gets Grandma's Yellow Pie Plate? www.1.extension.umn.edu
World Teach: www.worldteach.org

CREATING YOUR SHARED VISION

McLean, Pamela D., and Frederic M. Hudson. *LifeLaunch: A Passionate Guide to the Rest of Your Life*, 5th ed. Washington, DC: Hudson Institute Press, 2011.

Miller, Caroline Adams, and Michael B. Frisch. *Creating Your Best Life: The Ultimate Life List Guide.* New York: Sterling, 2009.

AFTERWORD

Bair, Deidre. *Calling It Quits: Late-Life Divorce and Starting Over.* New York: Random House, 2007.

Beer, Susan. *Move On Without Me: The Power of a Woman to Create a New Life After Widowhood.* Long Island City, NY: Hatherleigh Press, 2010.

Birnbach, Lawrence, and Beverly Hyman. *How to Know If It's Time to Go: A 10-Step Reality Test for Your Marriage.* New York: Sterling, 2010.

Bolen, Jean Shinoda. *Crones Don't Whine: Concentrated Wisdom for Juicy Women.* Boston: Conari Press, 2003.

Chambers, Pat. *Older Widows and the Life Course: Multiple Narratives of Hidden Lives.* Burlington, VT: Ashgate Publishing, 2005.

Culbreth, Judsen. *Boomers' Guide to Online Dating: Date with Dignity.* New York: Rodale Books, 2005.

Falk, Florence. *On My Own: The Art of Being a Woman Alone.* New York: Harmony Books, 2007.

Feldon, Barbara. *Living Alone and Loving It: A Guide to Relishing the Solo Life.* New York: Fireside, 2003.

Fleet, Carole Brody, and Lisa Kline. *Happily Even After: A Guide to Getting Through (and Beyond) the Grief of Widowhood.* Berkeley, CA: Cleis Press, 2012.

Ginsburg, Genevieve Davis. *Widow to Widow: Thoughtful, Practical Ideas for Rebuilding Your Life.* Boston: Da Capo Press, 1995.

Green, Janice. *Divorce After 50: Your Guide to the Unique Legal & Financial Challenges,* 2nd ed. Berkeley, CA: Nolo Publishing, 2010.

Healy, Kaye. *Coming of Age in our 50s and 60s.* Exeter, NSW: Kaye Healy Publishing, 2010. Kindle edition.

Klinenberg, Eric. *Going Solo: The Extraordinary Rise and Surprising Appeal of Living Alone*. New York: Penguin Books, 2013.

Lawrence-Lightfoot, Sara. *Exit: The Endings that Set Us Free*. New York: Sarah Crichton Books, 2012.

Lesser, Elizabeth. *Broken Open: How Difficult Times Can Help Us Grow*. New York: Villard Books, 2005.

Levine, Irene S., *Best Friends Forever: Surviving a Breakup with Your Best Friend*. New York: Overlook Press, 2009.

Mackler, Lauren. *Solemate: Master the Art of Aloneness and Transform Your Life*. Carlsbad, CA: Hay House, 2010.

Manfred, Erica. *He's History, You're Not: Surviving Divorce after 40*. Guilford, CT: GPP Life, 2009.

Shaner, Leslie Ann. *Divorce in the Golden Years: Estate Planning, Spousal Support, and Retirement Issues for Clients at Midlife and Beyond*. Chicago: American Bar Association, 2010.

Trafford, Abigail. *As Time Goes By: Boomerang Marriages, Serial Spouses, Throwback Couples and Other Romantic Adventures in an Age of Longevity*. New York: Basic Books, 2009.

Training, Workshops, and Seminars

PROVIDED BY DORI AND ROBERTA, TOGETHER OR SEPARATELY

Training for Professionals: Working with Couples in Retirement Transition

Retirement Transition Presentations and Workshops for Individuals or Couples

Corporate Seminars for Human Resources Professionals

Keynotes and breakout sessions for professionals, associations, and organizations

Seminars, workshops, and brown bag lunches for employees approaching retirement

Private consulting/coaching in person or by telephone

CONTACT DORI AND ROBERTA

Dori Mintzer: dorian@dorianmintzer.com
Roberta Taylor: rkt@pathmaking.com

Index

Q
Quiz, couple's, xxxi–xxxii

R
Reading guide, 273–274
Realistic optimism, 165–169
Relationships. *See*
   Communication; Family
   relationships; Intimacy and
   romance; Social life; Time
   together versus time apart
Religion, 130–132, 237–240
Relocating versus remaining
   in home, 21–24, 139,
   193–216, 219
ReServe, 230
Retirement, concept of,
   xxiii–xxiv
Retirement, postponing, 7, 8,
   9, 11, 24–26, 91
Retirement communities,
   203–211
Retirement timing. *See*
   Timing and options for
   retirement
Risk-taking, 14, 37, 59–63
Role modeling, 8, 64, 65,
   75–76, 134
RV communities, 210–211

S
Service Corps of Retired
   Executives (SCORE), 230
Service Opportunities after
   Reaching 55 (SOAR 55),
   230

Sex. *See* Intimacy and romance
Sexually transmitted diseases,
   112–113
Shared Vision, 257–263
Siblings, 143–146
Sleep, 170
Social life
   dating, 104–108, 112–113
   exercises/funwork, 232–234
   living in community, 226–229
   retirement communities,
      203–211
   retirement transition and,
      16–17, 69–71, 221–223
   talking about, 74, 217–226
   time together versus time
      apart, 23, 83–85, 222
Spirituality, 219, 237–240
Storytelling, 244–245, 247
Stress, 151, 170–172
Support groups, 71, 229

T
Time together versus time
   apart
   assumptions and
      expectations, 23, 84–94
   exercises/funwork, 96–98
   living separate lives, 94, 103
   overdependence, 80–81, 82, 222
   scheduling dates, 81, 101
   talking about, 79–84
Timing and options for
   retirement
   exercises/funwork, 27–29
   retirement transition and,
      16–18

Acknowledgments

This book is for and about couples in midlife and beyond at various stages of retirement transition. In order to understand the issues most relevant for couples in this phase of life, we facilitated several focus groups organized around the premise that common questions and concerns would emerge as couples talked together about their experience. *The Couple's Retirement Puzzle* could not have been written without the input of the couples who were willing to share their challenges, hopes, and dreams for the future. We want to acknowledge all of you who came together to talk about your life and relationship experiences, supporting and validating each other in the process. In addition, we are especially grateful to the many couples who, through their stories, helped make the book come alive.

In addition, we want to thank our guides and mentors who contributed to the book: Richard Leider, who exemplifies a true "thought leader" and has taught us so much about the importance of meaning and purpose in life; William Sadler, a strong and steady role model, researcher, and believer in all that's possible in the third age; the late Gene Cohen, an inspiring teacher and leader in the field of gerontology; Howard and Marika Stone, who continue to be 2young2retire and have totally walked their talk into Laughter Yoga and other ventures; and, of course, Meg

Newhouse, a dear and trusted friend, fearless Life Planning Network founder, and gifted and soulful presence. We deeply appreciate other colleagues who contributed words of wisdom and, through their own work, have inspired us: Helen Dennis, Connie Goldman, Jan Hively, Lisa Kramer, Carleen MacKay, Olivia Mellan, Rick Moody, Ruth Nemzoff, Gina Ogden, Ed Rogoff, Lin Schreiber, and Jeri Sedlar. In addition, we want to acknowledge friends and colleagues who offered feedback and encouragement along the way: Barbara Abramowitz, Ellen and Robert Ansel, Gene and Lois Arthur, Betsy Cole, Robin Dziuba, Lois Ernst, Evelyn Fowler, Harley Gordon, Lauren Gourlay, Elizabeth Jetton, Brian Kurth, Joe Pulitano, Skip Reilly, Judy Siegel, Penelope Tzougros, Hollie Vanderzee, Beth Wechsler, Deena Wynne, Chuck Yanikoski, and Paul Youd. With your help we have written what we hope is a comprehensive and useful guide for couples transitioning to the second half of life. We want to give special thanks to Fred Mandell, who has been a mentor and supportive presence throughout the process, generously sharing his gifts of creativity, wisdom, and friendship.

Much appreciation goes to Peter and Hinda Schnurman, two wonderful role models, who shared how their volunteer experiences in remote parts of the world brought meaning and purpose to their lives. And to Charlotte Savage, who told her personal story of discovering how, through her determination and tenacity, she had made a difference in the lives of many children and families.

Much gratitude goes to our many other dear friends who are part of the heart and soul of this book, especially those of you who contributed stories from your own retirement transition. You have been there from the beginning, witnessing our ups and downs, giving encouragement and support, and continuing to call even when we didn't have time to talk. We know that some of you were probably ready to give up on us when we were so absorbed with the book that we didn't have time for anything else. But you were always in our hearts, and we trusted that you would be there. Thank you for standing by us and knowing that there would be light at the end of the tunnel. Not wanting to inadvertently leave anyone out, we decided to thank all of you collectively. You know who you are!

We want to thank our primary readers, Fred Mandell and Susan Callahan, both accomplished authors who already had enough on their plates but generously made the time to read through the manuscript, give us valuable feedback, and support this project.

We also appreciate the ongoing support and encouragement from our friends and colleagues in the Life Planning Network (LPN), the LPN Business Development Group, the LPN Renewment Group, the Boomers and Beyond Special Interest Group, and friends in the Planner-Therapist Alliance. We are fortunate to belong to a community of so many creative and wonderful people who are traveling a similar path. Together, we are all creating a model of a new retirement transition that reflects our values and allows for creativity, ongoing growth, and the development of community.

We were fortunate to have worked with a talented "team" of professionals who helped us produce the first edition of our book: Mayapriya Long, our talented cover and book designer; Kristie Kelley, who helped with editing; and Christine Frank, who helped with our indexing. Special thanks to Fern Reiss, our publishing guru, who took us on as clients in spite of our huge learning curve, helped us to stay grounded, and moved us along so that the book would actually get done; Donna Gunter, who helped us think "bigger" about our book; and to Peter Meyer and his staff at Lincoln Street Coffee where we spent many hours working on the book.

Much love and appreciation to our supportive and extremely tolerant husbands: Bruce, Roberta's husband, our computer guru who tirelessly helped with some of the early editing and formatting of the manuscript; and David, Dori's husband, one of the early readers, who offered comments and feedback that enhanced the book. Last but not least, thanks to Dori's son, Louie, who came up with some terrific suggestions at strategic points when we were feeling stuck. We are so thankful for all of your support and love. We truly could not have written this book without knowing you were behind us all the way.

More than three years have passed since the first publication of our book. We are very excited to have this new edition published by Sourcebooks. We're grateful to our new team, and especially to Stephanie Bowen who believed in the importance of our book as soon as she read it and is working with us to take it to a larger audience. And to Jenna Skwarek, who has patiently helped with the editing and cover and title issues and to Katy Lynch for her publicity help. There are also a host of other team members "behind the scene," and we're grateful to all of you for your help and support in making this new edition a reality. With sincere appreciation and thanks to all of you at Sourcebooks.

—Dori Mintzer and Roberta Taylor

About the Authors

ROBERTA K. TAYLOR

Prior to working with individuals, couples, and single women in transition, Roberta had a successful career as a psychotherapist and clinical administrator. In her midfifties, with a desire to continue to learn and grow, and a curiosity about the possibilities of midlife and beyond, she became involved in the developing field of positive aging and midlife transition. Knowing this was her chosen path, she studied at the Institute for Life Coach Training and became a board-certified coach. She has a BS degree from the State University of New York and an MEd in developmental psychology from Rollins College. She is certified in several areas including money coaching, couples relationship coaching, wellness coaching, hypnotherapy, creativity, and elder mediation. She was trained by Richard Leider, the Purpose Project, at the University of Minnesota Center for Spirituality and Healing. She is a certified senior adviser.

Roberta is on the board of the National Speakers Association where she coordinates FAST Track, the educational program for NSA New England. She is a founding member and chair of the Boston chapter of the Transition Network. She is a former board member of the Life Planning Network and is a member of the American Society on Aging.

Roberta works with clients who want to clarify goals, develop their vision, and take action toward creating and living a fulfilling second half of life that aligns with their values and purpose. She helps couples work together to develop a shared vision for the next chapter of life. She enjoys working with single women who are reinventing themselves in their late fifties, sixties, and seventies. (Her upcoming book will focus on the issues, challenges, and opportunities for single women sixty and over.) Her developing programs include money coaching and working with women executives transitioning out of the corporate arena. She brings her background as a psychotherapist and expertise in adult development and life planning, as well as her own life experience, to working with individuals and couples who are asking themselves "What's next?"

Roberta facilitates workshops and seminars for community, corporate, financial, and professional groups on second half of life and retirement transition issues.

In addition to coauthoring *The Couple's Retirement Puzzle*, Roberta has contributed to *Live Smart after 50!* and *The Six Secrets to a Happy Retirement*. She has been quoted in the *Washington Post, Fiscal Times, Boston Globe, USA Today, MetroWest Magazine*, and several other publications.

Roberta lives in Waltham, Massachusetts, with her husband, Bruce. She has an office in Wellesley Hills, Massachusetts, where she sees individuals, couples, and groups.

Learn more about Roberta at www.pathmaking.com.

DORIAN MINTZER

Dorian (a.k.a. Dori) Mintzer, PhD, is a sought-after speaker, writer, teacher, coach, and therapist who is known to energize her clients and audiences. She received her BA from the University of California, Berkeley, her MSW from the University of Pittsburgh, and her PhD from Smith College. She was a lecturer in psychiatry at the Cambridge Hospital, part of the Harvard Medical School, for eighteen years. She's a licensed psychologist, licensed independent clinical social worker, board-certified coach, and certified senior adviser. She was trained as a coach through Mentor Coach. She has continued her training and education and has a variety of licenses, certifications, and advanced training in areas such as retirement transition, money and relationship coaching, mindfulness, creativity, positive psychology, spirituality, adult development, gerontology, family therapy, sexuality, and elder mediation.

Dori belongs to a number of professional organizations which include the National Speakers Association, the Life Planning Network, the American Society on Aging, the National Association of Social Workers, the American Psychological Association, and the International Coach Federation.

She has more than forty years of clinical experiences, initially working with community organizations and hospitals. She developed her private clinical practice in 1981 and works with men, women, and couples, individually as well as in groups. Her expertise in adult development, holistic life planning, and positive psychology, combined with her life experiences, has led to her passion for helping individuals and couples develop their own road map as they navigate the second half of life. She believes that clarifying values and priorities, making conscious and intentional decisions, and learning to communicate effectively helps people create more fulfilling lives for themselves and within their relationships.

She founded and facilitates two virtual communities: the Boomers and Beyond Special Interest Group for interdisciplinary professionals and the Revolutionize Your Retirement Interview with Experts Series for professionals and the public. Dori enjoys speaking to community, professional, financial, and corporate groups on a variety of topics related to "the changing face of retirement," midlife issues, important conversations, and living life with purpose and meaning. She also enjoys facilitating workshops for professionals, as well as for men, women, and couples to help them deal with their life transitions.

In addition to coauthoring *The Couple's Retirement Puzzle*, Dori has contributed to a number of books, including *Not Your Mother's Retirement, Live Smart after 50!, 65 Things to Do When You Retire* and its sequel *65 Things to Do When You Retire: Travel, 70 Things to Do When You Turn 70, The Six Secrets to a Happy Retirement,* and *Remarkable and Real.* She also writes online blogs and articles. Her continual goal is to do the things she loves and have a good life/work balance.

Dori has been quoted in publications such as the *Wall Street Journal, New York Times, USA Today, Washington Post, CNN Money, Fiscal Times, Forbes,* the ABC Evening News, and numerous blogs and articles. She was also a guest on NPR's *Talk of the Nation* and has been featured on other radio shows.

Dori lives in Brookline, Massachusetts, with her husband, David, and son, Louie. She works with individuals, couples, and groups in person in her Boston and Brookline offices and also works with clients by phone.

Learn more about Dori at www.revolutionizeretirement.com.